PIONEER JEWS

A New Life in the Far West

Edward Reinhart (left, on horseback) was a member of the Reinhart clan who followed the Central Pacific Railroad to Elko and Winnemucca, Nevada, in 1868. The Reinharts were active in commerce, banking, cattle raising, and public service for three generations. Courtesy Nevada Historical Society, Reno

PIONEER JEWS

A New Life in the Far West

Harriet and Fred Rochlin

Houghton Mifflin Company

Boston

1984

First published in 1984 by Houghton Mifflin Company
Two Park Street, Boston, Massachusetts 02108

Produced by Rosebud Books,
a division of The Knapp Press
5900 Wilshire Boulevard
Los Angeles, California 90036

Book and jacket design by Nan Oshin

Library of Congress Cataloging in Publication Data

Rochlin, Harriet, 1924–
Pioneer Jews.

Bibliography: p. 230
Includes index.
1. Jews—West (U.S.)—History. 2. West (U.S.)— Ethnic relations. I. Rochlin, Fred, 1923–.II. Title.
F596.3.J5R63 1983   978'.004924   83-12647

ISBN 0-395-31832-7

10 9 8 7 6 5 4 3 2 1

First Edition

CONTENTS

*I*NTRODUCTION

This work began as two individual quests. In the late 1960s, my husband Fred and I, both native westerners and Jews were impelled, independent of one another, to reconsider the communities where we were born, where we grew up, and which we left as soon as we could. We did not discuss what we were doing; we had no words to describe the nameless and—in the "here-and-now" sixties—anachronistic urge to look back. I have since come to see that the uprooted, whether by choice or by force, are often as driven to set the record straight about their native habitat as some adopted children are to pierce the mystery surrounding their birth parents.

In some respects, Fred's task was the easier. Little had changed in his birthplace, Nogales, Arizona, sixty miles south of Tucson on the United States–Mexico border, in the twenty years since he moved to California. The population still hovered around six thousand (it is close to three times that now), and the one- and two-story tufa stone and faded red brick buildings along Morley Avenue, the main street paralleling the railroad tracks into Sonora, boasted at most some new facades. Three miles east of town, on an otherwise uninhabited hillside, the territorial-style house where Fred was born still stood alone. Though shabbier, it was occupied, if not by the Rochlins who had built it, then by other desert lovers who also spent long hours sitting on the side porch gazing south across the expanse of Mexican hay, palo verde, and mesquite to the Siamese twin communities of Nogales, Arizona, and Nogales, Sonora.

Fred approached his unfinished business

with his hometown by resuming the historical research he had begun in high school on Nogales town founder and merchant Jacob Isaacson. Isaacson had spent three years on the Arizona-Sonora border, first as a lone storekeeper guarding against attack by hostile Apaches and then as an experienced settler guiding the newcomers who arrived when the Arizona & New Mexico Railroad and the Sonora Railway linked at the border in October 1882. From May of that year until approximately a year later, the settlement (later Nogales) was called Isaacson, and its namesake served as its postmaster. According to one newspaper advertisement Isaacson placed during that period, he was doing a large business in Sonora and could provide information "in regard to mines, ranches, and other valuable property, both in Sonora and that section of Arizona near the line." Then for no known reason, he sold his holdings and never returned.

Encouraged by the story he had uncovered, Fred began gathering material on other early Jews of Santa Cruz County, Arizona: prominent town builder Leopold Ephraim (he advertised himself as "the Fat Jew"); the Lulley brothers—Mark, Louis, and Moses; the Ezekiels brothers—Mark, Louis, and Alex; and William Rosenberg (self-dubbed "Rosie the Tailor").

The source of my interest in the past is more difficult to pinpoint. The social tremors that were making us all strangers in a strange land in the 1960s may have jolted me into a backward glance. Or maybe I had arrived at that point in life when abandoned parts of oneself demand to be reclaimed. For whatever reason, I began to feel like something of an impostor as a community-involved Sherman Oaks housewife who wrote part-time and on milestone occasions turned out to be Jewish. If that was not me, then who was? I began thinking about my birthplace, Boyle Heights, east of Los Angeles's industrial district. Between the world wars, Boyle Heights had flourished as the largest Jewish quarter in the Far West—some fifty thousand strong in 1930. Other ethnic groups shared this neighborhood, which was as large as a medium-size eastern city. The Mexicans were at least as numerous as the Jews, and there were also smaller Russian, Japanese, Armenian, and black enclaves, each occupying its own terrain. In school—looking like the kids in "Our Gang" comedies—we were taught by our teachers to get along despite our racial, religious, and ethnic differences, and we did, at least more than we did not.

This interethnic existence ended for many of us with high school graduation. Some were centripetally pulled back into ethnic isolation. Others, myself included, began venturing daily out of Boyle Heights in search of educational, occupational, and cultural opportunities our community lacked. By the early 1950s most of the Jews of Boyle Heights, propelled by postwar prosperity or the fear of being left behind, had also moved on.

Eager to understand the rise and decline of my vanished village, and finding few historical records, I turned to Los Angeles Jewish history in general. Jews of diverse origins, I learned, had arrived with the first American settlers and had lived on equal footing with their non-Jewish counterparts for several decades. No Jewish quarter coalesced until the 1880s when hundreds then thousands of less welcome, and as such, more insular European Jews began arriving. During this period, previously open doors closed on both the early pioneers and their successors. The former, however, being better established, remained rooted among the general populace. These findings and my family history meshed, and I began to view both the earlier and the later pioneers as my predecessors.

As my perspective widened, so did the scope of my search. In time it became apparent that just as the history of Boyle Heights was entwined in the roots of Los Angeles, the history of Los Angeles was linked to the history of the entire region. Early western communities were remote from one another and remarkably distinctive in their environments; yet in other respects they were noticeably the same. Similar opportunities stimulated their growth: minerals and other natural resources, agriculture, trade, new roads, and railroads. Similar obstacles deterred them: hostile Indians and outlaws; economic instability; and the absence of government, transportation, and communications. Even in the early years, when travel in that vast and rugged region was arduous, expensive, risky, and time-consuming, pioneers were surprisingly mobile. The same peripatetic seekers moved in and out of one western settlement after another, and when they rooted, a number of them maintained enterprises in two and often more states and territories. Once these similarities became clear, what had appeared to me to be separate quests—Fred's in southern Arizona and mine in southern California—I began to see as different pieces of the same mosaic.

By 1980 I had filled a bank of file cabinets. Between us—Fred was still burrowing away at the pioneer Jews of Santa Cruz County and by then also parts of northern Mexico—we had accumulated two walls of books, journals, and monographs. In our efforts we were increasingly assisted by a growing number of new sources of information and new works directly and indirectly related to western pioneer Jews. Western Jewish historical societies and archives had sprung up in various sections of the West, most prominent among them the Western Jewish History Center of the Judah L. Magnes Museum, founded in 1967 in Berkeley, California; and the Rocky Mountain Jewish Historical Society, established in 1976 in Denver. New histories, bibliographies, monographs, and academic studies also attested to a ground swell of interest in the neglected western Jewish past. In October 1968 the premier issue of the *Western States Jewish Historical Quarterly,* now in its fifteenth year, appeared. Yet despite the efforts of a growing number of historians, archivists, librarians, and historical society members, the general public was still largely unapprised of western Jewry.

I began to think about writing a book—an illustrated social history on the Jews in the West. My motive for undertaking so potentially unwieldy a task was twofold. Continued research on the pioneer Jews and the region in general had added immeasurably to my sense of belonging. In the accounts of these pioneers' lives I had discovered a usable past on native ground and spirited predecessors who were daring, persistent, enterprising, change oriented, and whose hallmark was optimism. Having grown up in Boyle Heights and close to immigrant grandparents, I am well acquainted with my eastern European Jewish roots. And I do more than revere this culture—I enjoy it. Yet I know that much of what I enjoy—the humor, folklore, rituals, and the intensely close family and communal ties—was forged to some extent as a defense against a menacing host community. I know as well that temperamentally and ideologically I have more in common with that questing spirit that prodded the pioneers to abandon their home soil and seek a new life in the Far West.

My desire to introduce these bold optimists to their less innocent and consequently less hopeful western successors and to others who would find their dreams worthy of note was one force impelling me toward this work. The other was plain willfulness. No one had (or, as far as I could see, soon would) set forth an account of these vibrant adventurers in its full length and breadth, or attempted to expose the singular character of this western ingathering. When allowed, these pioneers—the renowned and the obscure, the laudable and the lamentable—speak for themselves and project their own images. I wanted to help them do so. Fred, having already collected hundreds of remarkably expressive historical photographs and ephemera from early western Jewish life, agreed to provide a graphic narrative. We began gathering materials from all over the West, especially reminiscences, diaries, journals, letters, oral histories, and chronicles—data rich in authenticity even when superficially inaccurate. We also turned to the ever

widening range of published and unpublished works on the subject. Helpful as these were, it became clear that no existing approach was suitable for the regional study we had in mind. Foremost were the questions of chronological and geographical boundaries.

Committed to tracing the western Jewish pioneer experience to its roots, we decided to begin our study with the entry of the first Europeans—among them, secret Jews—in the late sixteenth century and to end it in 1912, the year the last two western territories were granted statehood. As for geographical perimeters, we opted to cover the Far West—from the Rockies to the Pacific—plus west Texas and the Black Hills of South Dakota, all of which developed simultaneously. Three factors prompted this choice. The boundaries of this region are real and definable, unlike those of the Old West, the Wild West, or the American West. The far western states and territories took shape from the same stimuli and during the same general period. And lastly, the various sections of this western third of the United States continue to share regional attributes and obstacles, and in the minds of many, an increasingly interrelated destiny.

Other questions arose, among them, who is a Jew? The offspring of Jewish parents or, at least, of a Jewish mother is the response according to traditional Jewish law. To record a full range of Jewish experience on the pluralistic western frontier, we decided to include as well the offspring of a Jewish father and a non-Jewish mother, and those pioneers who thought of themselves or who were thought of by others as wholly or partially Jewish.

Once I began piecing together shards of these pioneers' lives, new images and more questions emerged. The most persistent centered on the long-term effects of the Jewish presence in the Far West. Jews had contributed significantly to the development of the nascent region; that was abundantly evident. Less obvious were the effects of the far western experience on these Jews. I kept listening to their words and looking at their pictures searching for clues.

ACKNOWLEDGMENTS

The first to join us in our fascination with the untold story of the pioneer Jews of the Far West were Richard Kahlenberg and Don Ackland. They proposed this illustrated social history to editor Robie Macauley, who added his affirmative response and unflagging enthusiasm to the undertaking. For their part in transforming a notion into a work in progress, and to Macauley for the guidance that was our mainstay from conception to completion, go our heartfelt gratitude. We will also long remember the help we received from researcher Marybeth Hamilton, who worked with us for eighteen of the twenty-eight months this book was in the making. We thank her in general for her able assistance and in particular for her contributions to chapters four and six. We are equally appreciative of the energy and talent Elizabeth Ginsburg, Michele Kort, and Paul Lacques expended in the collection of data and in the preparation of the manuscript. Nor can we forget the numerous ways Melissa Bemel, Jeff Deneen, and Ruth and Dena Lohmann sped and cheered our task.

We were also fortunate to contact interested and skillful researchers in other far western cities who filled our mailbox with rich material that may have otherwise eluded us. For their help we thank: Scott Cline, Mary Mason, Tim Purdy, Teresa Salazar, Barbara Sherrod, Carole Simon Smolinski, and Marianne Zarchin. We are no less indebted to descendants of pioneer Jews who provided us with biographical information on and photographs of their forebears. Most helpful was material donated by: Al Alschuler, Marjorie Cerf, Loggie Carrasco, Peggy Stern Cole, Sylvan Durkheimer, Bessie Falk, Dorothy Feldman, H. Leigh Gittins, Sylvia Ganz Houle, Dr. Fred Ilfeld, Audrey Kariel, Charles Lesinsky III, Annie Mitchell, Betty Ramenofsky, Max Schutz, Jr., Henry Schwartz, Michael Shainsky, and Dode McEwen Smith.

We initiated our work in spring of 1981 by sending a letter requesting information to 150 repositories, most of them in the Far West. The response was as abundant as it was encouraging. Among the speediest to reply were the staffs of Jewish historical societies and archives. We were thereafter in continuous contact with these institutions. For this information, advice, and friendly support, we heartily thank: American Jewish Archives, Fanny Zelcer; Hebrew Union College Library, Harvey Horowitz; Seattle Jewish Archives Project, Howard Droker; Rocky Mountain Jewish Historical Society, Belle Marcus and Jeanne Abrams; and Western Jewish History Center, Ruth Rafael, Lauren Lasslaben, and Lynn Fonfa.

We also greatly appreciate the valuable assistance we received from: Arizona Historical Foundation, Susie Sato; Arizona Historical Society, Margaret Bret Harte and Heather Hatch; Arizona Historical Society, Elizabeth DeWitt; Bancroft Library, University of California at Berkeley, Estelle Rebec; Calaveras County Museum, Judith Cunningham; Colorado Historical Society, Catherine T. Engel; Huntington Library, Valerie Franco; Idaho State Historical Society, Karin E. Ford; Institute of Texas Cultures, Tom F. Shelton; Jefferson County Historical Society, Helen D. Burns and Debbie McBride;

Montana Historical Society, Delores Morrow and Patricia Dean; Museum of New Mexico, Richard Rudisell and Arthur Olivas; Nevada Historical Society, Robert Nylen; New Mexico State Records Center, Richard Salazar; Nez Perce County, Lora Feucht; Nimitz Library, U.S. Naval Academy, Alice Creighton; Northeastern Nevada Museum, Howard Hickson; San Diego Historical Society, Sylvia Arden; Silver City Museum, Susan Berry; Stanford University Library, Special Collections, Carol A. Rudisell; University of New Mexico Library, Jan Barnhart, Judy Pence, and Marianne Scholes; University of Nevada Library, Diane Nassir; University of Utah Library, Everett Cooley, Cindy Morgan, Judith Brunvard, and Marlene Lewis; University of Washington Library, Karyl Winn and Susan Cunningham; University Research Library, University of California at Los Angeles, Norman Dudley and the Special Collections staff; Utah State Historical Society, Steven Wood and Susan Whetstone; and William Andrews Clark Memorial Library, University of California at Los Angeles, Norman J. Thrower. In addition, we owe our thanks to the staffs of the Deadwood Public Library; Denver Public Library, Western History Collection; El Paso Public Library; and to Tom Owen of the Los Angeles Public Library California Room.

Julius Kravetz, professor emeritus of Hebrew Union College, New York, read and advised us on the portions of chapter eight dealing with the nature and practice of Judaism. Norton B. Stern, founding editor of the *Western States Jewish Historical Quarterly* and a one-man research center on the pioneer Jews, read the entire manuscript and most kindly pointed out errors and oversights. For the time they spent on behalf of this work, we are most appreciative.

We are also grateful to editor Taryn Bigelow for her unswerving determination to make this work coherent and accurate, as well as to copy editor Sylvia Tidwell and designer Nan Oshin for their contributions to this project. Finally, we wish to express our lasting gratitude to managing editor Pamela Mosher, who brought to this project steadfastness, good taste, and admirable grace under pressure.

Harriet and Fred Rochlin

Chapter One

LESS THAN A MINYAN

The story of Jews in the Far West began in the northernmost wilds of colonial Mexico on a sixteenth-century Spanish land grant. The square-shaped tract extended from steamy Tampico, on the Gulf of Mexico, north 200 leagues (about 600 miles) through arid wastes to what is now San Antonio, Texas, then west 200 leagues through portions of New Mexico to a point in the northern province of Chihuahua, and from there 200 leagues south through rugged mountains and dun-colored valleys to Chametla, on the Pacific Ocean. The New Kingdom of León, as it was called, was one of the largest, most dangerous, and potentially richest Spanish land grants ever chartered. King Philip II gave the right to colonize this vast tract to a New Christian of Jewish descent, Don Luis de Carvajal, described by historian Lesley B. Simpson as "the most enlightened and humane of the conquistadors." As governor with hereditary rights, Carvajal energetically developed the territory, peacefully subduing the "Chichimecs"—the Indian tribes of Chichimeca—and establishing orderly settlements, ranches, and mines. His prosperous, though troubled, ten-year reign ended when the Mexican Inquisition learned that many of Carvajal's colonizers were secret Jews. The subsequent persecution of the governor; his nephew, namesake, and for a time his heir apparent, Don Luis de Carvajal, the Younger; and more than 100 of his crypto-Jewish relatives and colonizers caused the grant to be dubbed the "Tragic Square."

The first settlers of Jewish descent to enter what is now the American Southwest were, in all likelihood, Carvajal's colonizers fleeing the collapsing "kingdom" and the fiery stake. These early secret Jews who settled in New Mexico and south Texas and who successfully concealed their identities and eluded arrest are, to date, largely lost to history. However, some insight into their dynamic Hispanic-Hebraic personalities may be drawn from the abundant Inquisition trial records of those arrested and tried in Mexico City. Among the most illuminating accounts are those of the Carvajals, whose family history paralleled that of tens of thousands of Iberian Jews.

From the first to the fourteenth century, their antecedents experienced more tolerance than tyranny in Spain and Portugal. During the Golden Age—a liberal Arab reign that lasted from the eighth to the thirteenth centuries—Jews, mingling harmoniously with Moslems and Christians, rose to unprecedented heights. But tolerance waned after 1250, when the Christians gained control of Spain and mounted a drive to turn the culturally diverse country into a Catholic nation. Enforced conversions were inaugurated in 1390, and the Spanish Inquisition in 1480. Then, in 1492, the Church and Crown issued an ultimatum ordering the Jews to convert at once or leave. Some 50,000 Jews joined the 250,000 who had already converted, while another 200,000 fled.

"She was accused [of Judaizing] by a heretic who was one of our people," wrote Don Luis de Carvajal the Younger of his widowed sister Isabel Rodriguez de Andrada, shown before Inquisitors. Illustration by P. Miranda, from Vicente Riva Palacio, El Libro Rojo *(Mexico, 1870)*

Don Luis de Carvajal, governor of the New Kingdom of León, a Spanish land grant delineated above, developed the grant from 1579 until 1589 when the Mexican Inquisition learned that more than 100 of the governor's colonizers were secret Jews. The subsequent arrests, trials, and executions caused Carvajal's "kingdom" to be renamed the "Tragic Square." The drawing is superimposed on an 1880 Johnson and Ward map of Mexico.

The families that accepted baptism, like the Carvajals, however, suffered a new torment. Not all the converts, called *conversos* by the Old Christians, and *marranos* ("swine") by the Jews, were sincere. Large numbers—many in high posts—donned the trappings of Christianity but secretly clung to the Jewish faith. Often within a single household, devout New Christians, crypto-Jews, and an occasional heretic who rejected all religion lived together unaware of each others' true beliefs.

Born in Mogadouro, Portugal, in 1539 to parents who were ostensibly Old Christians, as a youth Don Luis had no inkling of his Jewish ancestry. He was in his twenties, an important wholesale merchant who had been for a time a sea captain, when he learned of his Hebraic origins. The discovery was a devastating blow to Carvajal, a man aspiring to high Spanish and Portuguese circles. Possibly as a result of his new knowledge about his identity, Don Luis formed a close business relationship with another New Christian, the wealthy and influential Don Miguel Nuñez. In 1566, the young merchant made

the tie between them permanent by marrying Nuñez's daughter Doña Guiomar de Ribera. Not long after the wedding, Carvajal learned to his dismay that Doña Guiomar was devoted to the Jewish faith. Frustrated by his failure to persuade his wife to forsake Judaism and distraught over a substantial business loss, in 1568, Carvajal set out alone for New Spain. Throughout his adventurous and highly remunerative early years as a conquistador, Carvajal continued his association with his father-in-law. A year after Nuñez's death in 1577, Carvajal decided to settle permanently in the New World. He sailed for Spain bearing a petition to colonize a huge tract of land, much of which he or his agents had already explored and knew to be fertile and rich in resources. He presented his impressive credentials at the court of Philip II, and for six months advanced his case. During this interval Carvajal also recruited colonists, primarily among his own relatives, but also among his wife's. Doña Guiomar, however, refused to accompany her husband to the New World.

An equitable balance of privileges and obligations between the conquistador and the Crown was at last struck. The charter, issued on May 31, 1579, named Carvajal the governor of the New Kingdom of León and granted him the customary right to emigrate colonists at his own expense. No number was specified, but historians estimate that between one hundred and two hundred families went to New Spain with him. The charter also contained an unusual clause that exempted these emigrants from having to present *limpieza de sangre* certificates—legal proof of four generations of Catholic ancestry. Since 1449, the *limpieza* had been mandatory for Spaniards in key posts and for all but a few decades was required of settlers embarking for New Spain. (Carvajal insisted he did not know that many of his colonizers were crypto-Jews until a decade after their arrival.)

Among the new settlers were Carvajal's sister, Doña Francisca; her husband, Don Francisco Rodríguez de Matos, purportedly a rabbi; and eight of their nine children, including young Luis, the governor's namesake. The oldest son, Gaspar, a Catholic priest, was already in New Spain when the remaining Rodríguez Carvajals arrived in 1580. They settled in Tampico on the Gulf of Mexico in the humid, mosquito-ridden, and isolated Pánuco region. The family would later complain that in Pánuco they became even more impoverished than in Spain and that the governor failed to provide promised financial aid. Like so many pioneer Jews after them, Don Francisco and his sons started their new lives peddling goods at nearby mining camps. In their misery, the family turned all the more fervently to their religion, sustaining their morale with a round of secret Judaic rites.

One of the five Rodríguez Carvajal daughters, Isabel, had promised Doña Guiomar before leaving Spain that she would beseech the governor, on his wife's behalf, to return to the laws of Moses. When Isabel revealed to her uncle that she and her family practiced Jewish rites and implored him to join them, the governor flew into a rage. He knocked the girl down and ordered her never to mention the subject again. Thereafter, the governor shunned his sister's family, except for his teenage nephew, Luis.

Impressed with his nephew's brilliant mind and commanding ways, the childless governor hoped to make the boy his heir. The youth's father, the alleged rabbi, had also earmarked Luis as his successor. Torn between materialistic desires and mystical leanings, the boy anguished over whether to emulate his wealthy and powerful uncle or his pious father.

When Luis was nineteen, his father died. While the rest of the family moved to Mexico City, Luis decided to remain in Pánuco with the governor. Lonely and confused, the young man loyally worked for his uncle but when alone, pored over Jewish texts. One day, after reading that Abraham had circumcised himself to ensure his place in the Book of Life, Luis, similarly inspired, seized blunt shears and rushed to a ravine near the Pánuco River where he "cut off nearly the entire prepuce." In his autobiography, he would wryly note that once he had "received the seal of his holy sacrament upon his flesh, it served as a bulwark against lust and an aid to chastity."

A year later, Luis went north to develop mines in the San Gregorio Mountains and to help establish new settlements for his uncle. Living with the constant danger of Indian attack, he spent two harrowing and solitary years on his own. During this period, his administrative skills grew, as did his doubts that as a crypto-Jew, he could protect himself from attempts by civil authorities to usurp power on the competitive frontier. This feeling was reinforced when his uncle was arrested in 1586 for mistreating the Indians, one of many trumped-up charges raised against the governor. Abandoning his hopes of succeeding his uncle, Luis rejoined his family and a good-sized crypto-Jewish community in Mexico City.

Despite official prohibitions, by means of bribes and counterfeited *limpiezas,* a significant number of Iberians of Jewish descent had emigrated to New Spain. For more than fifty years following the Mexican conquest in 1521, they lived there relatively unmolested. The Holy Office of the Inquisition commenced operation in Mexico City in 1571, but for the first decade it focused mainly on bigamists, blasphemers, and pirates. As the number of crypto-Jews increased

The Jews and the Indians

In the early years of the Spanish conquest, speculations about an aboriginal Jewish presence in the New World took hold. Spanish explorers and settlers encountering a large, well-organized native population warily pondered its origin. One unsigned manuscript, written in the early sixteenth century in Cuba and quoted by Friar Juan de Torquemada in *Monarquía indiana* (Seville, 1615), claimed that the West Indian languages were rife with Yiddish and Hebrew. Indians, like the Jews, he said, had long noses, guttural voices, shaven heads, and side curls. He noted that among other similarities, both peoples divided themselves into tribes; built temples; and practiced circumcision, marriage, divorce, and polygamy. He explained the disquieting "Jewishness" of the Indians by adding a new link to the chain of speculations on the whereabouts of the lost Israelites. After the ten tribes of Israel were uprooted by the Assyrians in 772 B.C.E., he theorized, they wandered through Asia, then walked across the Straits of Anían (Bering) to become the first dwellers on the American continent and the forefathers of the Indians.

Torquemada believed the manuscript had been penned by Friar Bartolomé de las Casas, the renowned author of *Brevísima relacíon de la destruccíon de las indias*, and other works. Whether las Casas was the for-

Manasseh ben Israel was an eminent seventeenth-century Portuguese-Dutch rabbi, scholar, and author of many works, including Esperança de Israel, *a tract purporting that the lost Israelites were the first inhabitants of the North American continent. From* Hope of Israel *(London, 1652). Courtesy, Library of Congress, Washington, D.C.*

Mordecai Manuel Noah (1785–1851) was an American Jewish journalist, playwright, office-holder, and ardent Ten Tribist. In 1825 Noah tried to start a Zionist colony in New York for the Jews and their supposed descendants, the American Indians. Courtesy, American Jewish Historical Society, Waltham, Massachusetts

mulator of what became known as the Ten Tribes, or Indian Israel Theory, or that distinction belonged to another, the theory stuck. For many years, settlers throughout the Spanish New World noted similarities between the Indians and the Jews, and scholars, principally friars, systematically gathered evidence and debated the theory in writings of their own. Hubert Hugh Bancroft paid tribute to the concept's popularity in *Native Races of the Pacific States* (San Francisco, 1886), noting, "The theory that Americans are of Jewish descent has been discussed more minutely and at greater length than any others." Bancroft then devoted twenty-five pages to discrediting works on the subject.

The Hispanic ethnohistorians fueled an already burning interest in the origins of the New World aborigines in western Europe and North America. From the mid-seventeenth through the nineteenth centuries, scholars, philosophers, and ecclesiastics studied Indian Israelism and employed their findings to promote various causes.

The renowned Portuguese-Dutch rabbi Manasseh ben Israel used Indian Israelism as a foundation for his *Hope of Israel* (London, 1652), a plea for the readmission of the Jews to England. English millennialist Thomas Thorowgood penned *Jews in America* (London, 1650) to help raise funds to send Christian missionaries to convert the (Jewish) American Indians. Elias Boudinot, once the president of the Continental Congress, composed *Star of the West* (Trenton, 1816) to hasten the Indians' return to their Jewish homeland. Mordecai Manuel Noah, noted Jewish-American journalist and playwright, in 1825 attempted to found in New York the first Zionist colony for Jews and what he believed to be their Indian descendants. Among the most zealous of the later Ten Tribists was Lord Kingsborough (Edward King) who expended his fortune—dying in a debtors' prison—to write and publish between 1831 and 1848 a magnificent nine-volume folio called *Antiquities of Mexico*. King analyzed ancient Mexican paintings for new evidence supporting the theory.

The most far-reaching offshoot of the Indian Israel Theory was the work of Joseph Smith, founder of the Church of the Latter-Day Saints. In 1827, the then-youthful visionary—claiming the aid of the angel Moroni—discovered golden plates buried in a New York hillside. According to Smith, they were inscribed with a New World Bible prepared by Israelites and brought by them to the American continent. He read the ancient Egyptian script, asserted Smith, with the aid of a translating device he found with the plates. The contents, a description of the Israelites' journey to and mission in the New World, described in this ancient script, was published in 1830 as the *Book of Mormon*. Smith was murdered in 1844, but in 1847, his persecuted followers carried the belief that Israelites were the first inhabitants of the American continent into the far western wilderness and gave it a permanent home in their new Zion, and in Mormonism, now the faith of five million.

Mariana de Carvajal, convicted of Judaizing, was burned at the stake at an auto-da-fé in Mexico City in 1601 when she was twenty-nine. Illustration by P. Miranda, from Vicente Riva Palacio, El Libro Rojo *(Mexico, 1870)*

(to 20 or 25 percent of the population, according to one authority), so did the Inquisition's interest in ferreting them out. By the time Luis arrived in Mexico City in the middle of 1586, the Holy Office had organized a full-scale investigation of the secret Jews of that city.

In the heart of this active underground Jewish community, Luis's dedication to his faith bloomed. Eager to practice Judaism openly and aware of the increasing danger from the Inquisition, Luis and his brother Baltasar decided to flee to Italy. But their plan was thwarted when their sister Isabel was denounced as a Judaizer and, on March 13, 1589, was arrested. The information that Isabel gave under torture prompted the Holy Office to put her uncle, the governor; her brother Luis; her mother, Doña Francisca; and her sisters Catalina and Leonor in the Inquisitional jail.

After a hard-fought trial, in 1590 the governor was convicted of harboring Judaizers and was sentenced to one year in prison and six years in exile. The proud conquistador died before the year was out. The jailed Rodríguez Carvajal family refused to answer Inquisitors' questions until the screams of Doña Francisca, subjected to the rack and cords, broke their determination. In his confession, young Luis named as crypto-Jews 116 people who had come from Spain with his family to settle Pánuco.

In the next four years, Luis completed his training for martyrdom. As penance, the court assigned him to work in a hospital and in a monastery Indian school where he had access to a well-stocked religious library. As his knowledge of Judaism grew, so did his commitment. He secretly renamed himself to suit his emerging identity: Joseph ("he who was sent to aid his captive people") Lumbroso ("bearer of light"). Under this appellation he wrote *Autobiography of Luis de Carvajal, the Younger,* which, along with his letters and will, are the foremost documents of Jewish persecution in colonial Mexico.

After the family was released in late 1594, Luis/Joseph, ablaze with religious fervor, openly proselytized in crypto-Jewish circles. Three months later, he, his mother, and three sisters were rearrested and, as *relapsos,* sentenced to death. On December 8, 1596, in the Grand Square in Mexico City at an auto-da-fé, the largest to date in New Spain, Luis; Doña Francisca; Doñas Isabel, Catalina, and Leonor were burned at the stake. Mariana, another sister, was saved for the auto-da-fé of 1601. Anica was executed at an auto-da-fé in 1649. Leonor, the daughter of one of the martyred sisters (Catalina) became a Catholic and several of her descendants took holy orders. Two brothers escaped—Baltazar to Italy, Miguel to Salonica. Friar Gaspar, the oldest brother, did penance for harboring Judaizers.

The drive against the crypto-Jews raged for the rest of the seventeenth century. It is not known precisely how many victims it claimed. One leading authority, historian Seymour B. Liebman, has noted that throughout the Spanish colonial period: "The number of Jews who were burned at the stake are almost one hundred, and a like number died or committed suicide in the Inquisition cells, and a third hundred were consigned to the galleys for periods from three to ten years." According to Liebman, approximately three times that number were tried. Most confessed and did penance; a few were judged innocent and released. Numerous others fled to the West Indies and to the British-American colonies or to the remote southern or northern provinces of New Spain. Of those who went north, an unknown number trickled into what is now south Texas. (Archivist-historian Richard G. Santos completed his 1973 study with the conviction that descendants of these early crypto-Jews number in the hundreds, if not in the thousands in south Texas.)

Some of the persecuted also settled in New Mexico after the Spaniards founded their first feeble settlement there in 1598. For the next eighty-two years, civil and ecclesiastical authorities in the tiny new communities fought each other for dominion. On the losing end of some of those bitter engagements were New Mexican settlers denounced as Jews or Judaizers. Among the first was Juan Gómez Barragan, who came to New Mexico as a soldier-escort between 1613 and 1616. In 1626, he was arrested by the Holy

A seventeenth-century cartographer's rendering of the southern section of North America, then in the possession of Spain and France. Courtesy, Library of Congress, Washington, D.C.

Office and charged with speaking Hebrew. He died in prison a year later.

Another was Francisco Gómez, a native of Portugal, who came to New Mexico in 1604. Father Angelico Chávez, author of *Early New Mexican Families,* called him "the most outstanding military official in New Mexico during his lifetime." Gómez's Portuguese origins (numerous Portuguese of Jewish descent came to New Spain after 1580) and his criticism of certain clerical policies aroused the suspicions of his associates. "It is very possible that he was of Jewish extraction," noted Chávez. His soldier son, Francisco Gómez Robledo, born in Santa Fe in 1628, was similarly suspected.

Gómez Robledo played a minor role in the most well-examined Inquisitional case involving early New Mexicans. The leading figures were Don Bernardo López de Mendizával, governor of New Mexico from July 1659 to August 1661; his wife, Doña Teresa de Aquiler y Roche; and four of his soldiers, including Gómez Robledo—all had been accused of Judaizing and other crimes. This convoluted episode is hard to decipher even with the help of *Troublous Times in New Mexico* by France V. Scholes, Inquisition historian. What follows, consequently, is but a rough map through a labyrinth of slander, bribery, embezzlement, fornication, and Indian exploitation, all of which were endemic to the unstable northern frontier in that period.

López came to the governorship at the age of forty with suitable credentials. Well educated in the arts and canon law, he was a native of Chietla in southern New Spain and a member of a family well known for government service. López's reputation, however, was blemished. His maternal grandmother had been tried as a Judaizer and sentenced by an Inquisitional judge. The future governor had defended himself successfully against a similar charge in 1648.

As mayor of Guaiacocotla, New Spain, López, a bellicose man, had enraged the Catholic clergy by challenging their methods of Indian administration. Traveling to Santa Fe to assume the governorship, López quarreled about the treatment of the Indians with the Church custodian heading the caravan. The custodian later would claim that López intended from the start to usurp his jurisdiction over both his order and the entire Hispano-Indian community. The two were archenemies before López was installed as governor on July 11, 1659.

Early in his administration, López lost support among the New Mexican colonists by raising the Indians' wages from a half *real* to one *real* a day. He then incensed the clergy by ordering them to pay the Indians wages, though he himself paid his workers nothing. The churchmen, in turn, accused López and his wife, Doña Teresa, of religious laxity. Don Bernardo responded by denouncing one friar as a murderer, another as a thief, and yet another as a fornicator and by mocking members of the clergy and their religious practices before the Indians.

Charges and countercharges mounted, until the central authorities in Mexico City interceded. As a result, López was replaced as governor in August 1661. His successor, Diego de Peñalosa, offered to overlook the complaints against López for 10,000 pesos. But López refused to pay the bribe, assuming he would be vindicated of the charges. The new governor responded by placing López and his wife under house arrest and ordering servants and guards to report on their "Jewish" domestic practices.

An *audiencia,* an official hearing, in Mexico City assessed the evidence sent from Santa Fe and found López guilty of accepting bribes, having Apache males killed and seizing their women and children to sell, confiscating livestock for export, shaming friars, forcing women to submit to improper advances, oppressing both ecclesiastics and laymen, and other crimes.

On October 6, 1662, shackled and bellowing obscenities, López was locked in a cart in a departing caravan. His destination was the Inquisitional prison in Mexico City, where he had been summoned to answer to charges of Judaizing and other offenses. Also accused, and traveling with him, were his wife and four of his soldiers, including Francisco Gómez Robledo.

When he arrived in Mexico City, Don Bernardo was too ill to respond to the 257 charges against him, 30 of which dealt with religious laxity and 4 with Jewish practices. But Doña Teresa fought the allegations and attempted to indict their accusers. Her husband died in jail on September 16, 1664, and was buried in unconsecrated ground in the corral of the secret prison of the Holy Office. Doña Teresa, however, continued a long and reckless battle to disprove the Jewish charges. The proceedings finally were suspended on December 19, 1664, and after having been held in jail for twenty months, Doña Teresa was released.

Of the four soldiers tried, the most likely to have been of Jewish descent was Francisco Gómez Robledo. At the time of his arrest, he was thirty-three and *sargento mayor* of the local militia, a position his father had held. Like his father, he supported the civil authorities in their controversies with the clergy. Gómez also assisted the jailed governor in his war with the friars and—significantly—counseled him to allow the Indians their native ceremonies.

Gómez's trial began on May 16, 1663. Of the eighteen charges against him, the core articles were those accusing him of being a Jew. Witnesses testified that his father, who had arrived in Santa Fe only a few years after the town was founded, was similarly suspected, as were his wife and children. One of Gómez's brothers, it was reported, bore the nickname "Colita" because he had a small, demonic (Jewish) tail, spotted while he was swimming. During the trial, the sergeant was examined by a physician and was found to have circumcisionlike scars on his penis. Gómez was able to convince his Inquisitors that the scars were the results of ulcers, and with equal skill, that he and his entire family were unblemished Catholics.

In 1680 the New Mexican Indians, fed up with the oppressive and inconsistent Spanish rule, staged the Pueblo Rebellion, which temporarily displaced the Spaniards. The Spanish did reconquer the territory between 1692 and 1694, but thereafter the settlers were too occupied with pacifying the Indians and guarding against intrusion from the north by other nations to bother with the discreet crypto-Jews among them, many of whom in time forsook their ancient faith. No new "Jewish" cases emanated from New Mexico in the eighteenth century. The last edict prohibiting the entry of Jews into New Spain came from the colonial Holy Office on September 16, 1802, and probably was partially inspired by the per-

ceived threat of foreigners on the California coast and in the northeastern borderlands.

By 1800, a total of twenty-five thousand Americans, including a handful of Jews, were living in Spanish Louisiana and Texas as illegal aliens. The Spaniards, being too weak to eject the Americans, ceded Louisiana to the more powerful French on the condition that they never allow the territory to fall into the hands of an English-speaking government. Three years later, France broke the pledge and agreed to the Louisiana Purchase, giving the United States forty-three-thousand square miles of land between the Mississippi River and the Rocky Mountains.

While the expansion-minded Americans were inclined, and probably would have been able, to evict the Spanish from their colonial territories, they were spared the trouble by the colonists of New Spain. Determined to be freed of foreign rule, the Mexicans revolted. The revolution commenced on September 16, 1810, with an insurrection led by Father Miguel Hidalgo y Costilla. It came to an end on September 27, 1821, when Colonel Augustín de Iturbide liberated Mexico City from the Spaniards, only to recapture it less than a year later, self-styled as "Emperor" Iturbide.

After the revolution, the Republic of Mexico cautiously opened its doors to strangers, hoping to develop its empty territories as the United States had done, with immigrants and foreign capital. Between 1821 and 1846, Jews entered the Mexican West—Texas, New Mexico, and California—not as banished and despised members of Hispanic society but as Americans or as the Europeans who came with them. The Jews, like their non-Jewish companions, were registered guests, welcome as long as they complied with the many regulations governing their residence. Indeed, when conflicts did erupt, they were despised not as "Judíos" but as aggressive and usurpative "gringos."

The first Jews settled in east and central Texas in the 1820s and 1830s. They were forerunners of the Jewish pioneers who made their homes further west several decades later. They, like the other Americans who settled in Mexican Texas, set out in good faith, intending to abide by the laws governing their residency. But cul-

Noted for his sense of humor, Adolphus Sterne would amuse his friends by imitating an auctioneer, bidding off articles in rapid English, German, French, Spanish, and several Indian dialects in which he was fluent. During one unusually dull session of the Texas legislature, Sterne—in derision of the proceedings—rose and solemnly made a speech in Choctaw. Courtesy, Hoya Memorial Library & Museum, Nacogdoches, Texas

tural differences quickly created discord between the Hispanics and the Yankees, living side by side for the first time. Once the gringos became sufficiently powerful, fighting with the "greasers" appeared simpler than trying to get along with them.

The first Jew in Texas is said to have been Samuel Izaacs. He came with Stephen Austin's original party in 1821, and his name appears among "The Old Three Hundred," Texas's "Mayflower" immigrant list. Izaacs received one land grant in Fort Bend County from the Mexican government and a second in Polk County from the Republic of Texas for his services in the fight for Texas independence. In 1831, Abraham Cohen Labatt, a Sephardic Jew of New Orleans, visited Velasco, a settlement on the Gulf of Mexico, and found there two Jewish merchants: Jacob Henry from England and Jacob Lyons from South Carolina.

Between 1826 and 1836, a clique of German Jews gathered in Nacogdoches, a small, cattle-raising settlement between the Neces and Sabine

rivers. Living there during, or immediately after, the Mexican period were physician Joseph Hertz and his brother, Hyman, a merchant; as well as Simon M. Schloss, Simon Weiss, Albert Emmanuel, and Sam Maas—all also merchants.

Possibly the most colorful of this group was Adolphus Sterne, whose two-volume diary provides a valuable depiction of pioneer life in East Texas. Born in Cologne in 1801 of a Jewish father and Lutheran mother, he migrated to the United States in 1817 and to Nacogdoches in 1826. Bright, multilingual, and gregarious, Sterne threw himself exuberantly into frontier life and, with political acumen, switched sides as required.

One of his first actions was to support a group of Americans in the Fredonian Rebellion, an early Texas uprising. The Mexicans captured him selling munitions to their enemies and sentenced him to death. Sterne waited in chains for two weeks while the International Order of Masons negotiated his pardon. Before his release, he was required to swear allegiance to the Mexican government, after which Sterne became a valued citizen in Mexican Nacogdoches, serving as mayor, councilman, and city treasurer. In 1828 he married Rosine Ruff of Natchitoches and raised a family. When the Texas revolution erupted, Sterne circumvented his promise not to bear arms against Mexico by going to New Orleans, where he raised funds and recruited troops for the American cause. After Texas became a state in 1845, he served as a member of both houses of the legislature and was a state senator when he died in 1852.

Chafing under the restrictive Mexican rule as much as their fellow Texans, other Jewish settlers were fiery partisans in the fight for Texas independence. One, Dr. Moses Albert Levy, originally from Richmond, Virginia, raised a contingent of sixty-six young men in New Orleans to aid in the "Texian" cause. Levy was assigned the post of surgeon-in-chief of the Volunteer Army. From his battle station he wrote to his sister describing the sentiments that inspired him, and surely others, to join the conflict:

It is now a few weeks since I last address [sic] and I do it now with feelings keenly alive to this conviction that I am engaged for the first time in my life in the real, stirring, and precarious struggle of man with

Left: *Nathan Benjamin Appel (1828–1901), a native of Hochstadt, Germany, pioneered first in the New Mexico Territory and then in the Arizona Territory. In 1863 he served as a delegate to the First Arizona Territorial Legislature. Appel earned his living as a merchant and as a freighter until the railroads arrived in the 1880s and put him out of business. He was Tucson chief of police from 1883 to 1884, then moved to Los Angeles where he was a popular court bailiff. Courtesy, Arizona Historical Society, Tucson*

Right: *Henri Castro angered almost everybody involved in the promotion of his west Texas settlement. He considered himself a European aristocrat, maintaining a regal distance from the daily struggles with the raw land. On one occasion, when a rainstorm drenched Castroville, he wrote, "Even I was wet." Courtesy, Barker Texas History Center, University of Texas, Austin*

man, & should I succeed, I shall at once be elevated to such a standing in society as must ensure me independence aye even a fortune, & an immortalized name. Should we fail, my life falls a sacrifice to outraged liberty.

Under the command of Colonel Ben R. Milam, on December 4, 1835, three hundred men, including Levy, attacked the Alamo, a San Antonio mission and fortress. The physician later described their hard-won victory:

After a regular storm of five days and nights duration, during the whole of which the enemy kept up incessant firing we forced them to surrender, our men fought like devils (even I fought). I worked in the

This illustration is from Commerce of the Prairies, *a classic, firsthand account of the early Santa Fe trade written by merchant Josiah Gregg (New York, 1844).*

ditches, I dressed the sick and wounded, I cheered the men, I assisted the officers in their counsels, for five days and nights I did not sleep that many hours, running about without a coat or hat, dirty and ragged, but thank God escaped uninjured.

The Alamo was retaken by Mexican forces on March 6, 1836, as they marched east to San Jacinto, where they finally were defeated by the Texians under General Sam Houston.

After the war, two hundred Jews, a number of them proud veterans, had settled in Texas and would struggle to see it annexed to the United States. None cut a wider swath than Henri Castro, a French Jew who had responded to General Houston's pleas for financial aid during the fight for independence. In 1842 Houston offered Castro a tract of land between San Antonio and the Rio Grande.

The grant was situated in an arid, danger-infested Indian stronghold. With glowingly descriptive maps and pamphlets, Castro attracted to his colony an initial 700 settlers (eventually increased to 5,000), principally from Alsace Lorraine, and the bordering German provinces. During the first crucial year, Castro spent

$150,000 to house and feed the newcomers and supply them with implements for farming, viticulture, and a livestock industry. When his contract expired in 1847, Henri was living in the first settlement, called Castroville. By then, his large personal resources and those of his wife were exhausted. For his colonizing efforts and expenditures, Castro had expected to receive half the land awarded each colonist. But the state of Texas overruled Castro's claim and granted all the acreage to each of the 2,210 colonists still in residence. Castro received 38,400 acres, worth approximately ten cents each at the time. A more lasting reward came posthumously. In 1876, in recognition of his pioneering contribution, Texas officials named a Panhandle county, Castro, in his honor.

Mexican authorities had permitted the first American trappers and traders to enter New Mexico in the early 1820s. From the outset, the welcome was provisional. Minute regulations governed their arrivals and departures, the number and kinds of animals trapped, the type of merchandise sold, and the customs duties paid. (Bribes were customary and off-the-record.) Despite these substantial obstacles, the Americans kept coming—trappers in decreasing, traders in increasing numbers.

During the golden era of the Santa Fe trade, between 1821 and 1841, hundreds of itinerant merchants transported millions of dollars' worth of manufactured goods from the United States into Mexican territory. While profit was their main motive, there were other benefits as well. Westward trails, first to New Mexico, then to Chihuahua and California, rapidly improved, as did techniques for transporting large cargoes long distances in covered wagons. Traveling mile by mile through the territory, Americans saw how feebly governed the Mexican West was. The more familiar they became with the potentially rich and sparsely inhabited land, the more undeserving its rulers appeared. Before long, they were as covetous of New Mexico as the Yankee traders and farmers in California or the American missionaries and farmers in Oregon were of those choice regions of the Far West. By the mid-1840s, a strong political faction had picked up this acquisitive impulse and was promoting it as the nation's manifest destiny.

It is impossible to say how many Jews were among these traders. Some undoubtedly concealed their identities in a Hispanic country where the word "Jew" had been for centuries synonymous with "criminal." Some names drawn from church records listed by Father Angelico Chávez in *New Names in New Mexico, 1820–1850*, during those years hint at a discreet Jewish presence: Blumter, Prussia; Framel, Missouri; Fuchs, United States; Simon Levi, origin unstated; Mayer, Germany; Newman, origin unstated; Rubin, New York; and Sanserman, France.

There are descriptions of the Santa Fe Trail that suggest the presence of Jews, too, although none are named. In *Commerce of the Prairies*, Josiah Gregg wrote of a thirty-four-man caravan leaving Independence, Missouri, in the spring of 1839 with "representatives of seven distinct nations, each speaking his own native language." Among the immigrants, he noted a tailor, a silversmith, and a German peddler, who were ready to travel a thousand miles "in the hope of doing the 'Spaniards,' as the Mexicans are generally styled in the West, out of a little surplus specie."

It is possible the tailor mentioned was Jacob Frankfort, who was almost certainly a Jew. Frankfort was living in Taos, New Mexico, in 1841, where he was identified as thirty-one, a bachelor, and a native of Germany. Throughout his stay in New Mexico, he remained well behaved and unattached; his name appears in

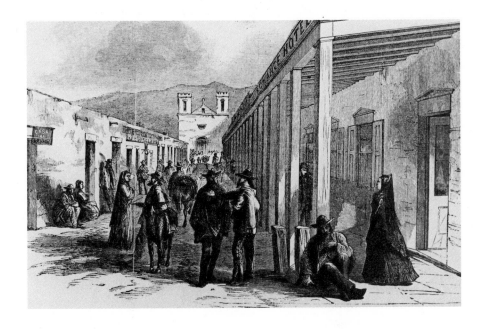

In 1866 San Francisco Street in Santa Fe was lined with hotels (the Exchange Hotel is on the right); stores selling groceries, clothing, furniture; and blacksmiths', carpenters', and saddlers' shops. Most crowded of all were the saloons and gambling halls where faro and monte games were in progress day and night. Drawing by Theo. R. Davis, from Harper's Weekly *(April 21, 1866)*

This drawing of the town of Los Angeles was executed in 1853. Courtesy, The Bancroft Library, University of California, Berkeley

neither Church nor civil records. He may be imagined stitching garb for a few well-to-do New Mexican ranching families, although it is more likely he trapped or traded. About Frankfort's departure from New Mexico there is no need to speculate. He left hastily in September 1841 with other non-Hispanic Taos residents thought to be conspiring with a party of Texans to seize control of New Mexico. The group, joined by an eight-man scientific expedition and three Mexican families, formed the historic Rowland-Workman party, the first of its kind to travel overland from New Mexico to southern California. They arrived in Los Angeles on December 12, 1841.

Unusually well outfitted, well provisioned, and well led, its members were also uniquely well educated. Among the forty travelers were two physicians, two prosperous traders, a naturalist, a mineralogist, an engineer, a musician, a gunsmith, and a tailor—Frankfort. Two members of the party left descriptions of the journey. Both writers mentioned Frankfort, but nothing he did or said excited further comment.

Of a flamboyant Prussian Jew named Albert Speyer, however, quite the opposite was true. His swashbuckling style and large-scale, sometimes controversial business practices earned him a prominent place in the diaries and reminiscences of his trail companions.

Speyer operated on the Santa Fe Trail and throughout Mexico as early as 1843. His confidence and the scope of his enterprises have been linked to the resources of the House of Speyer, an important international banking firm, although no connection, other than familial, has been established. The most famed of his numerous exploits in the Mexican West took place during the turbulent days at the opening of the Mexican War in the spring of 1846.

Speyer at the time was in Independence, Missouri, preparing for his spring trip down the Santa Fe Trail. More than the usual number of traders were similarly engaged. On May 15, 1846, the *Daily Missouri Republican* reported: "Nearly double the number of goods will be taken out this year to any previous year. It is thought that upwards of four hundred wagons will leave Independence for Mexico this year, and they may be safely set down at four thousand dollars [worth of merchandise] per wagon." The reason soon became apparent. President James Polk, overriding widespread opposition, had mustered an army to conquer the Mexican West. The additional traders were there to provision part of that force: General Stephen Watt Kearny's "Army of the West," which was preparing to invade New Mexico and Chihuahua.

Speyer's twenty-five wagons hastily de-

deliver his controversial cargo and sell off his more than $100,000 worth of goods before the traders in Kearny's train got to Mexico with their postconquest and duty-free merchandise.

Moving as swiftly as mule-drawn wagons could through summer storms, steep sand hills, and trade stops, the Speyer party arrived in Penol, forty miles north of Chihuahua City, on August 25. There they were accosted by Mexican forces who relieved them of the two wagons of weapons and then disarmed and jailed the entire party.

During his six weeks' imprisonment, the single-minded trader repeatedly petitioned Mexican authorities for his release, eager to get to San Juan de los Lagos, Jalisco, in time for the annual pre-Christmas fair. The government finally freed him on the condition Speyer would dismiss his American drivers and hire Mexicans. Speyer agreed, and his wagon train, carrying one hundred tons of goods, arrived in San Juan on November 27 in time for the fair. After selling all of his merchandise, he reloaded the wagons with Mexican goods—mainly silver curios and sugar—and returned to Chihuahua.

Several days after he arrived, American troops led by Colonel Alexander W. Doniphan entered Chihuahua City. Speyer was detained and ordered to answer for the weapons he had delivered to Governor Trías and for the American wagoneers he reportedly had abandoned. Trader James Josiah Webb, who was traveling with him, reported:

Mr. Speyer kept "open house" and entertained liberally. Whist parties with wine were held every night in his rooms, and many articles of bric-a-brac which he had bought at the fair disappeared from his shelves. And after a couple of weeks he was tried before a court-martial and honorably acquitted.

While the exceptional Albert Speyer followed profit on the Mexican side of the border, a few Jews were among the American forces that waged the campaign to take the Mexican West. Some were with the long supply and merchant trains. At least one, and probably others, served with the volunteer soldiers—farm boys or immigrants attracted by the promise of free land and wages of ten dollars a month.

parted on May 22, before most of the other traders, partly because he was carrying secret cargo— two of his wagons contained Yager rifles and matching ammunition ordered the year before by Angel Trías, the governor of Chihuahua. When Kearny learned the contents of the two wagons kept mysteriously apart in the Speyer train, he sent a detachment of dragoons to overtake the trader and seize the Mexico-bound weapons. Aware he was being pursued, Speyer ordered his men to drive the mule-drawn wagons at top speed. Covering eight hundred miles in thirty-eight days, the trader's party eluded the soldiers and arrived in Santa Fe early in July. By then, the main body of the American invasion force had left Fort Leavenworth, Kansas. As described by soldier William E. Connelley, ". . . long files of cavalry, gay banners fluttering, and the canvas-covered wagons of the merchant train glistening like banks of snow," headed toward New Mexico. New Mexico's Governor Manuel Armijo reacted at once to the news that "a serpentine line as far as the eye could see" was traveling his way. He charged Speyer an unprecedented $750 per wagon in duties and unloaded his own merchandise on the Chihuahua-bound trader for cash in case he (the governor) was forced to flee.

Speyer started south at once, determined to

Ever embroiled in controversy, Albert Speyer took his Far West trading profits to New York. There, established as a gold broker, he became involved in the 1869 conspiracy with Jay Gould, James Fisk, and other tycoons to corner the national gold market. Amidst curses, death threats, and physical abuse on the trading floor, Speyer continued to make inflated bids for any remaining gold. When the scheme collapsed on Black Friday, September 24, 1869, and the price of gold plummeted, Speyer was a mocked and ruined man. Gould and company denied any connection with Speyer's buying spree. Courtesy, American Jewish Archives, Cincinnati, Ohio

Bernard Latz served little over a year as an army private under Colonel Alexander W. Doniphan. Latz came to the United States from Posen, Prussia, in 1842 and was working in St. Louis, Missouri, when Kearny issued a call for volunteers. Latz had a horse—not a good one (he had to abandon it in Mexico) but good enough to qualify him as a private in Doniphan's First Regiment of Missouri Mounted Volunteers. The unit left Fort Leavenworth on June 22, 1846, traveled to Bent's Fort, then to Santa Fe for the bloodless capture of New Mexico's capital on August 18. On orders from Kearny, they spent two more months in Navajo country trying to negotiate treaties with the Indians. After numerous sorties, a few casualties, and much talk, Doniphan gave up and set out with his restless men and grumbling merchant train for Chihuahua, a city of ten thousand and their prime target. Capturing the capital of Chihuahua Province, on February 28, 1847, proved easier for Doniphan than maintaining peace among the conquerors.

He finally pleaded for orders to return home, asserting that his men "despised all carefulness, all order, and all restraint."

By the time Latz was discharged with his regiment in New Orleans on June 22, 1847, he had traveled fifty-five hundred miles, mostly through barren and rugged terrain, subsisting on half rations and battling disease, hunger, bad water, hostile Indians, and quarrelsome comrades when not engaging with the enemy.

Latz settled in New Mexico and started an Indian trading post in San Miguel. He was quickly known as a man who dealt knowledgeably and fairly with the Indians. In the spring of 1851, on orders from Governor James Calhoun, Latz brought six chiefs of the Jicarilla and Mescalero Apache tribes to discuss a permanent peace treaty with the governor. Several months later, he embarked on a more venturesome expedition further west. The noted New Mexican Franz Huning,

Solomon Jacob Spiegelberg founded Spiegelberg Brothers in Santa Fe in 1846, then encouraged his younger brothers to join him. Painting by Constant Mayer; courtesy, Museum of New Mexico, Santa Fe

The Spiegelberg brothers spent fifty years in territorial New Mexico as merchants and bankers. Pictured here, from left to right, are Willi, Emanuel, Solomon Jacob ("S. J."), Levi, and Lehman Spiegelberg. Courtesy, Museum of New Mexico, Santa Fe

who had clerked for Latz, recalled in his memoirs that in the fall of 1851 he had accompanied his employer on an expedition to trade with the western Apaches, the Gilas Coyoteros, and the Pinalenos in the future Arizona Territory, "then a complete wilderness." Latz remained a southwestern trader and adventurer until his death in June 1864. *The New Mexican* eulogized him as a man insensible to fear and danger.

Two other young Jewish immigrants—both later well-known in the Far West—launched their New Mexico mercantile careers during the Mexican War. A decade later, both were gone: one to a raw new settlement plagued by hostile

Apaches, in what became the Arizona Territory, the other back to Europe and "civilization."

Nathan Benjamin Appel was born in 1828 at Hochstadt, Germany. He arrived in New York when he was sixteen and after a few months headed for St. Louis. Physically strong, intelligent, and genial, Appel was already fluent in French and German; he soon picked up English and Spanish. He had an opportunity to join Kearny's volunteer dragoons, Appel later wistfully recalled, but he lacked a horse. So he did the next best thing—he drove a wagon in a merchant train. When the New Mexico campaign ended, he went to work for the firm of Tully &

ESTABLISHED 1846.

SPIEGELBERG BROS.,

SANTA FE, · · NEW MEXICO,

(PALACE STORE.)

WHOLESALE MERCHANTS AND IMPORTERS

◄►—IN—◄►

GENERAL MERCHANDISE.

We offer special inducements to the trade, and invite Jobbers and Retail Merchants to examine our stock and prices.

Special Inducement given to Cash Customers.

This announcement was included in the 1882 Business Directory and Gazetteer of New Mexico *(Santa Fe, 1881). From the Rochlin Collection*

Ochoa, running trading posts, first in Santa Fe and then in Socorro, New Mexico Territory. Five years later, ready to start his own enterprise, he settled in Mesilla, New Mexico, where he opened a store in partnership with Charles Hoppin and in 1852 married a New Mexican named Victoria Torres. In 1858, Appel moved with his wife and two children to Tubac, on the Santa Cruz River, where a group of intrepid trailblazers had launched a silver-mining operation. The Appels remained in Arizona and were one of the territory's first American families.

The other young immigrant was Solomon Jacob Spiegelberg, the oldest of the ten children born to Jacob and Betty Spiegelberg of Westphalia, Prussia. S.J., as he was later known, was

twenty in 1846 when he arrived in New Mexico. Judge Joab Houghton later recalled his arrival:

About the commencement of the war in New Mexico, there came to this city a rosy-cheeked youth who sought and found employment in the mercantile house of E. Leitendorfer [Leitensdorfer] and Company of which firm I was at that time a member. This was Solomon Jacob Spiegelberg . . . as a clerk he was faithful, intelligent, energetic, and industrious; very soon acquired the language of the country, and ascertained its commercial wants. In the winter of 1847–48, General Price marched his army on Chihuahua [Colonel A.W. Doniphan was in command]. Jacob, thinking there would be an opening for a successful venture, much to the regret of his employer, left his situation. Upon closing his account, there were found just three hundred and sixty-five dollars due him . . . he had credit and obtained from a countryman of his in Santa Fe, an outfit of goods and transportation for the Mexican southern trade.

Appointed a sutler, at Fort Marcy, New Mexico, after the war S.J. had the best customer in the new territory—the United States Army—to help him launch his general merchandising firm. Once off to a promising start, he urged his younger brothers to join him. Levi arrived in 1848; Elias in 1850; and subsequently Emmanuel, Lehman, and Willi. S.J. returned to Europe in 1854 but remained an active partner in the business he founded. The other Spiegelberg brothers spent nearly fifty years in territorial New Mexico and achieved prominence in retail and wholesale merchandising, mining, real estate investment, and banking.

The few stories that have surfaced about Jews who reached far-off California during the Mexican period reflect the irresistible draw that territory—called a scenic paradise, a climatic wonderland, America's shining destiny—had on Americans and Europeans. The first Jew known to have lived on the Pacific Coast was Lewis Polock. Like many restless American youths in the 1830s, Polock went west in search of adventure and gain. Some of these young men tested their mettle, then settled into conventional manhood. For others, Polock included, the California fantasy hid an abrupt and grim end.

Polock was born in Philadelphia on February 14, 1819. His parents, Rebecca (Barnett) and Hyman Polock, natives of Amsterdam, Holland, married in London and emigrated to the United States in 1811, possibly with the assistance of Rebecca's uncle Aaron Levy, the founder of Aaronsberg, Pennsylvania. Lewis was the fourth of twelve children, four of whom died in infancy or early childhood. His father, a jeweler, was a pillar of the Jewish community. One son, Moses, became a noted book dealer—the first in the country to specialize in Americana. A daughter, Isabella, was a leader in Jewish charitable and religious educational work. Three sons strayed from this righteous mold, Lewis among them.

In 1837, when he was seventeen, Lewis left home without a by-your-leave for Nantucket, where he signed on the *Harvest,* an American whaler bound for California. In Yerba Buena—present-day San Francisco—he jumped ship. From late 1837 to the spring of 1840, he worked in the tiny port for several merchants and, as he later wrote, was "in a fair way to accumulate handsome property" when his "fond hopes and prospects" were abruptly blasted.

On April 9, 1840, Mexican authorities, fearing encroachment by foreigners, seized Polock and fifty or sixty others of the two hundred Americans and Englishmen in California. They were marched to Monterey to appear before Governor Juan Alvarado, who charged them with conspiring with an American indigent named Isaac Graham to take over California. The incident became known in diplomatic circles as the "Graham Arrest."

The prisoners vehemently denied the charge. Polock wrote:

A more absurd thing could not be imagined. The fact is they have long looked with envy on the foreigners and thought they were making money too fast. These people are not only very indolent but also ignorant and covetous and the foreigners were too persevering and industrious to live amongst them. They had long threatened to turn them out of the country and they conceived it a good time to put their threats into execution.

In Monterey, a visiting American attorney, Thomas J. Farnham, later a prominent Califor-

nia booster, promised to work to obtain their release. From Monterey, the men were sailed to Santa Barbara and incarcerated in crude quarters for another week before being taken to San Diego, where they were driven into the hold of the *Joven Guizpucoana,* which departed for San Blas, Mexico, on May 9. For ten days, the duration of the journey, they lay in enforced silence, chained to a bar in prone position. From San Blas they were marched fifty miles in blazing heat along a mountainous road to Tepic.

When they arrived, to their joy, they discovered Farnham had preceded them to Tepic and had arranged to have them released to the British consul until they had been cleared of the charges and remuneration claims had been filed. (It took eleven years for the Mexican authorities to make restitution. On April 15, 1851, Polock received $4,603.50, the full amount he requested for confiscated merchandise, personal possessions, and other losses.) The prisoners were allowed to leave on October 29, but Polock, ill at the time, remained in Tepic. Upon recovery, he went to work in a cotton mill there and reported to his family that he was doing well.

During the Mexican War, he and his brother Solomon turned up in Mexico City in the train of the American army at the Battle of Chapultepec, September 8, 1847, a crucial victory for the Americans.

As soon as news of the gold discovery at Sutter's Mill reached New Orleans, where Polock was then living, he speedily returned to California. He may have tried some mining—he was in Sonorian Camp in the San Joaquin District in August 1849—but gambling soon became his main endeavor. In October 1849 his brother Barnett, who had joined him in California, was shot dead on a San Francisco street by a belligerent stranger. Abraham Dyer, a friend of the Polocks, kindly lied in a letter to the family, saying Barnett had died of cholera. Nearly two years later, Lewis came to an equally disastrous and a more notorious end. The following story appeared in the *Alta California* on June 23, 1851, between columns that described the city's sixth horrendous fire:

Bell's Row (later Mellus's Row), at the corner of Aliso and Los Angeles streets, was the last known residence of Jacob Frankfort in Los Angeles. Also occupying spaces in the row in the 1850s were seven unmarried Jewish merchants: Abraham Jacobi (25) and Morris Michaels (19) from Poland; and Morris L. Goodman (24), Phillip Sichel (28), Augustine Wasserman (24), Felix Bachman (28), and Joseph Plumer (24), who were all from Germany. Courtesy, Southern California Historical Society, Los Angeles

A TERRIBLE AFFAIR—Last evening, about half past ten, a terrible affair occurred in a house of ill fame kept by Mary St. Clair in Merchant Street, just below the plaza. A man named Lewis Pollock [*sic*], a sporting man from Philadelphia, well known in this city, it seems was in bed with an occupant of the house, a girl named Jane Hurley. A man named Samuel Gallagher, who it seems had been living with the girl previously, went to the door and knocked. Pollock came out, and after some few words, in which Gallagher accused Pollock of having interfered with his rights in connection with the woman, Gallagher drew a pistol and shot Pollock through the head. This is the story that is told by inmates of the house. The brains and blood of Pollock were lying in a clotted mass upon the threshold of the room where he had been sleeping. Gallagher was arrested immediately and taken before the Vigilance Committee. The Coroner held an inquest upon the body, and the Jury returned a verdict that the deceased came to his death from the pistol shot wound inflicted by Samuel Gallagher.

Jacob Frankfort's life in early California was as tranquil as Polock's was tumultuous. He arrived in December 1841, eight months after the Graham Arrest. The antiforeigner furor had quieted by then, and Frankfort had no apparent trouble settling in Los Angeles (population eleven hundred). He was one of fifty foreigners, and probably the first Jew to reside in the City of the Angels. Frankfort kept almost as low a profile in Los Angeles as he had in Taos. A few notations in the Mexican civil records confirm that he was on hand and variously occupied. The Los Angeles Prefecture Records show the Mexican authorities employed Frankfort, possibly a merchant at the time, to appraise shipwrecked cargo. In the Mexican census taken in 1844, he reported himself to be a tailor and, as before, a bachelor.

Frankfort was still in residence the day the Mexican War reached Los Angeles (August 13, 1846), when Commodore Robert F. Stockton, Major John C. Frémont, and their men marched through the deserted streets, the army musicians blaring lively Yankee tunes. Whether tailoring or commerce, Frankfort's business almost certainly stood to benefit by the presence of the several thousand American soldiers who were stationed in the city after the Mexicans' capitulation in California on January 13, 1847. For a few months, streets and plaza were clogged with well-fed, well-disciplined men with money to spend enjoying Los Angeles's convivial social life and well-stocked stores. Apparently, improved business prospects did not overly excite Jacob Frankfort. He chose that eventful and potentially profitable period to take a year-long trip to Honolulu.

He may have tried living in San Francisco on his return. He bought a lot there in 1849 and joined the Society of California Pioneers but

Lewis Adler sat for this photograph in 1895, fifty years after his tumultuous wanderings. Standing on the left is Henry Bates, his nephew; on the right, his son Adam. Courtesy, Helen Shainsky, Sonoma, California

one year later was back in Los Angeles. On January 23, 1851, the first American census taker found him living and/or doing business in Bell's Row at the corner of Los Angeles and Aliso streets. No further record of Jacob Frankfort, alive or dead, in Los Angeles or elsewhere has been found.

More thoroughly documented were the adventures of another Jewish pioneer who arrived in pre-gold-rush California. He was born Ludwig Simon Draugott Adler in Düsseldorf, Germany, on February 7, 1820. His father, John Henry Frederick Adler, fought with the Germans during the Napoleonic Wars, hoping that victory would mean total emancipation for the Jews. Following a brief liberal period came a regime that restricted the Jews more than before. Lewis's father decided to seek another route to equality, one favored by a number of impatient German Jews—he converted to Christianity. Lewis, then nine, was baptized also and sent to a boarding school for converted Hebrew children in London. His schooling ended when he reached the age of fourteen and he became a cooper's apprentice.

At twenty-two, Lewis left Liverpool on a whaler. Harsh as the seaman's life was, for a few years he continued to ship out. When shipboard conditions became unbearable on one voyage, he and some shipmates jumped ship in Manila, only to be arrested and held in prison until the British consul arranged their release. Adler spent some time in the Hawaiian Islands and then went to Tahiti, where he ran a cooperage. He liked to tell how Queen Pomare, dressed in a green silk dress and wearing orange blossoms in her hair, used to drop into his shop early in the morning for a smoke from his pipe. A chief, impressed by the tall and attractive seaman, offered him his daughter, with an island and a herd of cattle thrown in. Adler politely refused. After the French took control of Tahiti, English citizens found themselves at a disadvantage, so Adler boarded the *Euphemia* and sailed to California. When he disembarked in Yerba Buena, the quiet little port had a population of two hundred, mostly foreigners. During his first year there, the flag changed from Mexican to American and the town's name from Yerba Buena to San Fran-

This 1846 view of Yerba Buena, renamed San Francisco a year later, was drawn when the quiet seaside village had a population of two hundred. Courtesy, California State Library, Sacramento

cisco, all with minimal attention from the residents. Adler had arrived with a thousand dollars and the energy of an enterprising firstcomer. He opened a small cooperage shop, but within three weeks gave it up to clerk at William Heath Davis's general merchandise store. After eight months, he moved on to manage the Bee Hive, a store owned by absentee Scottish investors. In the spring and summer of 1847, when the newly American town was subdivided and lot auctions were held, Adler dealt in real estate on behalf of his employers, expecting to share in the profits. His share not forthcoming, he undertook a lone venture. With two Hawaiians at the oars of a merchandise-laden longboat, Adler crossed San Francisco Bay and traveled up the Sonoma Creek to trade with various Indian tribes.

Trading turned out to be so profitable that in February 1848, Adler and Charles Meyers bought out G.F. Blume (possibly an even earlier Jew in the region) and undertook to supply Sonoma, Napa, and the surrounding country with "a large and choice selection of *Drapery, Grocery, and Iron Mongery Goods.*" The first advertisement for their Commerce House in Sonoma ran in the *Californian* on March 15, 1848, along with the first announcement of the gold discovery at Sutter's Mill (a coincidence that proved fortuitous for the new storekeepers). Situated between San Francisco and the goldfields to the north, Sonoma became a busy supply depot for gold seekers flooding into the area late in the spring of 1848. On June 11 of that year, the twenty-eight-year-old wandering ex-Jew showed signs of settling down. He bought a home site (where

Adlers would live for a century) and two days later revealed the reason for the purchase. On June 13, he married Ann Bones, a widow from Kentucky, five years his senior and the mother of three children. Shortly thereafter, in business on his own again, he was doing well enough to erect a new store in Sonoma, opposite the old Blue Wing Hotel. In the following year Lewis Henry was born, the first of the four children he would father, three with Ann and one with his second wife, Martha Winkle Adler.

Adler spent the rest of his long life enjoying the bounty of his surroundings. His long and circuitous journey from Düsseldorf Germany, to Sonoma, California, was eventually recorded by his son Adam under the straightforward title *Life of Lewis Adler by A. W. Adler, His Son.*

By 1849 hundreds of Jews had reached California and were laboring in the goldfields and supply centers. Native-born and naturalized American Jews were among them; others came directly from Europe. While some had advanced more than others, all were part of the long, slow march out of the ghettos of western and central Europe and the shtetls of eastern Europe. In varying degrees, each bore the imprint of centuries of European oppression: pogroms, expulsions, segregations, exploitative taxes, and barred occupations. As these firstcomers tested California, touted by boosters since the 1830s, Jews all over the world scrambled for their reports. Was it true that "Liberty, Equality, and Fraternity" flourished in a field of boundless opportunities? And if so, were Jews as welcome as non-Jews?

CALIFORNIA.

Golden Regions.

EMIGRATION TO
CALIFORNIA !

Do you want to go to California? If so, go and join the Company who intend going out the middle of March, or 1st of April next, under the charge of the California Emigration Society, in a first-rate Clipper Ship. The Society agreeing to find places for all those who wish it upon their arrival in San Francisco. The voyage will probably be made in a few months.— Price of passage will be in the vicinity of

ONE HUNDRED DOLLARS !
CHILDREN IN PROPORTION.

A number of families have already engaged passage. A suitable Female Nurse has been provided, who will take charge of Young Ladies and Children. Good Physicians, both male and female go in the Ship. It is hoped a large number of females will go, as Females are getting almost as good wages as males.

FEMALE NURSES get 25 dollars per week and board. **SCHOOL TEACHERS** 100 dollars per month. **GARDNERS** 60 dollars per month and board. **LABORERS** 4 to 5 dollars per day. **BRICKLAYERS** 6 dollars per day. **HOUSEKEEPERS** 40 dollars per month. **FARMERS** 5 dollars per day. **SHOEMAKERS** 4 dollars per day. Men and Women **COOKS** 40 to 60 dollars per month and board. **MINERS** are making from 3 to 12 dollars per day. **FEMALE SERVANTS** 30 to 50 dollars per month and board. Washing 3 dollars per dozen. **MASONS** 6 dollars per day. **CARPENTERS** 5 dollars per day. **ENGINEERS** 100 dollars per month, and as the quartz Crushing Mills are getting into operation all through the country, Engineers are very scarce. **BLACKSMITHS** 90 and 100 dollars per month and board.

The above prices are copied from late papers printed in San Francisco, which can be seen at my office. Having views of some 30 Cities throughout the State of California, I shall be happy to see all who will call at the office of the Society, 28 **JOY'S BUILDING**, WASH–INGTON ST., BOSTON, and examine them. Parties residing out of the City, by enclosing a stamp and sending to the office, will receive a circular giving all the particulars of the voyage.

As Agents are wanted in every town and city of the New England States, Postmasters or Merchants acting as such will be allowed a certain commission on every person they get to join the Company. Good reference required. For further particulars correspond or call at the

SOCIETY'S OFFICE,
28 Joy's Building, Washington St., Boston, Mass.

Propeller Job Press, 142 Washington Street, Boston.

Chapter Two
GOLD AND OTHER DISCOVERIES

When the gold fever reached Mackville, Kentucky, in the spring of 1849, twenty-six-year-old Louis Sloss, a "young man of small means and uncertain prospects" originally from Bavaria, was caught up in the excitement. He and a wheelwright named Smith swiftly departed for St. Joseph, Missouri, where parties were forming to make the overland journey to California. There they purchased places on the Turner and Allen Pioneer Wagon Train. The fare was $200, and the passenger list, recalled one traveler, included "sterling elements from the better families of the country." Among them were Dr. C. H. Swift and Dr. R. Frank McDonald, a native of Mackville, whose family Sloss knew.

Before the wagon train even departed, passengers began succumbing to the cholera epidemic raging at all the embarkation points on the Missouri frontier during the rainy spring of 1849. Of the 165 passengers, 42 died within the first month, including Sloss's companion, Smith. By the time the party arrived at Fort Laramie, Wyoming, the epidemic had abated.

No longer urgently needed, Dr. Swift and Dr. McDonald decided they could complete the journey more speedily on horseback and urged Sloss to go with them. Agreeing to settle disputes by a two-thirds vote, the trio set out together and quickly outdistanced the elegant wagon train. On their own, the men repeatedly withstood the cold hand of calamity, swimming their horses across the rushing South Platte River, eluding a

herd of stampeding buffalo, and traversing the seemingly endless Humboldt Desert, where mirage after mirage floated before their fevered eyes. The three entered California on July 18, 1849, near Nevada City, in the foothills of the High Sierra. Taking a nearly perpendicular road down the mountainside, they arrived in Steep Hollow at the base, where they delightedly encountered "a camp of miners with old-fashioned rockers working zealously to wash out gold." Sloss and the others wasted no time in joining them.

Many more Jews, traveling alone, in pairs, and occasionally in families or with mining companies, came to California by sea. In response to the gold mania, clipper ships and steamers, often barely seaworthy, were pressed into service. Some gold seekers sailed the Cape route, others took the land-and-sea Panama route. Both were long and horrendous trips from which few travelers emerged unscathed.

"If I had known before, nothing would have induced me to go," wrote Adolf Nachman in a diary during the tortuous, six-month trip around the Horn that began in Hamburg on May 15, 1850, and ended in sight of San Francisco on November 13. Traveling on the *Gellert*, a small vessel carrying eighty-eight German immigrants, the twenty-year-old youth had paid $200 for a place in steerage. Sensitive and homesick, he remained below in dark, crowded quarters, his space a bunk six feet long and eighteen inches wide. He refused to join the assertive steerage passengers, who "took every opportunity to get near the first class." Mealtime compounded Nachman's suffering:

From Fanny Palmer,
The Rocky Mountains:
Emigrants Crossing
the Plain, *Currier and
Ives Print, 1866; cour-
tesy, The Bancroft
Library, University of
California, Berkeley*

Peas, beans, lentils, salt cabbage and pork was all our meals consisted of; bad coffee in the morning and worse tea in the evening. Like prisoners, each of us had to take his plate to the cook to get it filled. Immediately afterwards, a tub with hot water was put down, the same tub that was used to cook the meat, and all the passengers had to wash their dishes in the same water.

The often wild and shark-infested sea terrified him: "Nobody can imagine how an immigrant feels during a storm. The wind is whipping the water against the ship which sometimes sounds like the explosion of a bomb, and we are almost waiting for the whole thing to burst." The *Gellert* required twenty-seven days simply to round the Horn, so huge were the waves. "What a life I have been living for three weeks," lamented the forlorn traveler.

More surprising than the misery and mishaps was the large number of Jewish travelers who arrived in San Francisco after months at sea—weary, sick, often nearly penniless—but nonetheless eager to get to work in San Francisco or rush to the goldfields. As early as the spring of 1849, "Israelites," detectable in numbers among the throngs of exotic strangers in San Francisco, were exciting comment. The same xenophobic eyes that saw "hideously tattooed New Zealanders; short, thick, clumsy Japanese; easy-principled, philosophical Germans; Italians

and Frenchmen of every cut and figure" noted "a particularly remarked number of thick-lipped, hook-nosed, ox-eyed, cunning, oily Jews."

Jews were also highly visible throughout the gold districts. The most readily identified were those who had recently arrived from Europe and were scratching out precarious livings as peddlers and marginal merchants. Their foreign appearance and alien customs inspired derision in some quarters. One observer described them as "the Jewish slopsellers" who "congregated at every new digging but never mined." Another, J. D. Borthwick, a noted chronicler, also recorded his displeasure:

I never saw a Jew lift a pick or shovel or do a single stroke of work . . . and in a country where no man, to whatever class of society he belonged, was in the least degree ashamed to roll up his sleeves and dig in the mines for gold, or engage in other kind of manual labor, it was a very remarkable fact that the Jews were the only people among whom this is not observable.

While neither universally held nor accurate, these acrimonious views are nonetheless valuable, since they confirm two important points. They show there was a significant number of Jews plying their European trades in gold rush California. Moreover, those who were acculturated, and many were, often were not perceived as Jews. They make clear as well that two age-old stereo-

"Between Decks on an Emigrant Ship—Feeding Time"; from "The Immigrant's Progress,"
Scribner's Monthly *(1877)*

types had survived the journey to far-off California: one, that of the "Jewish swindler," an enemy of honest work; the other of the "Christian toiler," daily cleansing himself in a bath of honest sweat.

One young forty-niner revealed the extent of his distaste for commerce, and presumably those who worked at it, in a letter to his sister shortly before he died of fever and exhaustion. W. Wilberforce Ramsey III wrote:

If I choose to keep a grocery, a gambling house, or any such low calling, I could make money faster and easier than by mining; but as I could not engage in such business without departing from the lessons of my youth, and sacrificing my principles of religion and morality, I cannot entertain any such a notion.

Most fortune seekers who rushed to California showed considerably more flexibility. The majority, Jews included, followed arrows of profit wherever they led, rushing from one field of endeavor to another, from site to site, and after the late 1850s, from territory to territory. When mining paid or held hope of paying, Jews mined, not as extensively or as overtly as they merchandised and banked—their names emblazoned on store signs and in advertisements—but in significant numbers and with considerable impact on the nascent far western mining industry.

Gold-district newspapers document their widespread mining ventures in California:

The Cohen claim at Vallecito made another whopping clean-up.

Nathan Rhine has one of the best ledges I have seen. He expended about $8,000 to develop it.

A Jew named Heyman and several others have . . . worked for some weeks some claims on the new ledge. These claims were jumped by a man named Moore.

On a vacant lot on State Street, Mr. A. Levy washed out eighteen pans of dirt on Thursday last and obtained $6.50.

Left: *Often derided and caricatured, the "Jew Peddler" journeyed alone from mining camp to camp and town to town, prey to the harsh elements and bandits. Mother lode newspapers in the 1850s regularly reported crimes against itinerant merchants: In Grass Valley a peddler named Jacobson lost $380 and his pack to two assailants; a teamster ran off with a wagon and $1,500 worth of merchandise belonging to J. S. Levy of Placerville; and at Chips Flat, Sam Rosenthal lost his money ($4,000), then his life. As soon as they were able, Jewish peddlers traded in the lonely and lethal roads of the mining districts for more permanent and protected occupations. Caricature from "The World in California,"* Hutchins *(Christmas, 1857); courtesy, California State Library, Sacramento*

Right: *News of a gold strike along the Fraser River in British Columbia reached San Francisco in the spring of 1858. Some twenty-five to thirty thousand gold seekers, mostly from California, rushed north only to discover the findings had been greatly exaggerated. Drawing by J. Ross Browne; from "A Peep at Washoe,"* Harper's New Monthly Magazine *(December, 1860)*

More evidence emanates from the biographies, diaries, letters, and reminiscences of California's pioneer Jews, prominent and obscure, who worked at mining. Among the most expressive was Bernhard Marks, born in Poland and reared in Medford, Massachusetts. Marks arrived in California eager to learn all he could about mining. "I came to see the gold in the process of being taken and I could not rest satisfied until I had my vague, uncertain notions replaced by more definite knowledge," wrote Marks in one of the eighteen letters he sent from California to his cousin Jacob Solis-Cohen in Philadelphia. While clerking in a small store in Placerville, a job he despised, Marks organized a public library and debating club. Hearing "ignorant hoosiers" allude sneeringly in debate to Jews as work shy, Marks wrote angrily, "I was . . . ambitious of giving them a practical demonstration that there were at least some Jews who were willing and able to work, when that proved as profitable as anything else."

Marks impatiently anticipated becoming a miner with calloused hands, a hickory shirt, cowhide boots, and a pick on his shoulder. A seasoned forty-niner took the eager tenderfoot on his first mining expedition in the summer of 1854. The excited neophyte wrote his cousin,

noting every item in his miner's pack, where they slept, and what they ate. In the following year, Marks became one-fifth owner of a promising gold mine at Spanish Hill. Convinced they were approaching a rich vein, he and his partners sank a shaft 180 feet deep, 70 feet of it through hard rock. Hoping to get to the ore before an adjoining company, they exhausted themselves working day and night. Shortly after the vein was uncovered, however, their tunnel caved in. Marks detailed these events and his losses— $3,000—during a subsequent three-month illness, but he was neither downhearted nor deterred. He wrote to his cousin: "We have already started from another direction to reach our best or richest ground and hope to compass it in about six to eight months. In the meanwhile, our pay will be modest, so that I will not be able to return east as soon as I expected." When the new attempt failed, Marks sold his share at a loss and left Spanish Hill but didn't abandon mining.

Marks's second big venture was only slightly less frustrating. In 1859 he entered a partnership with a seasoned prospector named Barrow, an uncle of his new wife, Cornelia. With his help, Marks formed the New York Tunnel Company and commenced drilling toward an even more promising gold deposit near Jamestown, in Tuol-

"Washing the Long Tom Near Murphys," from Harper's New Monthly Magazine *(May, 1859)*

umne County. A competing company, claiming a prior right, filed for an injunction and forced the New York Tunnel Company to cease work. Marks and Barrow sued. Over the next three years, the matter was tried in district court seven times, in the state supreme court three times. Just before the eleventh trial, Marks succeeded in having the case thrown out. After acquiring sole ownership and with the financial aid of new partners, he recommenced drilling. As soon as the tunnel was completed, the mine became profitable. In time Marks recouped his investment and sold out with a substantial gain. His notions no longer vague or uncertain, Marks's fascination with mining ended.

Equally vivid were the experiences of a down-on-his-luck baker-confectioner who left his wife and children in Pomerania and came to the New World to fight a personal war against poverty. Upon his return four years later, this Jewish Odysseus wrote *Interesting Accounts of the Travels of Abraham Abrahamsohn to America and Especially to the Gold Mines of California and Australia,* published in Ilmenau, Germany, in 1856. Detailed in the small volume are the battles he waged as a peddler, glazier, snack-shop merchant, *mohel,* or ritual circumciser, boardinghouse owner, and, for two intervals, as a gold miner.

Abrahamsohn arrived in San Francisco on April 8, 1851, and speedily set up a canvas-roofed store on the Long Wharf. He earned eighty-five dollars the first day and continued to do well until May 4, when a fire razed much of San Francisco. The erstwhile baker was left with nothing but ashes and advice. "Abrahamsohn, you have no other choice but to go to the mines," said a friend from Posen, who grubstaked him to warm woolen clothing, a pick, a spade, a pan, a strong, wide knife, and ten dollars in traveling money. As Abrahamsohn described it, "I knew well that digging for gold was not such an easy job, and that now I would have to do what in Germany the stone crushers do in the sweat of their brow. . . . But necessity forced me to bite into that sour apple."

Abrahamsohn became the tenth man in a group departing for the mines. Buoyed by colorful wildflowers during the day and by brilliant stars at night, his spirits rose. When the party arrived in Beavertown, a scattering of dwelling tents and tent stores flying American flags, Abrahamsohn found a claim. At the upper end of a mountain gorge (the lower one had already been dug), several hundred miners were at work. He picked his spot in accordance with the local law, a plot sixteen feet long by eight feet wide with another three feet for excavated earth. Emulating the others, he dug up the soil and wheelbarrowed it to a stream a half mile down a slope to wash it for gold.

The first day Abrahamsohn extracted enough gold to buy provisions at exorbitant prices. He cooked himself a meal and then, reveling in the magnificence of his mountain surroundings, lay down in the brush shelter he had made and slept until "the bushy partridges and larks" woke him.

Working in "temperatures glowing with heat," his eyes became bloodshot and his hands so swollen that he had to soak them in cool water at day's end. At night when he stretched out to rest, he slept fitfully. "Due to the large number of scoundrels and the unspeakable gambling fever," a vice to which the reminiscer quickly became addicted, "there was a great insecurity in the mines. . . . Everyday one heard about workers and merchants who had been killed, mostly in their sleep, and then robbed." At the end of three months in Beavertown defending himself against assaults and witnessing senseless murders (one victim fell dead in his arms), Abrahamsohn calculated his net profit: forty dollars.

Consequently, he abandoned the goldfields and went to work for a tailor in Sacramento while waiting for a better offer. That offer came from a countryman who knew Abrahamsohn was a certified mohel. The man promised him sixty dollars and traveling expenses to come to San Francisco to circumcise his new son. This work proved his most lucrative to date in America, for, as Abrahamsohn wrote, "Jews in that city rivaled the increase of their ancestors in Egypt." In six months he was able to open a boardinghouse on the Long Wharf with a French cook, three waiters, and a dishwasher. On April 1, 1852, another fire struck. Abrahamsohn, wiped out

This picture of Browntown, a mining camp on Althouse Creek (Oregon), was drawn by Sigmund A. Heilner, a native of Urspringen, Germany. Sigmund emigrated in 1853 and came west in 1855. He operated a dry goods store in Browntown, was a money lender, and was briefly a freighter. Courtesy, Heilner Collection, Sanford Heilner, Salt Lake City, Utah

again and desperate, gambled away his circumcision fees. Living contrary to his better instincts, he resolved to flee his bad luck in San Francisco's ubiquitous gambling saloons.

He eventually wangled passage to Australia, and there, alone in the remote reaches of the Bendigo goldfields, his luck changed decisively. As he recalled in his chronicle:

I arrived in a very swampy meadow, where there were many great water holes and puddles, and with my hands I lifted boggy directly into the pan. When I washed it out to my happy surprise, I found eight ounces of pure gold. . . . Now, who was happier than I?

He mined feverishly, warding off hostile Papus and concealing his "lucky strike" from newcomers. When his efforts at dissimulation failed and miners crowded in around him, Abrahamsohn took his earnings, $1,500, and moved on. At the Jurika mines near Pallad, he set up a bakery topped with a flag bearing the baker's insignia to attract the hungry miners. In eleven months, Abrahamsohn wrote:

I had amassed such a fortune that I was sure I could live with my family in the homeland free of financial cares. I had seen enough of roughness, wildness, and man in all his degradation. I felt the need to move again in a secure, quiet, companionable society.

From its inception, the California gold rush attracted superlatives—some glittering, some damning. It was the richest mineral rush in history: more than $500 million worth of gold was extracted during the first decade. It was the best attended, too: the population of California jumped from fourteen thousand to nearly four hundred thousand between 1848 and 1860. With 35 percent of that number from abroad, it was also the most international. Henry David Thoreau condemned its quick-money orientation and high crime rate as "the worst disgrace known to mankind," while Walt Whitman extolled egalitarian gold rush California as the long-awaited "true America."

By the late 1850s, "the poor man's gold rush," the only one, according to Carey McWilliams, where everyone who worked got something, was over. Thousands of gold seekers had by then already returned home to savor or suffer a slower, more predictable life. Others, unable or unwilling to go back to the lives they had left, responded to the new excitements that were erupting like geysers all over the Far West: in British Columbia (1858), Nevada (1858), Arizona (1859), Colorado (1859), Montana (1860), Idaho (1860), Utah (1860), and Wyoming (1868). Many of these early strikes were false alarms or superficial dig-

Traveling with Lieutenant John Bigelow's Tenth United States Cavalry Apache pursuit troop on June 5, 1886, was Frederic Remington, the famed western artist. Remington drew this sketch at the scene of the Goldbaum murder. From Lt. John Bigelow, Jr., On the Bloody Trail of Geronimo, *Westernlore Press (Los Angeles, 1968)*

gings. Others—the Comstock Lode in Nevada, Colorado's California Gulch–Leadville and Cripple Creek–Victor, Tombstone in Arizona, Deadwood-Lead in South Dakota, and Butte in Montana—were remarkably rich.

As the Far West's first major industry developed and spread, Jews were engaged in every phase, in every area, and at every level of mining. They worked alone or in small companies of itinerant prospectors and miners; they worked as engineers, assayers, and mine superintendents; as industrial mine workers; as independent mineowners and operators; and as developers, promoters, and investors. A few even fought their way to the elevated peaks of corporate mining, where the rewards were as tantalizing as the competition was ruthless.

Typical of that restless breed of lone itinerants responding to the call of each new strike was David H. Cohen. He arrived in San Francisco on June 16, 1852, on a cholera-ridden steamer; fifty-three of the six hundred passengers had died en route from Germany. Glad to be alive, Cohen headed for the goldfields in Jackson, Calaveras County. His complete ignorance of English impeded him only a little. He was soon earning from $80 to $100 a day in placer gold mining. Cohen worked in Jackson for three years, until a water shortage put him out of production. His next stop was La Porte, originally called Rabbit Creek, in the Sierra Nevada. Here the diggings were richer, and the water was more abundant. As soon as he had earned enough money, he gave up mining and bought a billiard hall. When, however, in the spring of 1858 twenty-five to thirty thousand gold seekers, mostly from California, hurried north to the Fraser River in British Columbia, Cohen could not resist. Six months later, with little to show for his trouble, he made the long, expensive trip back to La Porte.

When Nevada's Comstock Lode heated up in 1862, Cohen walked "over the hills," joining the tail end of a rush that in six months deposited twenty-five thousand people in Virginia City, Gold Hill, and the surrounding camps. Since the good claims were "all gobbled up," he moved on to Austin, Nevada, and the liquor business. By 1865 he was on the move again, to mine in Montana at Alder Gulch, at Virginia City, and then at Ophir City. Among the first to enter the stampede to McClellan Gulch, Cohen recorded the thirteenth claim. Mining and speculating in mining claims, by 1867 he was well enough cushioned to plan a wife-seeking journey to Germany.

Family life (he and his wife eventually had three sons) slowed him only a little. The Cohens spent six years in business in Nevada, first in Austin, then in Schellbourne. They moved back to Montana, however, when Butte, a prosperous placer camp in the 1860s, became a silver center in the 1870s. The erstwhile miner was prospering in Butte in tailoring, general merchandising, and the retail liquor trade when he was uprooted by one more gold strike—at Coeur d'Alene, Idaho, in 1883. Cohen rushed to Idaho and invested heavily in a camp called Eagle. When the diggings gave out, it became a ghost town, and Cohen became a big loser. Back in Butte, he

Adolph Sutro went to England in 1869 to raise funds to build the four-mile-long Sutro Tunnel in Virginia City, Nevada. While in London Sutro posed as a miner to publicize his mission. Courtesy, Nevada Historical Society, Reno

entered the "fruit and cigar trade in a small way" and roamed no more.

Some Jewish prospectors refused to give up. Unwilling to relinquish the hope of sudden wealth just over the hill, they continued prospecting despite repeated failures and perpetual danger. One such indefatigable seeker ultimately succumbed to the fate that lone prospectors feared most.

Born in Prussia in 1835, Marcus Goldbaum and his Bavarian-born wife, Sara, had lived in Kansas, Colorado, New Mexico, and California before they settled in Tucson, Arizona Territory, in 1869. They brought four children with them and had three more during their Arizona years. The family moved around the territory to Florence, Wickenburg—where in 1870 Goldbaum was justice of the peace—Harshaw, and then back to Tucson. Although a butcher by trade, Goldbaum frequently went out on prospecting trips in the southern Arizona Territory. During the summer of 1886, he was prospecting in the Whetstone Mountains when he was murdered by a band of Indians. His body was discovered by E. L. Vail, a soldier in a party led by Lieutenant John B. Bigelow, Jr., who was patrolling the area in pursuit of the famed leader of the Chiricahua Apaches, Geronimo, then on his last rampage. As Vail later recalled:

When I reached Apache Springs, close beside it I found the body of a man who had been murdered by the Indians, and as a grim joke, they had killed his little black dog and laid it by his side. They had also killed a large white burro which was still tied to its stake. The man's cabin nearby had been ransacked. Flour, beans, and everything Indians did not want were scattered about. I at once went back to the troop and told Bigelow what I had found. We all went to the Spring and the Lieutenant searched the pockets of the dead man and found a memorandum book, but it did not contain his name. We learned afterward that his name was Goldbaum and that he lived in Tucson and had been prospecting in the Whetstones.

When the craze moved beyond California, emphasis shifted from surface to hard-rock mining. New techniques had to be devised to gain access to the rich mineral veins that lay deep within the earth. Writing of the rush to the Comstock Lode in Nevada that began in 1859, mining historian Rodman Paul noted, "no California mining venture of the 1850s . . . had been conducted on such a flamboyantly large scale, and required such a rapid advance in engineering and technology."

If the Comstock was a testing ground for the new mining industry, Adolph Sutro was the embodiment of what a bold, self-taught engineer and financier could accomplish in this arena. His first achievement was an ore-extraction process. His second was an ingenious and costly four-

The Sutro Tunnel was a prodigious feat that was accomplished too late to be of use. Courtesy, The Bancroft Library, University of California, Berkeley

mile tunnel through Mount Davidson, upon whose eastern slopes the Comstock Lode was situated. The project took him a total of thirteen years to complete.

One of ten children, Sutro was born in Aachen, Prussia, in 1830. He remembered his birthplace as beautiful and peaceful and the Sutro household as commodious—thirty to forty rooms—harmonious, intelligent, and, in Jewish observances, liberal. A year or two after his father died in 1847, Adolph's widowed mother decided to sell the family's no longer profitable textile factory and move with her children to Baltimore. They arrived in October 1850. A week later Adolph set out for California, convinced he would have a better chance "in a new country than in a settled-up place." The open ambience of the Far West matched his own progressive spirit, and he quickly adapted. "Here it seemed to me like home," he later wrote.

By the time he was thirty, he was a successful tobacco merchant, had married Leah Harris, and was the father of three children, with three still to come. In 1858 he and his brother Gustave rushed to the Fraser River gold strike in British Columbia. Finding more seekers than gold, they quickly returned home. By July 1859, Adolph was caught up in a new excitement—the gold and silver strike in Nevada. He made an ex-

ploratory trip and wrote a report that was published in the *San Francisco Bulletin.* Returning to San Francisco, Sutro and a German chemist, John Randohr, developed a method for extracting silver from useless tailings. The pair then returned to Virginia City to build their reduction mill.

Once the ore-extraction process was in successful operation, Sutro attacked a more serious and extensive problem. Poor ventilation and accumulated water in mines slowed production along the lode and were a constant threat to the health and safety of the miners. Sutro came up with a practical solution—the Sutro Tunnel. His design called for a four-mile shaft to be drilled through Mount Davidson from Carson Valley to the Comstock Lode. According to Sutro, the passageway would provide ventilation and ease the hauling of ore and the draining of excess water from the mine. Some local owners of large mines opposed the tunnel, calling it a ploy to gain control of the Comstock. Sutro carried his cause to the United States Congress. Legislators were initially enthusiastic and granted him a charter; then, responding to political pressure, Congress denied him the promised financial aid. However, some miners and their pioneer unions supported the project, particularly after a Gold Hill mining disaster in 1869—the Yellow Jacket fire— claimed the lives of forty-five miners. Shortly after the blaze, Sutro staged a mass meeting at the Maguire Opera House in Virginia City. Eloquently assailing the bankers and mineowners who wanted to stop him, he enjoined the workingman audience to "crush out that hydra-headed monster, that serpent in your midst—the Bank of California." The miners supported him, subscribing $50,000 toward the construction of the tunnel. The rest of the funds eventually came from European investors.

The widely ballyhooed project was dedicated in August 1878, but ironically, it came too late. The Comstock Lode, the biggest silver strike in United States history, was by then in decline. Sutro benefited nonetheless. He sold out for $5 million in 1879 and returned to San Francisco with a reputation for inventiveness, persistence, and concern for workingmen.

As mining expanded, men with technological expertise and managerial ability were needed to supervise the increasingly large and often absentee-owned mining companies. Some Jews acted as mine superintendents, at times running several operations simultaneously.

Ben C. Levy, a native of France, arrived in Eureka, Nevada, in 1869, at the outset of a silver strike that launched the town and kept it prosperous for more than a decade. During the boom (the population peaked in 1878 at four thousand and included about one hundred Jews) Levy was active in several mining enterprises. He was superintendent of the K. K. Consolidated Mine, a member of the management of the Phoenix Mining Company, and later, superintendent of the Bowman Mine. He and his wife were also high-steppers in the desert town's surprisingly active social and political life and in its Jewish community. The silver began to wane in the 1880s, and by 1890, most of Eureka's population, including the Levys, had responded to the call of new mineral strikes elsewhere.

In 1880 Abraham Hyman Emanuel, who was a well-known mine superintendent, arrived in the silver-struck town of Tombstone, Arizona Territory, having already worked at mines in California and Nevada. Emanuel managed the productive Vizina Mine in 1880, and as a recognized mining authority, he also developed other claims during the boom years.

Elias Cohn of Colorado also had a long career as a mine superintendent. In 1910 he attracted attention with an ingenious method for repairing pumps at the bottom of flooded mines in Aspen. Cohn sent for two deep-sea divers from New York who for $100 per day went down to the floor of the flooded shaft and started up the

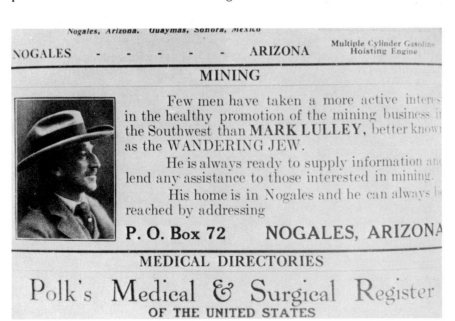

In 1875 Mark Lulley reopened the Alto mine, a southern Arizona mine worked by Spaniards in the seventeenth century. Around the turn of the century, he opened the Wandering Jew mine. Calling himself "Lucky" Lulley, the Wandering Jew, he advertised his services in business directories and mining journals. This advertisement appeared in the Arizona Business Directory *(Denver, circa 1900).*

stalled pumps. The operation worked, and so they were called back when the pumps broke down again. On the second visit, the divers trained a few miners to perform the operation in a company-owned diving suit.

Jews also worked as ordinary muckers and miners. A miner's wage in 1860 on the Comstock Lode was $3.50 to $4.00 for a twelve-hour day spent underground; surface and mill workers got less. Twenty years later, in Black Hills, Dakota Territory, the miner's wage was little better. A union organized to win fair wages fought from 1867 to 1872 for an eight-hour day. Consequently, miners tended to be immigrants—mostly from Ireland and England, nations with a lode-mining industry; after 1880, there was an influx of immigrants from China as well. An occasional Jew entered those ranks, and when one did, the newcomer's first experiences in mining were likely to be memorable.

"My father was a frontiersman, always going toward new districts," said Sam Aaron, the first Jewish boy born in Salt Lake City (1866). Sam launched his own career as a jack-of-all-trades in silver-rich Butte, Montana, when he was eleven. The twenty-five hundred inhabitants of that "town built [on] top of the mountains" were mostly miners, and "the money flowed like water." Sam sold apples in saloons, the fruit paid for by chips scooped off gambling tables. "It ruined me," noted Sam, for thereafter he "wanted to be a faro dealer." From Butte, he moved with his family to the town of Oakland in Oregon; they later moved to San Francisco. In 1881, Sam, then fifteen, set out on his own for Charleston, near Tombstone, Arizona Territory, the site of Ed Schiefflin's big 1877 silver strike. For several years Sam clerked by day and gambled by night. In 1884, after losing a thousand dollars belonging to his father, he was forced to resort to desperate measures—a job at the Tombstone Mining and Mill Company.

Three months later he was still at work, mainly at the smelter as wheel charger, pot wrestler (dumping slag), and tapper, during which time he "used to run [his] hand through the molten lava in front of the tourists while the lava was red hot—that was the way [they] took samples." Sam, however, stayed away from the most

Sam and Bertha Flax were married in Cripple Creek, Colorado, in 1909. Struggling to earn a living, the Flaxes moved from Cripple Creek to Denver, New York City, and Newcastle, Wyoming, then back to Denver where Sam eventually established a successful restaurant and hotel business. Courtesy, Rocky Mountain Jewish Historical Society, Denver, Colorado

dangerous tasks. Handling mercury caused ill effects in amalgamators, and arsenic poisoning took almost as high a toll in the furnace room as did fights between overheated workers. As soon as he could, Sam got out of mining and into work he preferred. As a faro dealer he earned the sobriquet "the Lucky Jew Kid." "I once had as high as thirty-two Chinamen playing against me at one time," he recalled.

As late as the 1890s and early 1900s, a few Jewish youths, new in the Far West and in need of employment, sought mining jobs. Sam Flax, a poor young Russian Jewish immigrant in love with a young beauty named Bertha, tagged along when her family decided in 1906 to leave New York City for Cripple Creek, Colorado. The morning after they arrived, Sam, who spoke nothing but Yiddish and had no money, discussed job possibilities with a junk peddler named Jaffa who had taken him in. His host led him to

This was the office of the Promontorio Mining Company, owned by Leopold Ephraim in Nogales, Arizona, circa 1890. Ephraim arrived in southern Arizona in about 1882 and opened the El Promontorio mine near the famous "Planchas de Plata" district, which had been mined by the early Spaniards. Photograph by Dinwiddie; courtesy, Smithsonian Institution Archives, Washington, D.C.

the rear yard and pointed: "See those rocks out there, this is what they call gold mines. Go down there; they pay three dollars a day."

Sam balked when he learned that the mines went thousands of feet into the earth. Instead, he took the only other job available, assistant bartender in a saloon in nearby Victor. His employer paid him so little and drove him so hard that as soon as Sam learned English and could speak with miners, he summoned the courage to seek an ore-house job. He was about to throw in his bartender's apron, when a miner he knew came into the saloon "all patched up," the victim of an ore-house explosion. Flax put his apron

back on, only later to learn that his employer had induced the fellow to feign injury in order to keep Sam on the job. By then, though, Flax was no longer in the mood to take chances. Bertha had at last succumbed to his pleas and had agreed to marry him.

Adventuresome, impatient, and well educated, Bernard Baruch had higher aspirations. He came west to "strike it rich—quick—in the gold and silver mines." Young Bernie and a friend traveled by railroad and stagecoach to Cripple Creek, Colorado, "a wide open mining town with saloons, dance halls, and gambling joints." Eager to make a start, Baruch bought some shares in

Henry Lesinsky spent an agonizing ten years trying to make profitable his Longfellow mine in the San Francisco Mountains, Arizona Territory. He eventually sold the company for $1.2 million. Courtesy, Arizona Historical Society, Tucson

the San Francisco Mine, the first shares he had ever owned. Then he got a job as a mucker and quickly earned his stripes in a fight with a fellow worker. He loaded ore until he was promoted to the blasting crew. His evenings he spent at the tables, watching small fortunes change hands. With skills that later would earn him a high place in the world of finance, he figured out a surefire system at the roulette wheel. Thus he added to his small wages until the management barred him from the premises. About his mining ex-

periences, Baruch noted, "I had learned my first lesson in moneymaking—in mining people often put more into the ground than they take out of it." With that nugget, Baruch was ready to return to New York and Wall Street, to embark on his career as a distinguished financier and honored public servant.

A few Jews did make industrial mining their lifelong trade. Sam Butcher, a strapping Hungarian Jew who came to Colorado in 1875, worked in Leadville and later in Cripple Creek hacking out a living and a reputation as an able hard-rock miner and blaster. Aware that miners could be abusively anti-Semitic—he had seen a man beaten for no other reason than that he was Jewish—Butcher took pains to conceal his identity. A Leadville tailor, however, gave away the Hungarian's secret. Challenged by a knot of rough miners to cite a single Jew in their line, the tailor could not resist naming his muscular coreligionist. By then, however, Butcher was an accepted member of the hard-rock miners' fraternity, and the revelation was received with nothing more than surprise and disbelief.

Some pioneer Jews owned and operated gold, silver, and copper mines as their primary endeavor. A great many more businessmen, such as Leopold Ephraim (Nogales, Arizona Territory), Ernest Kohlberg, (El Paso, Texas), E. E. Cohen (Browntown, Oregon), Lewis Behn and Felix Poznainsky (Helena, Montana), and Simon Bamberger (Salt Lake City), ran mining operations in addition to their other enterprises.

In 1872 southwestern entrepreneur Henry Lesinsky made a small investment in a newly discovered copper mine, thinking it might make a rewarding sideline. The venture turned out to be the most agonizing but eventually the most rewarding of his numerous enterprises. Lesinsky's cause célèbre was a ferocious, ten-year battle at the Longfellow Mine on the rugged slopes of the San Francisco Mountains in the Apache-menaced southeastern Arizona Territory. A small, contentious man with as many enemies as friends, Lesinsky shared his worries and rewards with his partners, his brother Charles and his uncle Julius Freudenthal, who was an early New Mexico pioneer.

Born in 1836 in Prussian Poland, Henry was

Left: *Samuel Newhouse parlayed his far western mining gains into worldwide ventures, publicized with his own flamboyant personality and spectacular lifestyle. Newhouse conceived and built the classic Flatiron Building in New York, gained first mineral rights in China (only to lose out with the Boxer Rebellion), and hobnobbed with the British Royal Court. Courtesy, American Jewish Archives, Cincinnati, Ohio*

Right: *Much more than an ornament, Ida Stingley Newhouse provided her husband with key contacts in his business career. During the early days of their marriage, while running a hotel with Samuel, Ida befriended a guest who provided Samuel with his first financial backing for a mining venture. Her own natural charm was further polished by her education; Ida was eventually presented to the English court and soon became a favorite of King Edward's and a valuable business ambassador for Samuel. Their long-distance marriage (Ida spent much of her time abroad) ended in 1914, as Samuel's empire was crumbling. Ida later lived at the Beverly Hills Hotel until her money ran out. She died in poverty in a nursing home in 1937. Portrait by Pierre Troubetzkoy; courtesy, Nolan Hardy, Salt Lake City, Utah*

sent at fourteen to London to learn a craft. Convinced he could never wrench himself upward from poverty as an artisan, in 1854 the youth accepted Anglican Society sponsorship to go to Australia where a mineral rush was in progress. Four years later, the somewhat more prosperous Lesinsky pushed on to California, where he mined briefly in the dwindling goldfields. That same year, news of a silver strike lured him to the New Mexico Territory, where his uncle Julius resided. The silver excitement, however, was short-lived, so Henry went into business with his uncle, first buying grain for the government, then operating general merchandise stores in Las Cruces and Silver City. During this period,

Lesinsky acquired some capital, took a trip home to Europe, married Mathilda (also née Lesinsky), and fathered several children.

In 1872 a new mining venture came his way. One of his employees, Eugene Goulding, brought Lesinsky a sack of copper ore located and extracted by Robert Metcalf from a site in the San Francisco Mountains about 220 miles from Las Cruces. Lesinsky remembered:

Not long thereafter I was in my saddle and accompanied by Goulding and the discoverer, together with a few armed men, started for the copper mines. . . . We were some six days in finding the place again. Rivers had to be crossed, mountains ascended, and a careful watch for Indians maintained.

In 1876 at the age of fourteen, John B. Newman worked on a ship for his passage to the United States. His first jobs were in mining; later he became renowned as a mine developer in Arizona and died a millionaire in 1927. Courtesy, Norton Stern, Santa Monica, California

The Indians eventually outwitted the prospectors and stole their animals and provisions, but the loss failed to cool Lesinsky's ardor, and with a $10,000 investment he bought a controlling interest in Metcalf's mine.

From the outset production problems curtailed the output of the potentially rich but remote mine. With the closest railroad twelve hundred miles away, the owners had to build their own smelter. Local Mexican miners constructed one of adobe bricks, but it was soon apparent that a more up-to-date smelter was needed. A Baltimore Copper Works crew spent two years experimenting, which cost Henry, who was in charge, "unspeakable anxieties" and cost the company $20,000. His patience and funds at an end, Metcalf sold his share to his Jewish partners, who continued to grapple with the smelter problem, this time with a German metallurgist. The expert took eight months to perfect a firebrick of local clay, only to have the furnace collapse within twenty-four hours of beginning operation.

According to Lesinsky's cousin Louis Smadbeck, superintendent of the Longfellow Mine, Lesinsky himself, in a moment of irritation, solved the problem. Unable to find anything else to back the furnace, Lesinsky ordered a workman to try a copper plate that was "lying around loose." This impulsive move led to the construction of a copper-sided furnace that was water coolable and capable of withstanding contact with the molten slag.

Production soared, but the battle was not yet over. The price of copper dropped from twenty-five to fifteen cents a pound in 1878, and the Longfellow remained in the red. Lesinsky asked the miners to accept a temporary cut in pay to avoid a shutdown. Although they maligned him bitterly, they did consent. In two years, copper was back to twenty-five cents a pound, and the Longfellow, employing six hundred, was showing a profit.

In 1882 a party of English and Scotch mining investors offered to buy the enterprise for $1.2 million. Physically and emotionally exhausted, Lesinsky quickly agreed. A decade later he recalled:

The ten years of agony were forgotten. My craving after mines that had inspired my work for seventeen years turned out to be the true lodestone that led the wanderer in the right direction. Forgotten the despair, the unspeakable sufferings, the mental torture. My heart went out and embraced all things, animate and inanimate. So it is when peace and contentment enter your heart.

As mining grew in scale and technological

complexity, ever larger companies developed. Initially, capital was supplied by local merchant grubstakers, individual investors and bankers, and in time, from the sale of mining stocks. Toward the end of the nineteenth century, the opportunities for mammoth returns attracted wealthy East Coast and European investors. Jewish mine financiers, developers, and promoters found important roles to play.

One flamboyant far western mining developer and promoter was a Gilded Age figure named Samuel Newhouse. Bold, innovative, and socially ambitious, Sam successfully promoted ventures for more than thirty years. Then he hit a long losing streak and fled the competition. A native of New York, Newhouse began his career in Leadville, Colorado Territory, in 1879. The twenty-five-year-old city boy started out in a Rocky Mountain freighting business, quickly learning about mules, heavy wagons, skinners, teamsters, and steep, narrow mountain toll roads. Accumulating some capital, he bought mines (Wheel of Fortune, Maid of Mist, and Lost Lode) and built extensively in Idaho Springs and Central City, including the Newhouse Tunnel. In 1883 he married Ida Stingley, the sixteen-year-old daughter of a boardinghouse proprietor.

The second and more notable half of Newhouse's mining career, however, took place in the Utah Territory. He arrived there in 1896, an experienced developer, millionaire, and international bon vivant whose partners were for the most part wealthy English and French investors. For more than ten years Newhouse developed promising Utah mines to sell to syndicates, frequently with Thomas Weir, a highly respected mine operator. They started with gold mines in Bingham Canyon, at the Southern tip of the Great Salt Lake, gathering a group of ten claims that spread over seventy-five acres. The enterprise was initially called the Highland Boy Mining Company; when English investors joined, the company name was changed to the Utah Consolidated Gold Mines Ltd. On October 6, 1896, the *Salt Lake Tribune* predicted a model development, but the operation ran into a snag. Gold was abundant, but copper was more so. This problem was overcome with the construc-

tion of the first copper smelter in Utah. Before the smelter was completed, however, the Rockefeller interests paid $12 million to obtain control of the company.

A second Newhouse-Weir undertaking in Bingham Canyon was a $300,000 copper mine, incorporated on May 14, 1898, as the Boston Consolidated Copper and Gold Mining Company Ltd. Expecting the mine to produce even more copper than the Highland Boy, the company invested heavily in a costly ($1.5 million) concentrator and new steam shovels that proved impractical for the site. The price of copper tumbled in 1905, and two years later the Panic of 1907 struck. In 1910 Boston Consolidated was forced to merge with the Utah Copper Company, a Guggenheim interest.

Another Newhouse development slowed by the panic was the Cactus Mine in Beaver, Utah, which the tycoon acquired in 1902 with the help of English and French investors. The project included a townsite (named Newhouse), a mill, and a short railroad line (Newhouse, Copper Gulch, and Sevier Railroad) connecting the mill and the mine. Mining and smelting problems, however, forced Newhouse to sell the entire project in 1910. These and other reversals drove him out of mining and into a new occupation: skyscraper construction.

The most lavish was the Newhouse Hotel, its opulence reflecting the owner's penchant for mansions, costly autos, private railroad cars, grand parties, and rich and titled friends. Yet before the hotel opened in 1915, Newhouse was bankrupt. He retreated to his sister's chateau outside Paris, leaving Newhouse watchers in Utah, still dazzled by his exuberant style, to speculate on the cause of his empire's collapse.

Another Jewish mine developer avoided publicity as much as Newhouse courted it. He rose from mucker to millionaire, his name virtually unknown outside the mining district in which he operated. A year after John B. Newman died on August 8, 1928, his biography was published for the first time in the *Mining Journal*. A brief banner described him as "a 'wizard' prospector of Arizona who participated in many successes and who died worth many millions though

Meyer Guggenheim had two goals: to have a large close-knit family and to make a lot of money. Of the eleven children he fathered, seven were sons, who joined him—with varying degrees of willingness—in Guggenheim enterprises. From left to right: *Benjamin, Murry, Isaac, Meyer, Daniel, Solomon, Simon, and William. Courtesy, Guggenheim Brothers, New York*

he could make but a mark for a signature but demonstrated a real 'nose for ore.' "

Born on April 8, 1862, of Polish-Jewish parents in Chorna, then part of the Austro-Hungarian Empire, Newman worked on a ship for his passage to the United States in 1876. Fourteen and on his own, his first jobs were in mining: coal in Pennsylvania, copper in Michigan. He arrived in Globe, Arizona Territory, in 1883, when it was a prime silver-mining camp on the border of the volatile San Carlos Indian Reservation, and went to work as a mucker at the Old

Dominion Mine. It was during this period that he was renamed Newman—no one could pronounce his long Polish name. He would later acquire the nicknames "J. B.," "Black Jack," and "Lucky Black Jack."

During the Spanish-American War, Newman enlisted in Company B of the Arizona First Territorial Regiment. According to his son Sam, Black Jack's most significant battles were fought at card tables, where he amassed a substantial bankroll. After he was discharged, Newman began locating, buying, and selling claims in the

Globe mining district and the surrounding area. During those years, he developed his reputation as an extraordinarily shrewd prospector and mine developer and as his own regulator. On one occasion, Black Jack argued with a partner he believed to be stealing from him, and the man pulled a knife on him. Newman drew the forty-five revolver he always wore and shot off the man's arm. He was later vindicated.

Newman scored his most renowned coup between 1904 and 1906 when he located the claims that formed the nucleus of the Inspiration Consolidated and the Miami Copper Mines. An account of how Newman discovered the ore body was related by Sheriff S. Henry Thompson. The sheriff, Newman, Inspiration Mine owner John S. Copeland, and a banker named Sieloff went one Sunday to inspect some potential properties situated on a flat six miles west of Globe. When the others were ready to leave, Newman, whose speech was heavily accented and characteristically spare, muttered something about remaining behind. Several days later, the prospector met the sheriff on the street and mentioned that he had filed thirteen claims in the area they had visited. Newman sold the assortment, along with some adjoining claims, to the Lewisohn brothers, important New York–based copper-mine developers.

Another incident from Newman's dramatic mining career pitted the illiterate expert against leading mining technologists and financiers. While the country was reeling during the Panic of 1907, Miami Copper bought a group of low-grade porphyry mines, the Oats-Newman group, from Newman for $180,000 in cash and $330,000 in stock. The company's engineer, Fred Alsdorf, noted mining geologist J. Parke Channing, and Newman, the local expert, initially disagreed on the location of a main shaft. Newman stubbornly argued his case, convinced the expert Channing, and the drilling began. The surface rock was uncompromising, and expenditures mounted. When the New York office finally wired a stop-work order, Black Jack refused to obey. Personally guaranteeing wages, he kept the work going until the drills hit the great Miami ore body at

three hundred feet. Throughout the drilling, Newman confidently acquired adjacent claims and was named as locator on a large number of the Miami Copper mines.

By 1900, although some mavericks continued to fracture their hearts, homes, habits, and pocketbooks to chase the elephant around the Far West, the craze, as such, was over. Mining had by then polarized into opposing camps: labor and big business. A miner was likely to be a strike-prone union man, his employers, members of a trust composed of large mineowners and absentee investors. Among the most powerful—and as on-site mine and smelter operators, the most knowledgeable—were Meyer Guggenheim and his sons.

As with most meteoric successes, the Guggenheim rise resulted from a collision of fortuitous givens. The first was timing. Mining caught Meyer's eye in 1880, just as eastern investors began scooping up opportunities and resources in the Far West and, in the process, started industrializing the new region. The second was Meyer's background. He was born in Lengnau, Switzerland, where Jewish wealth was restricted by special taxes, and marriage licenses were denied to limit Jewish offspring. In reaction to those restraints, when Meyer settled in Philadelphia in 1848 with his wife, Barbara Meyer, he wanted nothing more than to earn money and raise a large, tightly knit family. The third lucky given was the children he fathered: of eleven, seven were sons. For nearly two decades they bowed to their father's will (some more willingly than others), each playing a key role in the business during its formative years.

Meyer honed his style in Philadelphia. Starting as a pack peddler, he quickly moved up to merchant, then manufacturer, of stove polish, coffee essence, lye, and Swiss lace and embroideries. With each item he established a market for the product, then cut out the middleman by producing the goods himself. Enlarging on this pattern, the Guggenheim sons would outdo every mining tycoon in the Far West.

In 1880 Guggenheim entered mining through Charles H. Graham, a former Phila-

Numbers: Only Part of the Picture

By 1880 pioneer Jews were living all over the new region. One commonly used enumeration of Jews in the Far West was derived from the first national Jewish census, taken between 1876 and 1878 under the auspices of the Board of Delegates of American Israelites and the Union of American Hebrew Congregations (UAHC). The count found 230,257 Jews nationwide, with 21,465 living in eleven western states and territories. Of that total, 16,000 were reported in San Francisco, and another 2,000 lived in the growing cities of Portland, Oregon; Oakland and San Jose, California; Virginia City, Nevada; Helena, Montana; Denver; and Salt Lake City.

Hailey, Idaho, circa 1880; courtesy, Ben M. Roe Collection, University of Utah Library, Salt Lake City

Los Angeles, California, circa 1875; courtesy, California Historical Society/Ticor Title Insurance, Los Angeles

Left: *Las Vegas, New Mexico Territory, circa 1880; courtesy, Western History Department, Denver Public Library, Denver, Colorado*

Right: *Denver, Colorado, circa 1874; courtesy Western History Department, Denver Public Library, Denver, Colorado*

Since this was the only count taken of the early (pre-1881) pioneers, on that score alone it is valuable. It should be noted, however, that these figures are well under the actual number of pioneer Jews in the Far West at the time, a fact that can be attributed to the methods used in the survey. Data for the UAHC census was sent in by Jewish congregations and lodges or by important Jewish individuals in a locale. These affiliated and/or influential Jews tended to omit those not similarly situated. Moreover, entire communities were overlooked, either because no response was received or because their existence was not known. Numerous bypassed towns had dozens of Jews, many of whom were early pioneers and, in some cases, townfounders and leading citizens. A few had hundreds of Jewish residents. Historian Mitchell Gelfand, for example, using the 1880 United States census records, listed 418 Jews living in Los Angeles, a community not appearing in the UAHC survey. Also drawing on the 1880 census, Fred Rochlin conservatively counted 316 similarly unreported Jews living in Tucson, Phoenix, Tombstone, and other Arizona Territory towns.

More important than the quantitative omissions is a qualitative underestimation. To portray pre-1880 far western Jewry as smaller and more urban than it actually was minimizes the most unique aspects of these Jewish pioneers' frontier experience, namely, their swift entry into the mainstream and their consequent substantial participation in the creation of towns and cities all over the Far West.

What statistics fail to tell, ephemera do, and none do so more graphically than photographs. By the early 1880s the ubiquitous camera had captured a Jewish presence from Port Townsend, Washington, to El Paso, and from San Diego to Deadwood, Dakota Territory.

Holbrook, Arizona Territory, circa 1885; courtesy, Museum of Northern Arizona, Flagstaff

Wallace and Jackson streets, Virginia City, Montana, circa 1865; courtesy, Library of Congress, Washington, D.C.

San Diego, California, circa 1880; courtesy, San Diego Historical Society, San Diego, California

delphian. Graham had traveled east from Colorado seeking a loan to buy a two-thirds share of a pair of producing lead and silver mines near Leadville, Colorado. He set forth the potentialities of the two diggings, the A.Y. and the Minnie, so convincingly that Guggenheim loaned him $5,000 to buy one third, and bought the other third himself.

Not long after, Meyer traveled to Leadville, then a silver-boom mountain town of thirty-five thousand, with shanties and log cabins spilling down its ten-thousand-foot slopes. Following a bumpy ride to California Gulch, Guggenheim watched the third partner, Samuel Harsh, throw a stone to the watery bottom of the main shaft of the A.Y. Otherwise impressed with the mines and attracted to the get-rich-quick aura of Leadville, Guggenheim paid to have a Denver engineer pump the mines dry. Soon thereafter, ore production rose from two hundred tons a month to fifty tons a day.

In the year that followed, Guggenheim's misgivings about the mines grew as he spent between $30,000 and $70,000 to have the mines repumped and to buy out his insolvent partners. Then, in August 1881, a telegram arrived, erasing his doubts. His miners had struck a silver bonanza at the A.Y. Meyer's next act distinguished him from less daring and determined investors. Deciding to manage the mines himself, he turned over his lace and embroideries business, M. Guggenheim's Sons, to his four older sons, Isaac, Daniel, Murry, and Solomon. He then sent the three younger ones, Simon, Ben, and William, to learn the mining business at universities and on the job.

In 1888 Meyer launched the manufacturing half of his future mining empire. That year, loaded down with cost, labor, and production problems, the $500,000 Guggenheim smelter—the first in Colorado—opened in Pueblo with Ben and Simon in charge. A short time later Meyer turned over his company, the Philadelphia Mine and Smelter Company, to M. Guggenheim's Sons to operate. His older sons balked. They were prospering in Swiss textiles while their father's ill-functioning smelter was consuming the considerable profits the mines produced. Nor

did they gladly accept, then or ever, their three younger brothers as equal partners.

The objections of the four overruled, two years later the seven Guggenheim brothers were actively engaged in mining and smelting, guided by Meyer, who had retired. The next bold leap would carry the Guggenheims out of the regional and into the global realm. Their first foreign venture was in Mexico, where they went to buy ore for their Pueblo smelter. With encouragement from President Porfirio Díaz, they acquired mines, then built smelters in Aguascalientes and Monterrey. Guggenheim Exploration Company finds later drew them into Chile, Bolivia, Angola, and the Belgian Congo.

In 1899 the Rockefeller interests organized the American Smelting and Refining Company, ASARCO, a trust composed of the country's larger mine and smelter operators. Aspiring not to membership but to leadership, the Guggenheims refused to join. A battle of behemoths followed. When the dust settled in 1901, Dan, Meyer's successor, was chairman of the board of both ASARCO and M. Guggenheim's Sons. At that point, two brothers, William and Ben, withdrew from active participation. Their ostensible reason was that they objected to nonfamily partners. One biographer, William H. Davis, believed they were forced out to prevent them from interfering with their older brothers' management policies and from sharing in future profits. Both received substantial settlements and issued no protest for some years. (In 1916 William displayed his accumulated wrath in a lawsuit he filed against his brothers that was settled out of court for a rumored $5 million.) Consequently, when Meyer died in 1905, his dream of wealth had been realized, but his dream of family unity had been shattered.

Functioning for the next ten years through ASARCO and M. Guggenheim's Sons, the remaining quintet founded a kingdom of silver, copper, gold, and lead. Best known among their enterprises were Utah Copper Company (Bingham Canyon); Nevada Consolidated Copper Company; Ray Consolidated Copper and Gila Copper companies, Arizona; Santa Rita Copper Company, New Mexico; Kennecott Mine

Company, Alaska; and Chile Copper Company (Chiquicamata Mines), Chile. By 1912 the Guggenheims controlled 70 to 80 percent of the world's silver, lead, and, most important, copper, which was in great demand during World War I. By the end of the war, though, the tide was gradually turning. Government regulation and modern corporate practices had curbed the Guggenheims' power, and the lack of suitable and willing successors had snuffed out their "family only" business. Thereafter, noted Davis, instead of making money, the business of the Guggenheims became spending it on grand living and equally grand philanthropies.

Nowhere did the new winds reordering the United States blow harder than in the development of the Far West during the mining craze that raged between 1848 and 1900. Gone was the slow, single-file advance that gradually set-tled agrarian America, with the trailblazer in the lead, followed by the trapper, farmer or stock raiser, townsman, and, when summoned by special circumstances, city builder. In its place was a pluralistic, open, disorderly, top-speed assault on not one, but many widely separated frontiers. Shaped by the mining mania and the adventurous, free-for-all spirit it so aptly expressed, camps, towns, and cities rose seemingly overnight, some to wither, some to flourish. The initial enterprises, mining and supplying the miners, quickly splintered into a variety of paying pursuits. In a region whose population grew from less than 100,000 aborigines in 1848 to roughly 1.75 million in thirty years, Jews had found abundant opportunities to apply the skills they brought with them and to learn others, no less new to them than mining.

FOSTER,
LADIES & GENT'S
FURNISHING GOODS,
FOREIGN & DOMESTIC
DRY GOODS.

Levi Strauss & Co.

14 and 16 Battery Street,

SAN FRANCISCO, Cal.

SOLE PROPRIETORS
OF THE
PATENT RIVETED
OVERALLS.
It's no use they can't be ripped

SOMETHING NEW

AND ALREADY AN

IMMENSE   SUCCESS

PATENT RIVETED

Spring Bottom PANTS.

SAMPLE OF
MATERIAL ENCLOSED.

$ 13 50 Per. Dz.

Chapter Three

ENTERPRISING PEOPLE

Most Jews came to gold rush California prepared to trade or to fall back on trade should mining prove unrewarding. Few got off to a speedier start than young and nimble Morris Shloss, who docked in San Francisco on September 25, 1849, and made his first sale on the landing. The twenty-year-old Polish merchant had brought a wagon from New York, packed in a large wooden box. A buyer paid him $100 on the spot—not for the wagon; that Shloss could keep. All he wanted was the four-by-seven-foot box, for which its owner had paid three dollars. The buyer, a cobbler, unable to afford the high rents asked for the city's few available structures, wanted the box to use as a workshop by day and a bedroom by night.

Shloss used his profit to buy stationery, which, displayed on a stand in the plaza, brought him a 500 percent return. He also got a job playing the fiddle at night at the El Dorado, a gambling house on the corner of Washington and Kearny streets. For fiddling from seven to ten, his nightly pay was a sixteen-dollar ounce of gold; for an additional hour, he accrued an extra grab of silver from the monte table.

Shloss soon rented a minuscule store for $400 next to the El Dorado to house still another enterprise: buying trunks from arriving passen-

gers eager to unload their possessions before rushing to the mines. In the next two months the energetic immigrant claimed to have earned between $5,000 and $6,000, despite the more than fifty inches of rain making the streets all but impassable that year. Shloss and his fellow newcomers were also plagued by garbage, rats, and fleas, by shortages of drinking water, housing, and gas for lighting; topping it all was a cholera epidemic. Unimpeded by these hindrances, he bustled along until Christmas Eve, 1849, when the new city's first fire broke out in a hotel behind his store. It leveled the buildings around Portsmouth Square.

Wiped out, Shloss decided to give mining a try. He sailed north to Trinidad Bay near present-day Eureka, where, despite the rumor that had lured him there, neither gold nor other seekers materialized. Shloss survived on beans, crackers, and clams for four months until a passing schooner picked him up.

Though dogged by new disasters, thereafter he stuck to merchandising. In 1851 his brother Solomon, who had followed him to the Pacific Coast, was killed in the wreck of a steamer transporting Morris's merchandise to Oregon; he lost a second business to fire in San Francisco in 1852; and he suffered a third substantial loss in 1853 when his store in Redding, Shasta County, also burned down. Even so, Shloss was sufficiently prosperous to start still another business in San Francisco during the same year and to send for his fiancée.

Like Shloss, most pioneer Jews found the frontier—where all (white) hands were wel-

Men's flare pants aren't really so new. This is an advertisement for Levi's "spring bottom" pants, as they appeared in the 1880s. Levi's "spring bottoms" were designed to fit over boots with a gentle flare in the cut of the leg. Courtesy, Levi Strauss & Company, San Francisco, California

and departures in woe-filled letters to his uncle in Philadelphia. He noted that merchants Greenbaum, Baker, Nusbaum, and Rosenbaum had died in a fire (on May 4, 1851) and were buried in the same coffin; that Goldstine had the pox and was preparing to return east, as was Mr. Heiter; and that Mr. Berman, who was insane when he arrived in California, was leaving in the same condition. Mayer, too, would eventually return east after a series of setbacks in California, but the majority of these early pioneers, like Morris Shloss, while suffering repeated failures, reacted to each loss by starting a new enterprise. After a decade or so, the average seeker who had arrived with no more than a knapsack or, as in Shloss's case, a wagon had

comed—abounding in tasks for their talents. The mainstream open to them on arrival, they Americanized and regionalized with speed, energy, and élan. For these Jews, the range of opportunities was as unprecedented as it was fortuitous.

For centuries, their ancestors had been barred in Europe and to some extent in the United States from the more honored and rewarding undertakings. Pursuing work that others shunned, they earned their bread as traders, artisans, brokers, and moneylenders, often living hand to mouth. Then, just as they were becoming sufficiently emancipated to seek more than Europe would grant them, a burgeoning America in need of commercial skills threw open its doors.

Most Jews who responded to the glittering promises on the far western frontier and rose to its awesome obstacles were intrepid, resourceful, and individualistic. For the most part, they were also literate, sober, and driven to prove themselves. If they did not succeed in one place, they tried another, and then another. As soon as one enterprise succeeded, in pioneer fashion they proceeded to the next.

Of course, not every Jew persisted or even survived. Alexander Mayer, who arrived in San Francisco in February 1851, reported both deaths

The most catastrophic natural disaster to hit far western merchants was the San Francisco earthquake of April 1906. Here in the aftermath, the Hoffman Cafe—a refugee kitchen—feeds the hungry. Courtesy, California Historical Society, San Francisco

Upper left: *Julius Meyer was a merchant who initiated a successful trading business with western Indians in the 1860s, learning several native tongues. He became the chiefs' trusted interpreter and an honored guest at tribal feasts.* Left to right, standing: *Meyer and Red Cloud;* sitting: *Sitting Bull, Swift Bear, and Spotted Tail. Courtesy, Nevada State Historical Society*

*Opulence arrived in the Far West with the arrival of the White House. The glove depart-
ment is shown here. Proprietor Raphael was the brother of Alexandre Weill of Lazard
Frères. Weill was greatly responsible for introducing sophisticated buying habits to the San
Francisco public. Courtesy, Raphael Weill Collection, Western Jewish History Center,
Judah L. Magnes Museum, Berkeley, California*

cornered a piece of middle-class comfort and
was counting himself a big winner.

Understandably stirred at the sight of Jews
speedily prospering in pre-1880 California, some
nineteenth-century observers made extravagant
claims about the success of the Jews in the Golden
State. They were not, however, all wealthy, universally successful, or the backbone of the economy, as was claimed. Some, possibly 15 percent,
remained or became poor in the Far West; conversely, a like number soared into large-scale
merchandising, banking, or brokering, acquiring wealth, influence, and social standing. No

great fortunes comparable with those drawn later
from far western minerals, railroads, or land development were made at this time, but at least
three commercial empires were seeded that
would in time surpass their founders' wildest
fantasies. All of these were enterprises that were
founded by immigrant families in the early years
of the gold rush.

The group with the most panache were
members of the Lazard-Weill-Meyer families of
Alsace-Lorraine, who were linked by ties of blood
or birthplace. The first of this clan to arrive in
the United States were the Lazard brothers of

Sarreguemines, Lorraine: Alexander, Simon, and an unnamed brother who soon returned home. In 1847 in New Orleans, these three founded the first Lazard Frères, a small mercantile enterprise. The trio, assisted by their young cousin Solomon Lazard of Fromberg, Lorraine, operated their imported dry goods and clothing store in the Delta City for about a year. Shortly after news of the gold discovery at Sutter's Mill swept New Orleans, a fire destroyed the Lazards' store. Hoping to recoup their losses in California, the brothers wangled passage on the first steamer to depart for the Pacific Coast. Eager to launch his own enterprise, Solomon sailed too.

Alexander and Simon established the second Lazard Frères store in San Francisco in 1849 and in a few years had added to the partnership their younger brother Elie, a half brother Sylvan Kahn, and their cousin Alexandre Weill of Phalsbourg, Lorraine. Braving hardships, including the Christmas Eve fire of 1849, the partners established a beachhead selling imported goods from France, Germany, and Switzerland and exporting gold bullion. Other cousins and countrymen joined them in the Far West: Henri Weill, Alexandre's brother; Alphonse Lazard, Solomon's brother; and the brothers Eugene and Constant Meyer of Strasbourg, Alsace, who became as close as kin to the Lazard-Weill family. Assisted by the cousinhood, each added distinction to his own name and to that of the clan.

In the fall of 1875, with assets augmented in the gold market, the partners closed their store and reopened Lazard Frères as what the *San Diego Union* of September 3, 1875, called "one of the largest banks on the Pacific Coast": the London, Paris, and American Bank. In 1883 the partners summoned Eugene Meyer from Los Angeles to head the San Francisco office, freeing other members of the partnership to establish national headquarters in New York and to start or reinforce branches in New Orleans, London, and Paris.

The Seligman family also made decisive headway selling goods and gold bullion in California. Recalled Jesse Seligman, "In 1850, when the 'gold fever' broke out in California, I determined to leave the store [in Watertown, New York] in the hands of my brother Henry, so that I might venture out to ascertain whether we could not still further improve our condition."

The eight Seligman brothers, sons of a poor farmer of Stadt Bayersdorf, Bavaria, had come to the United States determined to do just that—improve their condition. The first to arrive was Joseph, the eldest, a graduate of Erlanger University who landed in 1837 with $100 to his name. A dozen years later, the eight, bound together under Joseph's leadership, had acquired dry goods stores in New York, Alabama, and Missouri and some surplus capital earmarked for investment. Jesse, who at twenty-one had accrued nine years of American mercantile experience, persuaded his brothers to invest in him and in California. He set out that spring with $20,000 worth of carefully chosen dry goods, foodstuffs, clothing, and liquor, accompanied by his nineteen-year-old brother Leopold, who was "still more artist than businessman."

They arrived in San Francisco in the fall, rented a flimsy frame building on Commercial

Jesse Seligman, who later became an international investment banker, founded J. Seligman and Company, Dry Goods, in San Francisco in 1850. Portrait from Harper's Weekly

Street, and founded J. Seligman & Company. According to Jesse, the goods flew out at astronomical prices: five dollars for a tin cup and plate that cost pennies; forty dollars for a blanket worth five; twenty dollars for a quart of whiskey. Having just lost his Watertown store to a fire, Jesse cornered the first available space in a brick building. It was in the same structure as the Tehama House, a new hotel at the corners of Sansome and California streets. His precautions were justified when a fire erupted on May 4, 1851; the Seligman store was the only one on the plaza to withstand the blaze.

In 1863 Leopold, Henry, and Abraham (Jesse had returned to New York in 1857) reported to Joseph that the value of their California enterprise had reached $900,000. With these and other assets, the next year the eight brothers entered international investment banking as J. & W. Seligman Company, with headquarters in New York. Branches soon followed: Seligman Brothers, London; Seligman Frères, Paris; Seligman Stettheimer, Frankfurt; and in 1867, J. Seligman & Company (investment bankers), San Francisco.

Of hundreds of Jewish argonauts, only one has been awarded a place in the folklore of the California gold rush. His fame grew out of the

Top: *From peddler to millionaire to household word around the globe: Levi Strauss of San Francisco; courtesy, Levi Strauss & Company, San Francisco, California*

Left: *Levi Strauss emporium, San Francisco, circa 1880; courtesy, Levi Strauss & Company, San Francisco, California*

legend created to advertise a modern version of
the work pants he manufactured, which his successors named in his honor—Levi's.

According to the tale, at the height of the
gold rush Levi Strauss was selling tent canvas on
the streets of San Francisco when he was approached by a miner in need of a really strong
pair of pants. Vendor and customer hit on the
bright thought that pants made of canvas would
fill the bill, and they dashed off together to find
a tailor. Soon a queue had formed to buy the
pants called Levi's.

More accurate is an account that credits as
creator Jacob Youphes, also known as Davis, a
Russian Jewish tailor living in Reno, Nevada Territory. On July 2, 1872, Davis wrote Levi Strauss
& Company, a prosperous San Francisco dry
goods firm. He had, he told the "gents," designed work pants, some made of ten-ounce duck
and some made of blue cloth purchased from
their company:

The secratt of them Pents is the Rivits that I put in
those Pockets and I found the demand so large that
I cannot make them up fast enough. I charge for the
Duck $3.00 and the Blue $2.50 a pear. My nabors are
getting yealouse of these success and unless I secure
it by Patent Papers it will soon become a general thing.

The company's decision to coventure is apparent in the patent assigned to Davis and the
Levi Strauss Company on May 20, 1873. By 1874
Davis and his family were living in San Francisco,
and the tailor was supervising the production of
duck or denim pants, made at first by seam-
stresses working in their own homes and later
in the company's factories.

The actual Levi Strauss story, however, is at
once less dramatic and more remarkable. A native of Bad Ocheim, high in the Bavarian Alps,
Levi briefly assumed the position his grandfather and father had held as clerk of the town
registry. When his parents died, one shortly after
the other in 1848, the lone seventeen-year-old
youth sold the family house and joined his two
older brothers, Jonas and Louis, in New York.
Levi did his basic training in peddling, then
booked passage and sailed for San Francisco with
merchandise supplied by his brothers. Selected

possibly on the advice of his sister, Fanny, and
her husband, David Stern, who already resided
in San Francisco, the goods he brought proved
to be much in demand. Merchants who rowed
out to his anchored ship to get a first crack bought
most of the stock he had in the hold. Levi, with
his brother-in-law as his business partner, was
soon monitoring other incoming ships and rushing aboard to buy. Not long thereafter, Levi began transporting merchandise by side-wheeler
and pack train to mining-town merchants. The
variety, quality, and reasonable prices of his goods
won him loyal customers, first in California and
then in the new communities east and north of
the Golden State.

By 1872 the Levi Strauss & Company sign
was affixed to a four-story brick building at 14–
16 Battery Street. Levi, the acknowledged head
and heart of the five-member family partnership, was a millionaire and prominent social figure. When this descendant of registry clerks died
on September 28, 1902, his holdings were valued
at $6 million, most of which went to his four
nephews, Jacob, Louis, Abraham, and Sigmund
Stern. Lengthy obituaries offered highlights of
his career as a "pioneer merchant and philanthropist," and flags flew at half-mast in the
wholesale district the afternoon of his funeral.

After 1858, when mining spread beyond
California, merchants rushed to new camps and
supply settlements springing up all over the Far
West. In these places, fast-moving speculators
caught demand on the rise, snapped up good
locations, and plunged into the heady task of
town building.

The first challenge was getting there with
the right goods. Occasionally a peddler footed
it into a new territory. A larger number traveled
on paddle-wheelers to camps along waterways.
Most frontier traders, however, hauled in their
merchandise by pack or wagon train. Their jour-
neys generally commenced along buffalo/In-
dian/trader trails widened and rutted by immigrants' wagons surging west and ended on a faint
cutoff to a new outpost. In transit for weeks, at
times for months, during a single journey these
goods-laden adventurers faced down a forbid-

William Zeckendorf, colorful frontier merchant; courtesy, Arizona Historical Society, Tucson

1870, the "irrepressible Zeckendorf opened the season with a display of fireworks." In April 1871 Zeckendorf, with ten Mexicans assisting, left Apache-menaced Tucson to chase down a gang of Indian cattle rustlers. His activities in politics were also reported: Zeckendorf served in the Eighth Assembly; was the influential chairman of the Pima County Democratic Committee for many years; and headed committees to promote railroads and wagon roads to connect Tucson to other southern Arizona centers.

Zeckendorf's business career was no less eventful. In 1856, when he was fourteen, this native of Hemmendorf, Hanover, Germany, joined his brothers Aaron and Louis, then merchants and army provisioners in Santa Fe. In the next six years, as he learned English and Spanish—he already knew German, French, and He-

ding environment—water and food shortages, muddy marshes, sand dunes, dizzyingly steep trails, hostile Indians, and outlaws.

Southwestern frontier merchant William Zeckendorf (grandfather of the real estate magnate) was as explosively colorful as the fireworks displays he set off at the merest hint of a special occasion. In February 1869 he arrived in Tucson with a wagon train of merchandise and an army escort and opened a branch of A. & L. Zeckendorf Company of Albuquerque, formerly of Santa Fe. (The *A* was for his brother Aaron, the senior partner, who ran the Albuquerque store; the *L* was for another brother, Louis, the firm's resident buyer in New York. William, unnoted in the firm title, was manager of the new branch.)

The name of the high-spirited and at times high-handed merchant appeared in splashy ads in local newspapers and often spilled over into the news columns. On September 4, 1869, "the excited Z. caught burglars in his store and firing his pistol, put them in flight." On Christmas in

Advertisement for L. Zeckendorf & Company; courtesy, Arizona Historical Society, Tucson

Fred Z. Salomon; courtesy, Western History Department, Denver Public Library, Denver, Colorado

result of an overextension of credit, fluctuating Mexican currency accepted from south-of-the-border customers, and the influx of inexpensive goods arriving by rail. Zeckendorf was soon able to reopen but never operated on a grand scale again. In 1891, after thirty-two years in Tucson, William sold off his entire stock and joined his family in New York City, where he lived until his death in 1906.

Fred Z. Salomon was as enterprising a frontier merchant as ever led the first large pack train into a rough far western settlement. He and his brother Hyman (they were both Colorado fifty-niners) were among the first dozen or so Denverites. (A third brother, Adolph, joined his family a few years later in Colorado, but not in Denver.)

Fred was born in Strelno, Posen, Prussia. Like so many Jews who came to the United States in the late 1830s and 1840s, he got his American business training peddling and clerking in the East, the South, and the Midwest. In 1858, investigating opportunities in Las Vegas, New Mexico Territory, a nascent trade center one day's journey east of Santa Fe, Salomon met J. B. Doyle, a veteran Santa Fe trader. Doyle invited him to become his partner and haul a load of merchandise to miners at the booming Pike's Peak country, in what was then called the Kansas Territory. Agreeing, Fred journeyed to Independence, Missouri, purchased and loaded goods on ox-drawn wagons, then set out with the train. The arrival of goods that would stock the first store in Auraria—soon to be Denver—was nostalgically described in the January 1, 1873, issue of the *Rocky Mountain News:*

A noise of cracking whips and "gee, whoa, haws," coming down the valley of Cherry Creek announced the arrival of an old-fashioned train of huge, white-topped wagons, each drawn by five or six yoke of oxen, and loaded with $30,000 worth of goods, marked J. B. Doyle & Co. The new store was not ready and the train "corralled" in front of Uncle Dick's [Dickie Wooton].

Hyman joined Fred, and both brothers swiftly acquired other partners and enterprises. Hyman and J. H. Ming hauled goods up to the new diggings in South Park on the Continental

brew—he became adept at southwestern frontier trade: selling American and imported manufactured goods, purchasing for resale local agricultural and livestock products, hauling freight, and supplying the army on contract. After three years in the Union Army during the Civil War as a lieutenant and quartermaster for the New Mexico Regiment, he began exploring opportunities in the Arizona Territory. He was a partner in A. & L. Zeckendorf Company until 1873, when Aaron died, then continued in partnership with Louis, as Zeckendorf Brothers, until April 1878. In May of that year he opened, with typical fanfare, the Tucson firm of Zeckendorf and Staab at the corner of Main and Congress streets (his partner, millionaire Zadoc Staab, was a prominent New Mexico merchant). The firm thrived until a disastrous fire and a general decline in trade upset its equilibrium. Staab withdrew, leaving William to continue on his own at the same location.

In February 1883 the business failed as a

This negative stereotype of a "crafty Jewish merchant" was printed in Police News. *Titled "Solomon Cohen—Custom Misfits," it depicts an unspecified Oregon incident. From Lucius Beebe and Charles Clegg,* The American West, *E. P. Dutton and Co. (New York, 1955)*

Divide, while Fred and a man named Taicher started a brewery, which, noted the ever-alert *Rocky Mountain News*, speedily decreased the local consumption of strychnine whiskey and Taos Lightning. In 1860 the brothers also started a water company, later incorporated as the Denver Water Company.

From arrival, Fred, a lifelong bachelor, was a city builder and booster. In 1859 he helped organize the Auraria and Denver Chess Club and Literary Society, later, the Colorado Pioneer Society, the Denver Public Library, and the Denver B'nai B'rith lodge. He also served a term as territorial treasurer.

As the stakes grew, so did Salomon's contributions. A key member of the chamber of commerce, he took part in the fierce fight to bring one railroad (Denver Pacific), then a second (Kansas Pacific) to his town. As cochairman of the Board of Immigration, he had prepared booster pamphlets in several languages and traveled constantly, often at his own expense, to draw desirable individuals and institutions to Denver. During those years as a pillar of his community, he dressed immaculately and, as a fastidious epicure, "ran the most lavish living establishment possible for a bachelor."

Salomon so completely linked his life with

that of Denver, his personal and communal goals became indivisible. One can imagine his pain when the elite Denver Club—a shortened name for the chess and literary society he had helped found—was reorganized in 1881 and thereafter barred Jews.

Before this period, anti-Semitism was individual and scattered. The most apparent restraints against Jewish merchants and entrepreneurs were seen in Sunday trading laws and in credit-rating policies. Ordinances against commerce on the Christian sabbath were enacted and obeyed in numerous western communities, while other towns that carried the law on their books rarely enforced it.

More pointedly anti-Jewish were the nationwide credit-rating practices of G. H. Dun & Company, a nineteenth-century predecessor to Dun & Bradstreet. Subjects were identified with disparaging intent as a Jew, Hebrew, Israelite, and often further described as tricky and untrustworthy. Those of unassailably high standing were set apart as a "White Jew" or a "Jew of a better class." These practices were undoubtedly damaging; it is difficult, however, to determine how serious a hindrance they posed. Merchants who were reasonably good risks could get credit from Jewish wholesalers. Others sought capital

The above cut represents the Mormon "Co-operative Sign"—called by the Gentiles the "Bulls Eye." At the Mormon conference, in the fall of 1868, all good Mormon merchants, manufacturers and dealers who desired the patronage of the Mormon people, were directed to place this sign upon their buildings in a conspicuous place, that it might indicate to the people that they were sound in the faith.

The Mormon people were also directed and warned not to purchase goods or in any manner deal with those who refused or did not have the sign,—the object seemed to be only to deal with their own people, to the exclusion of all others.

The result of these measures on the part of the church was to force many who were Gentiles or Apostate Mormons to sacrifice their goods, and leave the Territory for want of patronage. Some few, however, remained. Among whom was J. K. Trumbo, an auction and commission merchant, who procured the painting of what was known as the

"GENTILE SIGN."

This sign was placed in position on the front of his store, on the morning of the 26th of February, 1869, in a similar position to those of the Mormons. All day wondering crowds of people of all classes, little and big, hovered about the premises, and many opinions were expressed as to the propriety of the sign, and whether it would be allowed to remain by the Mormons; but at about 7 o'clock in the evening the problem was solved, by a charge made by several young Mormons, who, with ladders climbed upon the building and secured ropes upon the sign, while the crowd below tore it down, and dragged it through the streets, dashing it to pieces. This should be a warning to all "Gentiles" in future, not to expend their money in signs to be placed on their stores in Utah—*unless they have permission.*

A sign of the times: The attempted Mormon boycott of non-Mormon businessmen and the response of one merchant, J. K. Trumbo of Salt Lake City. From Leon L. Watters, "Great Transcontinental Railroad Guide," The Pioneer Jews of Utah, *American Jewish Historical Society (New York, 1952)*

from Jewish wholesalers. Others sought capital from their families or *landsmen* (as was the custom) or, if need be, from one of numerous Jewish moneylenders.

The most violent restraints against Jews in the pre-1880 period occurred in Salt Lake City, where for a few difficult years Jews were strenuously opposed, along with the other "Gentiles," as all non-Mormons were called. Animosity between the groups arose in Utah after the Gentiles, who were arriving in increasing numbers in the 1850s and 1860s, began to pose a threat to Mormon autonomy.

From 1866 to 1869 the Saints staged a last-ditch defense against the intruding population, including the Jews, whom they had initially welcomed. A few Gentiles were murdered, many were beaten, and all were subjected to strictly enforced commercial boycotts. The most successful drive against Gentile merchants came in 1868, when Brigham Young formed the Zion's Co-Operative Mercantile Institution and ordered Mormons to trade there. By 1869 development spurred by the transcontinental railroad

and by mining precluded all possibility of seclusion. Joining what they could not prevent, the Mormons traded polygamy for statehood, and hostilities gradually faded.

The conflict clearly was more an effort to protect an infant religious sect than to restrain competition or exclude those of another faith. This fact is illuminated in the experiences of Samuel Kahn, a pioneer merchant who spent twenty-six years in the City of Saints and was as prosperous and prominent as he was independent and outspoken. Born in Prussia in 1836, Kahn arrived in the United States when he was fifteen and quickly started trading and freight hauling. In 1859 he bought a load of merchandise and joined a wagon train en route to Salt Lake City, a seventy-five-day journey from Missouri. Kahn and his partner returned to replen-

Samuel Kahn; courtesy, Special Collections, University of Utah Library, Salt Lake City

ish their stock, during which time the partner was murdered by Indians. Even after that disastrous crossing, Kahn continued hauling merchandise across the plains despite an increase in Indian raids as traffic grew heavier and the Plains tribes became more adept at relieving the freighters of their valuable goods. In the early 1860s he entered a Salt Lake City partnership with Nicholas Ransohoff, a friend and business associate of Brigham Young. When the Mormon leader bought out Ransohoff during the anti-Gentile boycott, Kahn joined forces with George Bodenberg in the firm of Bodenberg & Kahn. Samuel dissolved this successful association when his younger brother Emanuel arrived in Salt Lake City. Together they founded Kahn Brothers, Wholesale Grocers; soon they were serving all of Utah, Idaho, and Montana.

The more gregarious and politically attuned of the brothers, Samuel helped raise funds for Salt Lake City's first non-Mormon meeting place, Independence Hall, a project violently opposed by the Mormons. He was also one of the organizers of the Liberal party, the first non-Mormon political party in Utah, and he ran for office on their ticket. These activities neither impeded him in business nor dimmed his reputation as a valued Salt Lake City pioneer.

Perceivable in the foregoing accounts are the prerequisites for commercial success on the far western frontier. Those most likely to thrive arrived with capital (their own or borrowed) and some—often extensive—mercantile experience. Strangers in a strange land, Jews frequently operated family enterprises led by the strongest member or found a reliable partner; when one arrangement didn't succeed, they tried another. While Jews generally preferred to work with other Jews, a number of congenial mixed-faith partnerships proved successful and enduring: Solomon & Wickersham (Arizona), Kaufman-Stadler (Montana), and J. B. Doyle & Salomon (Colorado). Most Jewish merchants had good connections with wholesalers in New York, Philadelphia, and, by the late 1850s, San Francisco; or they had a resident buyer, often a partner or a relative, in one of these urban centers making advantageous purchases. Those who advanced most rapidly were also those likely to uphold the conventional virtues and possess respected credentials: thrift, perseverance, education, self-restraint, and sobriety.

These triumphant men of property, however powerful and influential, were a minority. More plentiful were the thousands of less-visible Jewish merchants and artisans who arrived in the Far West lacking one or more of these keys to success. The most likely to be lacking was capital, essential for starting a venture and for keeping it going.

In 1866 Russia-born Julius Basinsky arrived in Helena, Montana, with one thousand cigars

David Livingston stepped off a boat from Germany in 1872 to try his luck in San Francisco. Four years later he opened his own millinery shop and, with brothers Samuel and Edward, expanded it into a general dry goods store. Today it is one of the last of the family-run San Francisco businesses. Courtesy, Livingston Brothers, San Francisco, California

Jicarilla Apaches "Pluma" and "Juan Largo" with employees of Lowenstein, Strousse & Company, Mora, New Mexico Territory, circa 1890; Carl Harberg is sitting, Isaac Appel is standing. Courtesy, Rio Grande Historical Collections/Hobson-Huntsinger University Archives, New Mexico State University Library, Las Cruces

to sell and not enough money to buy lunch in one of Helena's numerous saloons. In 1881 Leopold Ephraim, a Prussian, sent two trunks of merchandise by stagecoach to Isaacson (later called Nogales) on the Arizona-Sonora border. Lacking the fare, he walked from San Francisco to the new Arizona railroad settlement, where he sold the contents of one trunk to pay the freight charges for both. Morris Strouse of Württemberg, Germany, described as "no man to stay in built-up cities," in 1882 drove a wagonload of merchandise across the Continental Divide to the newly staked townsite of Grand Junction, in western Colorado, where he started a trading post and a store.

If the community thrived, the impoverished newcomer advanced, as did Basinsky, Ephraim, and Strouse. Once the undercapitalized Jewish merchant got a toehold, he spared no effort. With forethought or by instinct, he was racing to fortify his base before inevitable and assorted disasters assaulted his infant enterprise. The most difficult of enemies to combat were the elements. Every far western city had its great fires. The newer and smaller settlements built of wood, canvas, or adobe and lacking fire-fighting equipment or a reliable water supply were even more vulnerable. Whether he wept alone in the ashes of his own store or with others in a burned-out business district, the question facing a merchant was the same: Could he muster the resources to reestablish his business, or was he, as was Abe Rashovsky, forced to relinquish his good location (in Caribou, Colorado) and go back to peddling in mining camps to earn a new stake?

Floods were less frequent but no less devastating. On May 19, 1864, torrents of water swept into the usually dry Cherry Creek, inundating the five-year-old town of Denver. A Jewish clothier, Gumble Rosebaum, died in the disaster. Years later another Jewish merchant grimly recalled "standing on the eastern bank watching the raging flood bearing houses, wagons, and all kinds of furniture in its mad and foaming water."

Another threat was that of Indian attack. In fact, army records list 1,064 Indian engagements in the West between 1866 and 1891, some of which were fought by civilians. Few settlers were more vulnerable to marauding Indians than were the freighters forced to haul merchandise through their domains. Some of this beleaguered breed, like freighter-merchant Nathan Benjamin Appel, who worked in the Far West for nearly fifty years, died leaving no assets other than their Indian depredation claims.

Travelers and small storekeepers in remote spots were especially vulnerable to another far western plague, the ubiquitous bandit. In 1877 M. Cahn left the general store he was managing in Miles City, Montana, to go on a buying trip. En route he ran afoul of "Big Nose George" and his gang, who robbed and murdered him. In San Bernardino, California, in 1862 a desperado named Dick Cole entered a dry goods and clothing store owned by Wolff, Isaac, and Louis Cohn,

intending to empty the cashbox and flee. Wolff resisted and was killed; Isaac, in turn, shot and killed Cole. Such stories were commonplace in newspapers of the period.

No more avoidable than the elements or the outlaws was a far more pervasive hazard in the developing region, economic instability. Settlements shot up, flourished, then in a few years began to fade. The most likely to decline were mining towns. In 1883, when the silver boom was at its height, the cloud-veiled community of Leadville, Colorado, had in excess of twenty thousand inhabitants including some seventy-five Jewish merchants and their families and a like number of single men. A quarter of a century later, the population hovered around fifteen hundred and all but a handful of Jews had moved on.

Ill winds from afar could also knock down a healthy young business. The advent of a railroad, for example, brought jubilation to merchants of the depot town and gloom to its newly disadvantaged neighbors. Also losing out to the iron horse were the overland and riverboat freighters. National economic tremors—the panics in the years 1857, 1873, 1893, and 1907—upended thousands of far western businesses, too. The quickest to succumb were the smaller, undercapitalized enterprises.

Bankruptcies were frequent in this catastrophe-prone period and region; in fact, most merchants and entrepreneurs passed through one, and often several, as they traveled the road to success. Hyman Goldberg, Arizona pioneer merchant and territorial legislator, failed after a business fire in Yuma in March 1878. He then opened a store in Harshaw, where in a year he suffered a cave-in and a flood, followed by a fire in August 1881 that destroyed most of his stock. After settling with his creditors, he resurfaced in Phoenix. H. Goldberg & Company was growing fast on "Quick Sales and Small Profits" when, in August 1885, a citywide conflagration began in their warehouse. By then, though, neither fire losses nor a 1888 bankruptcy in a Tombstone branch store could uproot what had become one of Phoenix's leading dry goods and clothing stores.

Of the numerous obstacles, the most unrelenting and for some the most demoralizing

Top: *Samuel Goldstone (pictured here wearing the derby) of Petaluma, California, moved to Cottonwood, Idaho, in 1892 with his wife, Phoebe. A year later he opened his own general merchandise store. In 1896 Goldstone opened a larger store and, within five years, owned several large ranches and numerous properties in Cottonwood and Lewiston. A local historian noted: "Mr. Goldstone is an active Republican and is always found in the lead for any movement that will benefit the town and the country, being progressive and public minded, and he is highly esteemed by all." Courtesy, John L. Turner, Lewiston, Idaho*

Bottom: *"Painting the Town Red"; note the predominance of Jewish-owned stores lining the street. Drawing by Rufus R. Zogbaum; from* Harper's Weekly

was competition. No matter where (city, town, or outpost) or which business (dry goods, groceries, clothing, mining, or farm supplies), profits attracted competitors. Few merchants stated their plight more clearly than Alexander Mayer, who wrote from San Francisco to his uncle in a mixture of chunky German and minced English during the dismal spring of 1851: "It is very Dull here, at present time, Why it Can't get otherwise There are so many Jehudem Here in Business and Everyone Want to Sell and this Year are four

times as man Goods here as there has been Last Year. . . . I think there will be a Great Many failures here and in the North."

Friction between the first merchant in a town and those who followed also could and did cause failures. One such battle became part of the lore of early Genesee, Idaho. Aaron Levy came to Genesee on the Salmon River in 1885, in the wake of a gold strike at Coeur d'Alene. A twenty-five-year veteran of far western vicissitudes, Levy established the first store in the settlement, then

Aaron Levy made and lost several fortunes in French Gulch, California; (Russian-owned) Alaska; and Genesee, Idaho, before he and his wife, Esther, settled in Seattle, Washington. Levy and son-in-law Isaac Cooper formed a Cooper-Levy retail and mail order house in 1892, making their fortune outfitting gold seekers in the Alaska gold rush. Courtesy, Seattle Jewish Archives Project, Suzzallo Library, University of Washington, Seattle

sent for his family. Doing well as the only storekeeper, he soon bought a safe and became the only "banker," then the postmaster.

In under a year, a German-Jewish pack peddler named Jacob Rosenstein opened a store across the lane from Levy's. Rosenstein was amiable and well liked—"Everyone loved Jake Rosenstein," noted one Genesee yarn spinner. Everyone, however, did not include Levy, particularly after Democrat Grover Cleveland was elected president and Democrat Rosenstein wangled the position of postmaster away from Republican Levy.

The animosity between the warring merchants prevented both from enjoying the advantages of the railroad when it came. The surveyor offered to run the tracks adjacent to their stores if together they would contribute the acreage for the depot. As the pair wrangled, other Geneseeans plotted a new townsite and depot some distance from the firstcomers' stores. Levy eventually moved to Seattle, where he and his son-in-law, Isaac Cooper, established the highly profitable retail and mail-order business, the Cooper & Levy Company. Rosenstein moved his store from Old Genesee to New Genesee, where he stocked a new establishment with "almost any item a family could want."

Pioneer Merchandising and Manufacturing Come of Age

By the early 1900s many businesses started by pioneer Jews in tents, shanties, and adobe huts had grown into mature, enduring commercial enterprises. Among them were department stores from one to twelve stories tall situated on choice commercial blocks in western metropolises. Surrounding these emporia were diverse specialty shops offering fashions for the increasingly style-conscious westerners. Serving thinner pocketbooks and more modest tastes in urban neighborhoods, on the main streets of smaller cities and towns and on dusty rural roads were smaller and more mundane replicas of the giant retailers. Goods sold in these lesser retail establishments came, at least in part, from the metropolitan warehouses of Jewish wholesalers and distributors.

In urban industrial districts as well as in the surrounding countryside, other firms founded by these pioneers were processing and, in some cases, packaging for distribution imported products, as well as those produced by the Far West's fields, orchards, vineyards, ranches, fisheries, forests, and mines. Nearby, Jewish-owned factories were turning out clothing and shoes, as well as metal, wood, and leather goods for consumption in the region, the nation, and elsewhere in the world.

Encore Roast Coffee; courtesy, MJB Company

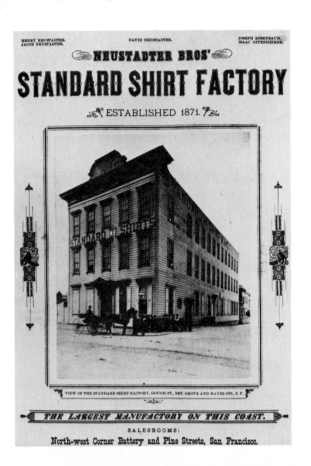

Left: *Neustadter Brothers, San Francisco, California; courtesy, Neustadter Western Jewish History Center, Judah L. Magnes Museum, Berkeley, California*

Below: *Point Loma Brand; courtesy, San Diego Historical Society, San Diego, California; and the Aguirre family*

Facing page and above: *These bank notes from Santa Fe, Phoenix, Tucson, and Seattle are evidence of the far-flung rapid gains made by Jews in far western banking. The Spiegelberg Hermanos note (top left) was not national currency but was backed solely by the Spiegelberg brothers' financial reputation. From the Rochlin Collection*

While present and prominent everywhere in merchandising and manufacturing, Jews were not confined to these endeavors. In a region that was mechanizing and urbanizing, every entrepreneur with a dollar in his pocket and an idea in his head could have a go at something he had never tried before. Jews found roles to play in banking, agriculture, ranching, rails and road building, real estate, and similar enterprises simply by responding to local or regional needs.

Many a Jewish merchant who provided rudimentary banking services as a courtesy to his customers—such as Levy and Rosenstein in Genesee—went on to operate full-service banks. I. E. Solomon of Solomonville, Arizona Territory, for example, who started out by keeping his customers' valuables in his safe, was soon making "handshake" loans to his friends in Graham County (a practice he would later find hard to give up) and then began dealing in drafts and checks. In December 1899 he and a group of southeastern Arizona businessmen opened the Gila Valley Bank in a corner of the Solomon Commercial Company's quarters. (From this institutional seed would spring the Valley National Bank of Arizona.)

By the early twentieth century, exploding industry had spurred the growth of two western

Jewish banking empires. One was headed by Bavaria-born Isaias W. Hellman, who came to Los Angeles in 1859, when he was sixteen. For six years he worked as a clerk and saved his earnings. When haberdasher Adolph Portugal decided to sell out and return to Germany, young Hellman had enough money to buy Portugal's store. He was already doing some banking in his store when he and two prominent Angelenos, William Workman and F. P. F. Temple, decided to start a full-fledged bank. On September 1, 1868, Hellman, Temple & Company was open and accepting deposits. Two years later the partnership was dissolved and Hellman established the Farmers and Merchants Bank of Los Angeles. During the next twenty years banker Hellman participated actively in every phase of Los Angeles life. Wrote Jackson A. Graves: "There was not a merchant, a farmer, a stock raiser whom he [Hellman] had not befriended or to whom he had not advanced money when they needed it." For himself, Hellman did especially well in real estate during the first southern California real estate boom in the 1880s. In 1890, I. W. moved to San Francisco to take over the financially troubled Nevada Bank. He later merged it with the Wells Fargo Nevada National Bank in San Francisco. In 1924 he added the Union Trust Company, creating the Wells Fargo Bank and Union Trust Company, parent of today's Wells Fargo Bank.

Another monetary marvel in San Francisco, then the financial capital of the West, was assembled by a group of California businessmen headed by the daring sons of Delia and Aaron Fleishhacker, Herbert and Mortimer. In 1908 the Fleishhackers and others acquired control of the Anglo-Californian Bank Ltd., organized in 1873 by J. & W. Seligman Company, and the Lazard Frères' London, Paris, and American Bank, organized in 1875. In the following year, the two were consolidated as the Anglo & London, Paris National Bank. With subsequent acquisition of new charters, branches, and services, the enterprise became one of the outstanding financial institutions of twentieth-century California.

From the 1870s on, banks owned completely or partially by Jews were launched in towns and

cities all over the Far West. Outstanding examples were the Bank of Daniel Meyer, founded by Daniel and Jonas Meyer, San Francisco; Puget Sound National Bank, by Jacob Furth and Bailey Gatzert, Seattle; Portland Trust Company, later called the Oregon Bank, by Benjamin I. Cohen, Portland; National Bank of Arizona, by Sol Lewis and Martin Kales, Phoenix; the Merchants National Banking Company, by Lewis Herschfield, Helena, Montana; and the bank of A. Levy, by Achille Levy, Oxnard, California.

Achille Levy, an Alsatian Jew, entered banking in Hueneme, a Ventura County community. He settled there in 1874 and started a general merchandise store with Moise L. Wolff, a distant relative. After six years Levy sold out, traveled to Paris, where he married Lucy Levy, then returned to Ventura County. In 1882, he became an agricultural broker in Hueneme, selling grains, peanuts, beans, barley, honey, fruits, and livestock to Ventura County growers. His suppliers asked him if they could bank their surplus profits until they needed cash to plant or to buy additional land or equipment. Levy continued to operate his own commission and banking business even after he became an incorporator and a founding vice-president of the Bank of Hueneme in August 1889. When a new sugar-beet industry brought growth to inland Oxnard nearby, Levy decided to give his personal banking enterprise a name and a facility there. In 1902 he built a brick building to house the Bank of A. Levy of Oxnard. The bank advanced for twenty-five years under the founder's direction and later, guided by his successors, continued to grow, advertised as "the bank that lima beans built." There are currently six branches of the bank in Ventura County.

To some western pioneer Jews, owning and cultivating the soil was more tantalizing than any other endeavor. Barred from the land for centuries in most of Europe, observant Jews daily revisited the fields and pastures of their ancient homeland—ever greener in separation—by reading the Holy Scriptures, written by farmers for farmers. Not surprisingly, a number of Jews exercised their newfound right to own land as individual homesteaders (after the passage of the Homestead Act of 1862), as agricultural colonists, as large-scale growers, or as agricultural financiers. The outcomes of these ventures ranged from destitution to agricultural duchies.

In 1865, when the gold gave out in California Gulch, Colorado, Simon Nathan, his wife, Anna, and their four small children wagoned down the eastern slopes of the Rockies from California Gulch to Beaver Creek in the Arkansas Valley, where they farmed and raised livestock. For the capable and hardworking Simon and Anna, one problem loomed above the many: the threat of Indian attack. After their baby daughter was kidnapped and held for ransom, Anna was never easy when the men were in the fields or on the range. As she later recalled, to conceal from the Indians that she was alone, she used to crawl on the ground to the barn to milk the cows, then inch back on all fours dragging a full pail behind her. By 1867 the Nathans had had enough of agrarian hardship and had moved to nearby infant Pueblo, where Simon opened the town's first store.

Agricultural colonies sprang up between 1881 and 1912 in Colorado, Wyoming, Utah, Oregon, Washington, California, and Montana. These experimental agrarian undertakings were started for a variety of reasons. Immigrant aid societies helped organize a few colonies in an effort to move eastern European immigrants—arriving in large numbers after 1881—from overcrowded eastern seaboard cities and into the less-populated West. Back-to-the-land political and philosophical movements inspired the formation of other colonies.

Some colonists, such as Ukrainian Jew Joe Cohen—who was part of the thirteen-family group that settled at Cotopaxi in 1882—simply wanted to farm, according to his son Max P. Cowan, a prominent far western cattle raiser. Cotopaxi lasted three disastrous years. Failure has been attributed to fraud on the part of the landowner Emmanuel Saltiel, a Portuguese Jew; the inexperience of the colonists—most were Hassidic merchants and artisans; and the negligence or ignorance of agents from the Hebrew Emigrant Aid Society. Unable to cultivate the rocky soil, the newcomers sought jobs in nearby

mines or on the railroad. Cohen and a few others eventually found considerable success as independent ranchers and farmers, as did other Colorado Jews. Like a storekeeper listing the other merchants on Main Street, Cowan named other Jewish ranchers and farmers in Colorado: William Handelman and "wheat king" Simon Fishman, both veterans of the Atwood Colony, which lasted from 1859 to 1899; long-bearded Yosel David Mandell "riding on his plow behind a team of horses"; and the Robinsons and the Ledermans, who were dairy farmers. There was also a colony of Orthodox Jews farming near Derby; Cowan's uncle, Aaron Gardenswart, "whose pretty daughters raced their ponies in the farm lanes"; Abe Morantz, who raised sugar beets with Cowan's father; and Alter Cohn, who spent his entire life in farming.

For Arizonan Michael Wormser, farming was more than an occupation, it was an obsession. Born the son of a poor butcher in Mittelbronn, Lorraine, when Wormser died in Phoenix on April 25, 1898, he was the sole possessor of a $250,000 agricultural kingdom. He spent thirteen years in the Arizona Territory, wrestling with mining, merchandising, and cattle raising, all with minimal success before he tried farming. His first crop in the Salt River Valley in 1876 was profitable, so he expanded his lands (at one point he controlled 23,000 acres) and invested in irrigation projects and sugar-beet refineries.

French, Yiddish-speaking, a bachelor, and interested in little but business, Wormser hardly could have been counted as "one of the boys" in late nineteenth-century Phoenix. His dealings with Mexican sharecroppers, who called him Don Miguel, El Judío; his passion for litigation—no debt was too small to press—and his miserly disregard for creature comforts earned him ugly adjectives. Business associates who knew him well, however, called him hard but fair and counted him a creative and a significant contributor to the agricultural advancement of the Salt River Valley. Although he was never a joiner, Wormser gave his coreligionists what he most loved—land—for the Phoenix Beth Israel Cemetery.

A few Jews combined the high-stakes games of international commodities and large-scale

Michael Wormser arrived in Phoenix, Arizona Territory, in 1874. When he died in 1898, he owned approximately 8,000 acres. Courtesy, Arizona Historical Society, Tucson

farming. The earliest and most swashbuckling was a freethinking German Jew named Isaac Friedlander, who was dubbed "the Grain King" in the early 1850s while most of his fellows were concentrating on gold and goods. Friedlander, who stood six feet seven inches tall, arrived in California in July 1849. After a fruitless spell mining in Yuba, he settled in San Francisco, where he soon found an open arena for his speculative bent and developer's vision. Friedlander, according to one biographer, was the first to see the agricultural possibilities of the San Joaquin and Livermore valleys and was the man most responsible for their early development.

By 1852 he had made his mark in the grain market. At the height of his career, he owned thousands of acres of wheatland, financed numerous other wheat growers, and maintained twenty vessels for shipping grain abroad. His first big setback came with the 1860 drought, and other reverses followed. The most significant was the repeated and ultimately successful drive to crack his near-monopoly of the grain market. A long-standing heart condition, worsened by his nerve-stripping undertakings, took his life at fifty-four. By then his vast lands had passed into other hands.

The makers of a 1920s movie *Der Yiddisher Cowboy* were going for laughs when they put a ghetto Jew in a Stetson and chaps. The city-bound Jewish stereotype bears a seed of truth, but so does the Jews' long and rich pastoral history. From Genesis 13:2 ("Abraham was rich in cattle") to First Chronicles 5:9 ("their cattle multiplied in the land of Gilead"), the Holy Scriptures abound with Hebrew herdsmen. As consumers

WAITING FOR A CHINOOK

Louis Kaufman, a German Jew, emigrated to San Francisco in 1864, then to Helena, Montana, mining until 1872 when he formed the Stadler and Kaufman Meat Company with Louis Stadler. Charles M. Russell, American western artist, managed their ranch for many years. The winter of 1886–1887 was a disastrous one for the region, and Stadler and Kaufman asked Russell for a report on how their herd was holding up. Russell's famous sketch, Waiting for a Chinook (Last of the 5,000), *was the grim reply. Courtesy, Montana Stockgrowers Association, Helena*

of beef and sheep products and domesticated fowl, Jews continued to raise, butcher, and buy and sell livestock in Europe, later in America.

Numerous pioneer Jews entered the livestock industry in the Far West and worked in every capacity, from cowpoke and shepherd to cattle tycoon and sheep baron. One of those who did time on the trail was penniless Alexander Rittmaster (later a prominent businessman), who in 1867 walked from Council Bluffs, Iowa, to Colorado, spending eight months en route occupied as a cowhand.

Among the first ranchers in Idaho was Meyers Cohen, a Prussian Jew who came west in the early 1860s and opened a store in Malad City,

Idaho, near the Utah border. Excited by the rich soil, luxuriant grass, mild climate, and full streams in nearby Marsh Valley, Cohen homesteaded there and acquired some livestock. By the time the Union Pacific and civilization reached Bannock County, Cohen was an established rancher and farmer; later he spurred the community to establish an irrigation company and to institute other improvements that made Marsh Valley an agricultural center.

Sol Floersheim developed a passion for ranching and passed it on to his son Milton and grandson David, both graduates of Colorado State College in animal husbandry. In 1880 Hamburg-born Floersheim went to work for the

Charles Ilfeld Company in Las Vegas and quickly became a valued employee. He was a small man—five feet tall and 110 pounds—but remarkably feisty for a flyweight. When he was sixty a customer half his age and nearly twice his weight pulled a knife on him. Floersheim relieved him of the weapon, gave him a beating, and collected the money the man owed him as well. Sol was also a spellbinding raconteur and a self-taught physician. He delivered three hundred babies, performed simple surgeries, and enjoyed a wide reputation as a diagnostician. Starting in 1884 he spent four years as Ilfeld's *partido* clerk and collector. Touring the territory each June and October and gathering wool and sheep from ranchers raising ewes for Ilfeld, his knowledge of and interest in ranching grew.

By 1889, having married Emma Blumenthal and fathered four children, Sol, with a bit of capital tucked away, was ready to go out on his own. He started a store in the northern New Mexico Territory, on the new Atchison, Topeka and Santa Fe line, first at Watrous, then at Ocaté, and finally at Springer, on the prairie near the Colorado border. His heart set on sheep ranching, merchant Sol built his reserve capital and waited for the right property. In 1897 with Harold C. Abbott as his partner, he bought the Jaritas Ranch, thirteen miles east of Springer with twenty miles of the Canadian River curling through the property. During bad years Sol was forced to add partners to keep going. By 1912 the Floersheim family were the sole owners of Jaritas, all sixty-three thousand fenced and well-watered acres. Tens of thousands of sheep, eighty-eight thousand in a peak year, grazed on Floersheim grass, until Sol's successors switched to Herefords.

Henry Altman, a Cheyenne pioneer, was a well-established businessman and member of the city council when he was attracted to cattle raising. In 1887 Altman and Dan McIlvain bought what had been Wyoming's most prestigious cattle ranch, the Swan Land and Cattle Company Ltd. Run by Alex Swan and financed by British stockholders, the company was widely known for its herd of purebred Herefords acquired from

stud farms in Herefordshire. The firm failed in 1887 because of a series of misfortunes, including an outbreak of Texas fever that killed thousands of Swan longhorns, and the historic blizzard of 1886, which wiped out 75 percent of the remaining stock. Altman and McIlvain rebuilt the herd and began filling orders for their prize steers. The head of the operation for twenty-six years, Altman was widely commended for holding together what was then America's largest herd of choice Herefords.

After the Civil War, no single group of enterprises generated as much excitement as modern transportation—transcontinental, regional, and urban—mostly rail and, to a lesser extent, water. In the unformed West, it shaped some communities, obliterated others, and completed the Americanization of the region. Jewish go-getters scrambled to get on board as financiers, promoters, builders, and operators, and they succeeded, except at the highest levels. (No Jews made anything close to the more than $100 million California's Big Four cleared on the construction of the western section of the first continental railroad.) Closest to the top were the ubiquitous Seligmans, at the time the country's leading financiers.

The company's chief, Joseph Seligman, initially hung back from the iron horse invasion, wary of railroad investments. Demand for financial backing proved too profitable to resist, though. At first the cautious Seligman confined his firm to selling railroad bonds. Once involved, however, the company was obliged to guard its investments by owning and operating railroads as well. Between 1866 and 1872 Joseph invested his concern's money in three competing railroad companies and simultaneously was a director of the South Pacific Rail Road; the Missouri, Kansas & Texas Railway (the Katy), and the Atlantic and Pacific Railroad. In 1872 he wrote his brother William, "We have made a fortune in the new R. Roads in the last six years." Even so, he still believed the house of Seligman had too many railroad bonds for comfort.

The Panic of 1873 wrung new complaints from the wearying moneyman, who at fifty-three was feeling the strain of "unconscionable" competition. He was disgusted with all railroads and would never, he swore, be tempted to undertake the sale of another railroad bond. His vow proved to be short-lived.

The next year, enchanted by his own sales pitch, Joseph was once again touting the Atlantic & Pacific Railroad (chartered in 1866 to run along the thirty-fifth parallel from Springfield, Missouri, via the Southwest, to Needles, California) as the "only line [to the Pacific] never obstructed by snows." Despite Joseph's efforts the A. & P. failed in 1875, and its franchise went to the new St. Louis and San Francisco Railway, "the Frisco." In 1880 the Frisco ran out of steam and was forced to sell a half interest in the A. & P. to the Atchison, Topeka, and Santa Fe. Using the A. & P. and the Frisco franchises, the Santa Fe finally completed the thirty-fifth-parallel route. Joseph Seligman never had the satisfaction of seeing the southwestern line in operation. He died in 1880 at age sixty, five years before the A. T. & S. F. reached Los Angeles.

During the iron horse era, dozens of Jewish investors built narrow-gauge railroads, short lines, and extension lines to speed the growth of their stores, mines, farms, ranches, and townsites or simply to share in transportation profits. Simon Bamberger, who in 1917 became the first non-Mormon governor of Utah, fought for eighteen years to complete a thirty-mile interurban railroad between Salt Lake City and Ogden, Utah. Opposition stemmed mainly from the two existing railroads using the route, whose owners were determined to block a third.

Bamberger began by building a line to Beck's Hot Springs. Several years passed before he acquired a franchise to continue to Farmington, where he built and operated Lagoon, a successful resort on an artificial lake. It took him another five years to win permission for a third section. To enter Ogden entailed crossing over Union Pacific tracks. No short-line promoter in western railroading ever fought so strong and unyielding an opponent as the powerful U.P. and won. On August 4, 1908, the first train of the Bamberger Railroad cheerily chugged from Salt Lake City to Ogden. The line underwent electrification in 1912 and was soon the most successful of the future governor's numerous business undertakings.

One little big man towered over Colorado transportation, a Russian Jew named Otto Mears. He arrived in the Far West in 1851, a twelve-year-old orphan with only his lively wits and clever hands to support him. During his long career, he earned the sobriquet "Pathfinder of the San Juan," a rugged, mineral-rich region in southwestern Colorado.

As Mears liked to tell it, his entry into transportation resulted from a chance encounter in 1867 with William Gilpin, an early Colorado governor. Mears's wheat-laden wagons had turned over on the two-mile-high Poncha Pass. Riding past on horseback, Gilpin stopped to suggest that the distressed freighter build a much-needed toll road. Mears decided to heed the suggestion. His first attempt, a seven-mile road costing $14,000, started at Saguache—a settlement Mears was developing—and ran over Poncha Pass to Nathrop, connecting the Arkansas and San Luis valleys. For eleven years Mears continued to cut roads through previously all-but-impassable terrain. Nine important roads and dozens of lesser ones brought once-isolated camps and towns into contact with one another and with supply centers, opening the area and converting numerous losing mines into money-makers.

In 1888 Mears embarked on a new and even more unlikely mission: constructing a narrow-gauge railroad seventeen miles long across the San Juan Mountains through the Red Mountain Pass, 11,075 feet high. Incorporating the Silverton Railroad Company, he raised the required $725,000 and had his chief engineer, Arthur Ridgway, lay out tracks from the junction of the Denver and Rio Grande Railroad near Silverton alongside Mears's toll road to Ironton. The design included the famed Chattanooga Loop and a unique roofed turntable to make return trips possible during heavy snows. It was completed in 1889, largely by Ute Indian laborers working solely by hand.

The next year Mears built a short line, the

Far Western Jewish Cattle Brands

Pioneer Jews became ranchers and stock raisers for a variety of reasons. Wolf Sachs, a native of Russia, emigrated to central Arizona, where he simply continued the farming life he had been born into and knew best. Others, like David Levy, new to farming, saw that ample inexpensive land, a large, skilled labor pool, and a growing market represented a promising investment. Merchants like Levy & Koshland accepted cattle instead of cash, and found themselves *de facto* cattlemen. Henry Jastro distributed beer to the towns around Bakersfield, California before becoming involved in ranching. He became a major figure in the California livestock industry.

Aztec Land & Cattle Company
Holbrook, AZ

D. Levy & Company
Prescott, AZ

Bella Jacobs
Tucson, AZ

William Koshland
Signal, AZ

Hannah Jacobs
San Diego, CA

Jacob Bergman
San Diego, CA

Samuel Barnett
San Bernardino, CA

M. Brandenstein & Company
Winnemucca, NV

Reinhart Land & Livestock Company
Winnemucca, NV

Charles Ilfeld
Las Vegas, NV

Nate S. Bibo
Grant, NM

Mrs. George Schuster
Thoreau, NM

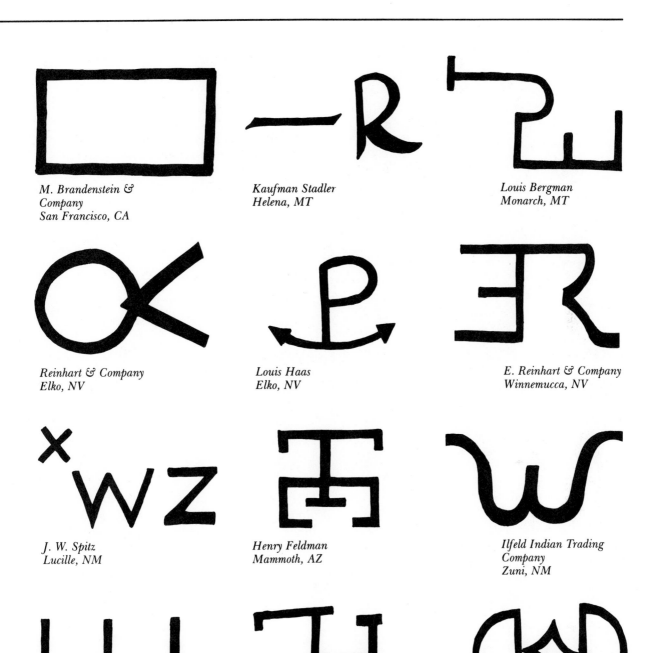

M. Brandenstein &
Company
San Francisco, CA

Kaufman Stadler
Helena, MT

Louis Bergman
Monarch, MT

Reinhart & Company
Elko, NV

Louis Haas
Elko, NV

E. Reinhart & Company
Winnemucca, NV

J. W. Spitz
Lucille, NM

Henry Feldman
Mammoth, AZ

Ilfeld Indian Trading
Company
Zuni, NM

Albert Lindauer
Deming, NM

Lina Badt
Wells, NV

Goldsmith & Fisher
Cheyenne, WY

Otto Mears (far left) and his narrow gauge Silverton Railroad; courtesy, Richard A. Ronzio

Silverton Northern, which traveled four miles into Animas Canyon to serve the mines there. His third venture was the Rio Grande Southern, running from Ouray to Ridgeway and from Silverton to Durango over Lizard Head Pass, with a high point at Lizard Head, altitude 13,113 feet. The breathtaking scenery and the Ophir Loop make this line one of the most exciting narrowgauge railroads in the country. Two years later, jostled loose by the Panic of 1893, the Rio Grande Southern and the rest of Mears's roads and railroads, except the Silverton Northern, fell into the hands of receivers.

Drained of wherewithal and morale, Mears retreated to Maryland, where he spent six years building and operating the Chesapeake Beach Railroad. By the turn of the century he was rehabilitating the Silverton Northern and gingerly trying out new transportation plans. In 1906

Mears moved back to Colorado with an overly ambitious scheme for a motor-age network of highways to radiate from Denver and to be built with prison labor. In 1907 he settled his family in Silverton and there continued to pursue his various interests.

Throughout the period, a slender but influential file of Jews speculated in land and developed communities. Arizona land claimant Solomon Barth was commended for and accused of a number of things, but never of being a small thinker. During the first decade of his long and varied Arizona career, Barth was a miner, pony express rider, sutler, and Indian trader. During this period he allegedly concluded a treaty with Navajo tribal chiefs that granted him title to nearly all of the northern Arizona Territory, including the Grand Canyon.

More plausible was his claim to the town of

Michael Reese arrived in California in 1858, when 23,000 San Franciscans left for the Fraser River in British Columbia during a short-lived gold rush there. Many of the departing were willing to sell their city property for a fraction of its value, as were large eastern investors, believing booming San Francisco was possibly a "bust." Reese purchased as much land as possible, and his faith in the future of the city was repaid in a few months, as land values quickly rebounded. Courtesy, The Bancroft Library, University of California, Berkeley

St. John's, which Barth, grubstaked by poker winnings, founded in 1874. He and his brothers Nathan and Morris dammed a section of the nearby Little Colorado River and began to farm and raise livestock. In 1877 a party of Mormons bought twelve hundred acres from Sol and settled down to create a Mormon community without hampering Barth's standing as St. John's founder and leading politico.

More representative were the experiences of David Kaufman, who arrived in Seattle in 1868 from Victoria, British Columbia. In an optimistic mood, the thirty-five-year-old tailor agreed to pay $100 for forty acres of land in the Green Lake district. Friends called him foolish, but Kaufman scrimped, first to pay off the seller and then to acquire another twelve-acre site, for which he laid out an exorbitant $200. Two decades later

This bookplate from the Sutro Library depicts Adolph Sutro's mining and real estate ventures. Courtesy, Sutro Library, San Francisco

both parcels were among the most valuable in Seattle. Kaufman retired from tailoring to manage his properties, help build Temple de Hirsch, and deliver homilies on thrift and foresight.

In that great economic whirlpool called California, all enterprises—gold, commerce, agriculture, ranching, and oil—generated land speculation and development. Upon arrival in San Diego in 1850, Louis Rose envisioned the old pueblo emerging as a modern port city and the terminus of a transcontinental railroad; he began gathering land for the town he named Roseville. His first purchase was eighty acres in the center of present-day Point Loma, now a genteel San Diego residential district. He continued to acquire adjacent acreage until he had enough for his townsite, Roseville-on-the-Bay.

To advance his dream community, he added a 472-foot wharf; invested heavily in one railroad and then a second; and widely touted the future community's unsurpassed bay, mild climate, and good water. Unluckily for Rose, and possibly for San Diego—Rose's site was more scenic—Alonzo Horton spirited more newcomers to his development three miles south of old San Diego, where the first railroad terminated in 1885.

From the gold rush days forward, Jews helped shape San Francisco and its environs. One early Jewish realtor, Michael Reese, whose eccentric miserliness was as widely noted as was his acumen, made millions ($8 million, according to his will) in Pacific Coast real estate. He arrived in San Francisco in June 1850 with $150,000 earned in land development in St. Paul,

Minnesota. After a losing fling at merchandising, Reese returned to real estate. He got his start buying San Francisco properties from gold seekers rushing to the Fraser River in 1858.

A 250-pound, six-foot bachelor, Reese began each day at four in the morning with a swim in the chilly Pacific. The rest of the day he spent tending his multiplying properties and dining and playing high-stakes poker. At his death on August 2, 1878, his holdings were listed, taking up a full column in a San Francisco newspaper.

At the close of the depressed 1870s, Adolph Sutro made a triumphal return to San Francisco from the silver mines of Nevada with $5 million to invest. His heroic ingenuity, energy, and appetite for astounding feats undiminished, he soon found an unlikely real estate development to occupy himself and his money. Its matrix was a 1½-acre property with a panoramic view of the Pacific Ocean. Sutro bought it in 1881 for $15,000 and acquired 22 acres of surrounding land to create Sutro Heights, his private estate. To this he added 1½ miles of beach land, including Cliff House; the shoreline and bluffs facing the Golden Gate; San Miguel Rancho, a 1,150-acre spread encompassing Twin Peaks; and sandy stretches bordering on Golden Gate Park.

With his usual flair he transformed the windswept bluff at Sutro Heights into intricately designed gardens, which he opened to the public in 1885. Of the then run-down and disreputable Cliff House he made a family resort; nearby he constructed the sumptuous Sutro Baths. He covered Mount Parnassus and Mount Olympus with fir, pine, and eucalyptus trees and planted the denigrated dunes ("Sutro's sandlot folly") with bent and Bermuda grass. Improved and subdivided, these former wastelands earned Sutro a new fortune.

Flimsy or substantial, handsome or hideous, exploiting the setting or obliterating it, by 1912 a network of communities spanned the Far West. To the delight of some and to the despair of others, in sixty-four years the region had been irrevocably transformed from a vast and largely untouched Indian/Hispanic domain to a self-sustaining section of twentieth-century United States. From the outset Jews had worked shoulder to shoulder with the rest of the pioneer population to achieve that end; like the non-Jewish majority, they had given what they had and had taken what they could.

Imbued with enthusiasm for the beauty, the economic potential, and the relative lack of civil and social constraints, most Jews in the Far West quickly decided to settle there permanently. As soon as they were able to scratch out any kind of living, these pioneers, most of whom had come west as footloose young bachelors, began to think of finding mates and starting families. For many, this second challenge required no less energy, persistence, and enterprise than did the first.

Chapter Four

OF ONE FLESH AND SEVERAL CULTURES

I have ceased to wonder that their little heads are turned as fast as they get here. . . . If a Gent wished to be distinguished by the honor of accompanying a lady to a Ball, they are of frequent occurrence nowadays, and has not the extraordinary fortune of securing a *grown* lady, i.e., from 12 upwards, he cannot secure a *young* lady, i.e., from 6 to 12, without at least offering an invitation a week beforehand.

In the early 1850s in California, when Bernhard Marks wrote the above, finding a dance partner was difficult, but obtaining a wife seemed close to impossible. This problem plagued all men who arrived on the raw frontier unattached but was particularly difficult for Jews, who found themselves in a perplexing situation. Many came out of Jewish communities that viewed a bachelor as "no man at all," and one who married outside the faith as dead. Yet the nearest Jewish women, for the most part, were thousands of miles away.

A few Jews, relishing the distance from what they saw as outmoded Old World traditions, married whomever they chose. Others wedded a woman of another faith but remained emotionally tied to their own heritage. More—probably the majority—clung to their religious identity, a bulwark in an alien atmosphere. When

Denver had only one huppa *(wedding canopy) in 1892, the year Ann Korch and Sam Grimes decided to marry. So Ann and Sam had to coordinate their plans with those of another Jewish couple whose wedding was scheduled for the same day, June 26. Courtesy, Rocky Mountain Jewish Historical Society, Denver, Colorado*

marrying, they chose Jewish women or didn't marry at all.

Louis Felsenthal was one of a number of pioneer Jews who remained bachelors. A native of Prussia, he arrived in New Mexico Territory in 1858, when he was twenty-six. During his forty years in the territory, Felsenthal worked as a legal and commercial clerk, his grasp of many languages aiding him in the multicultural frontier town. He served as a Union officer in the Civil War and further demonstrated valor by twice raising a volunteer infantry to defend the Santa Fe Trail against assaulting Pueblo Indians. Deeply fascinated with the developing Southwest, he was a founding member of the Historical Society of New Mexico.

Felsenthal's rich and varied experiences, however, never included marriage. His biographer, Jackie Mekata, speculated about his reasons. His family in Prussia, she noted, was Orthodox, and Felsenthal himself retained a strong attachment to what little Jewish communal life existed in Santa Fe. Lacking the resources to send for a Jewish wife from Prussia or to travel east to find one for himself, he had no choice but to remain single. However, despite his bachelorhood, Mekata pointed out, "there was no reason to assume that Felsenthal was celibate, since Santa Fe was a 'wide open' town with a somewhat casual attitude toward non-married people living together."

These easygoing views concerning intimate relationships prevailed throughout the Far West in the nineteenth century. As a result, pioneer Jews and frontier women participated in various

In 1861 lifelong bachelor Louis Felsenthal was leading a comfortable life as a clerk for the New Mexico territorial government when he volunteered, possibly out of a desire for adventure, for the Union army. After four years of battling Confederate Texans and then Indians, he was more than ready to resign his commission and return to civilian life. Courtesy, Museum of New Mexico, Santa Fe

kinds of unions: marriages and cohabitations, as well as brief encounters.

In the earlier or more remote settlements, where Americans and Indians were in close contact, some Jews took Indian women for wives. Isadore Meyerwitz was one. Described variously as a Russian or Polish Jew, Meyerwitz apparently journeyed to San Francisco from Alabama in 1849. In the early 1850s, he gained prominence as the companion of explorer Peter Lassen on the latter's treks through California. Together they established trading posts and ranching settlements at the foot of the Sierra Nevada in California, settling in 1855 in the Honey Lake Valley near the California-Nevada border.

At some point during those years, Meyerwitz married an Indian woman, whose name unfortunately has not been preserved. They lived in a long, low log house on Meyerwitz's ranch

until the summer of 1856, when they met with a mishap. Their story is recounted in Asa Merrill Fairfield's *Pioneer History of Lassen County:*

In the month of July, 1856, Isadore and his Indian wife were drowned in Honey Lake. He and Sailor Jack built a sailboat out of a wagon box or some old boards, something more like a box than a boat. It was a crazy affair, and their neighbors warned them against risking their lives in it. Evidently no attention was paid to their advice, for soon after it was finished, Isadore and his wife, George Lathrop, R. J. Scott, Reed, and Sailor Jack took a sail in it, starting out from near Isadore's ranch. When they had reached quite a distance from the shore, a sudden gust of wind upset the boat and threw them all into the water. They all managed to get back to the boat, and some of them clung to it, the others getting up on the bottom of it. The Indian woman kept slipping from the boat, and every time she did this, Isadore would put her back. Finally, he got tired out, and she drowned. Soon after this, he gave up and let go of the boat.

Documenting another Indian-Jewish marriage is a painting of a venerable Indian woman with the curious name of Sken-What-Ux Friedlander. According to local history, Sken-What-Ux was a Colville Indian born in Keller, Washington Territory, a direct descendant of the tribe's female chief, Kar-Ne-Za, and the daughter of Standing Cloud. She married Louis Friedlander, an early Jewish trader in the Washington Territory, and became a respected member of the general community. In her later years Sken-What-Ux became affectionately known as "Grandma Elizabeth" Friedlander.

Much more is known about the life of Solomon Bibo, born August 29, 1853, the sixth of eleven children of Isak and Blümchen Bibo, in Brakel, Westphalia, Prussia. Following the lead of his older brothers Nathan and Simon, Solomon arrived in New York on October 16, 1869, and journeyed from there to Santa Fe, New Mexico, where he joined Nathan and Simon in their merchandising business.

The brothers' trading operations put them in close contact with local Indians, and Solomon grew fascinated with their culture. He ultimately became the trusted advisor of the Acoma Pueblo Indians near Santa Fe. The Acomas had been fighting an uphill battle for years to regain lands taken from them under Spanish rule and passed

Sken-What-Ux (Elizabeth) was a direct descendant of Colville Indian chiefs. She married Isadore Friedlander, a trader in the Washington Territory. Courtesy, William D. Hardwick and the Maryhill Museum of Fine Arts, Maryhill, Washington

onto the United States after the Mexican War. Fluent in Keres, the Acoma language—a rare ability for a white man—Bibo helped the tribe fight its case in court. In this battle he was not entirely successful, earning himself the hostility of the United States government and even a government-initiated suit accusing him of attempting to defraud the Indians. (He was eventually cleared of all charges.) Yet the tie between Bibo and the Acomas remained strong.

In 1885, Solomon married twenty-one-year-old Juana Valle, granddaughter of a former Acoma chief. Two marriage ceremonies took place—an Indian one before a Catholic priest on May 1 at Acoma and a civil one before a justice of the peace on August 30. Bibo was now officially a member of the Acoma tribe. In addition, several times in the late 1880s (the exact dates are uncertain) Bibo was appointed pueblo governor, the Acoma equivalent of a tribal chief.

Embracing Indian culture did not mean that Bibo abandoned his Jewish heritage. A cantor's son raised in an observant home, Solomon valued Judaism too highly not to pass it on to his children. After their marriage in 1885, the Bibos moved first to nearby Cubero, New Mexico, then to San Francisco to provide for their children's secular and Jewish education.

As for Juana, she adapted to the world of her husband, learning to speak English and developing a good sense of business. Though they were temperamental opposites—Juana calm and imperturbable; Solomon mercurial and volatile—the marriage was a happy one. Their good friend librarian-historian Charles Lummis described their union reverently as "so beautiful an example and so rare an inspiration." The couple remained together until Solomon's death

Juana Valle (right), granddaughter of Martin Valle, governor of the Acoma Pueblo Indians, and Solomon Bibo (left), New Mexican merchant and Indian trader, married on May 1, 1885. Courtesy, Carl Bibo, Santa Fe, New Mexico

in 1934; Juana died seven years later. Their ashes were interred at the Home of Peace Mausoleum (Temple Emanu-El) in Colma, California.

Mexican women—appealing and, more important, present—attracted many frontiersmen in the Southwest. A Jew who succumbed to their charms was likely to find himself the father of Catholic children, and possibly a Catholic himself if he did not take strong measures to preserve his own religious identity. Nevertheless, a number of early southwestern Jews claimed señoritas of their own.

Such was the case in the colorful Jewish-Mexican union of Isaac Levy and Magdalena Riise, who married in Yuma, Arizona Territory, in 1880. Levy, born in 1847 in Chalon sur Marne, France, came to the United States at age twenty-one, spending a short time in San Francisco before heeding the call of the Arizona goldfields. He traveled to Arizona City (now Yuma) via river

steamboat and became great friends with its captain; when offered a job on board as steward, Levy happily accepted.

In 1878, while attending a dance in town, Levy spotted a dark-eyed young woman across the dance floor and fell instantly in love with her. She was Magdalena Casares Riise, who despite her youth already had seen a good deal of life. In 1874, barely fourteen years old, Magdalena had married Albert Riise of Denmark with her family's grudging consent. The marriage had ended in tragedy. A year after their wedding, while visiting his family in Europe, Riise suffered a fatal fall from a horse, and Magdalena was left a fifteen-year-old widow with an infant son.

When Magdalena met Isaac Levy, she was a blooming eighteen and apparently as attracted to him as he was to her. She agreed to wait for two years while Levy returned to France in 1879

One Jewish-Mexican marriage that gave rise to a dynamic southwestern family was the union of Alex Levin of Bahn, Prussia (with his son, Henry, at the left), and Zenona Molina of Sonora, Mexico. The Levins were among the first families to settle in Tucson after the Civil War. A brewer, Levin foresaw demand for a good, cold lager in that extremely arid Arizona climate. Also an audacious entrepreneur and impresario, in 1869 Alex started Levin's Park. The three-acre entertainment center eventually included lushly landscaped gardens, a restaurant, a dance pavilion, a theater, an opera house, riding stables, an archery range, and other recreational facilities. During its heyday it was the site of every important social and communal event in Tucson. Descendants of this energetic, imaginative pair include violinist Natalie (Levin) Echavarria, singer-actress Luisa (Ronstadt) Espinol, and singer Linda Ronstadt. Courtesy, Arizona Historical Society, Tucson

to hire a substitute for his French army service. They married on his return and, after a brief residence in a nearby mining camp, where Levy ran the camp store and served as justice of the peace, the couple and their family returned to Yuma; there Levy soon became the town's principal merchant.

The Levy household was a relaxed, open place. It ultimately held eleven children including Charles, Magdalena's son from her first marriage, and Magdalena's sister Eulalia. The ménage was served by two Indian men, José Yuma and José Mohave, who with their wives and families lived on the Levy property. Besides tending the Levy house, the Josés served as the children's guardians on summer trips to Los Angeles. On such jaunts, the men's bare feet and long braided

hair attracted much attention, but eyes forward and silent, they would ignore all questions and would not let anyone near the children. The offspring of the three families—Levys, Yumas, and Mohaves—grew up together and became devoted to one another, so much so, in fact, that the children of the two Indian families would later take the surname Levy.

Magdalena was pregnant with their eleventh child when, on January 4, 1898, Levy died in San Francisco following an operation. He was interred, according to his wishes, in Home of Peace Memorial Park in Los Angeles.

It was also entirely possible for these frontier busters to cohabit with an Indian or Mexican woman without damaging their status as upright citizens. As a consequence, lonely pioneer Jews living in scrawny new towns or in remote mining camps occasionally engaged in extended and often fruitful relationships with local women. Some of these unions lasted a lifetime; others, only until the frontiersman was ready and able to settle down with a Jewish wife. Barron Jacobs of Tucson, Arizona Territory, a pioneer businessman, fell in love with a Mexican woman who bore his illegitimate child, yet he remained one of Tucson's most prominent citizens, serving as territorial treasurer in the 1870s and acting as a leader in the town's social and literary life. When Jacobs ultimately did send for a wife, he chose sixteen-year-old Yetta, a Jewish girl who, her hair still in braids, journeyed to Tucson from New York City. She learned of the child shortly after her arrival and, sensible and fair-minded be-

yond her years, ensured that he or she was properly raised and educated.

Others who lived in communities where Hispanic customs prevailed were at times inspired to maintain simultaneously a *casa grande* and a *casa chica*. From 1872 until his death seventeen years later, Bernard Cohn, a prominent Los Angeles businessman, had a Mexican mistress and family. For a time, he maintained two separate households: one an Orthodox Jewish home with his wife, Esther, and their three children; the other staunchly Catholic and housing Delfina Verelas and their four sons. The arrangement was hardly secret—even Cohn's rabbi knew of it—but Cohn was nonetheless respected as a pious Jew and civic leader.

The problem of finding a suitable mate was

Lillie Solomon, daughter of Anna and I. E. Solomon, was born in Solomonville, Arizona Territory, in 1879. Lillie went to school in New York but preferred the bucolic southeastern Arizona Territory. In 1904 Lillie married merchant Max Lantin of Globe. Courtesy, Arizona Historical Society, Tucson

German-born Hedwig Kaestner was working as a domestic when she and Boise, Idaho, merchant Moses Alexander felkl in love. She converted to Judaism and, after they married in 1876, she became Helena Alexander. She was at his side during his long, successful career as a merchant and public servant. Alexander was the mayor of Boise from 1897 to 1899 and from 1901 to 1903 and served as Idaho governor from 1915 to 1919. Courtesy, Idaho Historical Society, Boise

not limited to the lonely first generation of western Jewish settlers. Their children faced troublesome dilemmas as well. Raised in pluralistic western settlements and given liberal educations, they often felt as strong a tie to the democratic openness of American society as to their Jewish heritage. Some, despite their Jewish upbringing, fell in love with local Anglo-Christians and sought to marry them. Family opposition, however, could be adamant. Having managed to preserve their Jewishness against great odds, without synagogues and at times without coreligionists, many Jewish frontier parents were determined to see their children do the same.

Anna and I. E. Solomon, who founded Solomonville in the southeastern Arizona Territory, succeeded in realizing that desire, although not without taking a strong stand. Around the turn of the century, their daughter, Lillie, then in her early twenties, fell in love with a young non-Jewish lawyer of the town. The pair wanted to marry, but Mother Solomon intervened. William Brooks, another Solomonville attorney, recorded the result in a letter of August 7, 1904:

The Solomon family are busy preparing for the approaching wedding of their daughter Lillian. The event takes place next Sunday and the lucky man is a Hebrew haberdasher from Globe. My predecessor in this office was one of her greatest admirers, and it was reciprocated on her part. They would have been married had not her mother raised a big hullabaloo that he was not one of the chosen people. Miss Lillie really loves him but she must marry into her own race at the command of others.

In other cases, love-stricken young Jews convinced their betrotheds to convert to Judaism. Moses Alexander, for example, who would later become the governor of Idaho (1915–1919), married Helena (formerly Hedwig) Kaestner in 1877. Helena had spent several months studying Judaism under the direction of a rabbi. In late 1876 she was converted in a St. Louis, Missouri, synagogue and given her new name.

For the most part, however, when faced with parental disapproval of their intended Christian mates, young Jewish men and women simply weathered the storm. That disapproval could be formidable: outright prohibition, disinheritance, snubs, and even violence. When the daughter of Solomon Nathan of Denver married her non-Jewish suitor in 1871, the girl's distraught father strode into a Denver bank and attacked the Christian minister who had performed the ceremony. In his defense, the minister maintained the girl had intended to run off with the man whether the ceremony were performed or not. Nathan, pleading temporary dementia, got off with a forty-dollar fine.

In 1897, Arizona's Mose Drachman married Ethel Edmunds, a Christian woman originally from Virginia. Mose was born in 1870, the second of the ten children of Philip and Rosa Drachman. His parents were among Tucson's earliest settlers and had struggled to establish both a living and a Jewish household in the rough, dangerous pueblo.

Mose floundered in a variety of jobs for seven years until he became an independent salesman for a coffee company. This successful venture

Early California and Utah pioneer Abraham Watters married widow Rebecca Steeg in San Francisco in 1862. From Leon L. Watters, The Pioneer Jews of Utah, *American Jewish Historical Society (New York, 1952)*

shy, ill-at-ease young man in front of Zeckendorf's store to help her back on her horse.

I was ready to mount and told him when I counted three I would jump and he was to hold my foot. Well, I jumped, but he just stood there and I went over the saddle, my arms hanging on one side and my feet on the other. My hat rolled in the sand. I was furious. "Why didn't you hold my foot?" "I never helped a lady on before." "You needn't tell me, I know it."

Mose was intrigued—he enrolled in a dancing class Ethel taught, feigning clumsiness, though in truth he could cavort like an 1890s Fred Astaire. Outraged at first, Ethel soon discovered that Mose's "crude" exterior concealed a kind heart and a warm, easygoing nature. They fell in love, agreed to marry, and ran into a new, unexpected obstacle—the Drachman family. Mose recalled:

My marriage did not please the rest of my family. We were Jews—not very strict Jews, of course, but they thought that I should have married a Jewish girl— strange as it may seem, not one of them married Jewesses and only one of my sisters married a Jewish man.

The couple decided to brave the disapproval and in December 1897 sneaked off to California to be married. Mose and Ethel's married life—their home a boardinghouse filled to the rafters with colorful characters—has been lovingly preserved in their daughter Rosemary Drachman Taylor's books, *Chicken Every Sunday* and *Riding the Rainbow.*

Although intermarriage did occur, most western Jewish settlers avoided mixed unions. In Los Angeles County between 1850 and 1876, less than 25 percent of Jewish marriages were with Gentiles; in Portland, Oregon, during the same years, there were practically none. Even on the newly opened frontier, where women of any kind were scarce, the majority of Jewish settlers chose to marry within their faith. A few early pioneer men came with wives. Rosina and Simon Koshland, Fanny and David Stern, and Rosa and Joseph Newmark were some of the couples who came together to the Far West in the late 1840s and early 1850s. A far greater number were bachelors, many of whom, defying the odds, found Jewish brides when and how they could.

gave him confidence, and he decided to propose to Ethel Edmunds, with whom, in his words, he was "madly in love." A native of Danville, Virginia, Ethel came to Tucson in 1889 to visit her brother, a stay that was intended to last only six weeks. Once she arrived, however, she was intrigued by the raw western town and remained.

Her first meeting with Mose was especially memorable to Ethel. Still a prim Southern belle sitting sidesaddle in her new green riding habit, Ethel had journeyed into town to do some shopping. When she finished she sweetly asked the

Some quickly snapped up the daughters of those few Jewish prospectors and merchants who brought their families with them to the rough western settlements. Isadore Strassburger met sixteen-year-old Rachel Cohen in the mining camp of Virginia City, Montana, in 1867. When her family decided to leave the town, the shrewd Isadore persuaded them to let Rachel depart in his carriage. Riding at a safe distance behind her parents, Isadore managed to convince Rachel to marry him; quickly he turned the carriage around, they returned to town, and were immediately married by a judge.

But such girls were hard to come by, and most frontier busters in search of a Jewish bride had to find one outside the Far West. Lonely and

Diminutive Bertha Angleman was born in Waxahachie, Texas, and raised in Kansas City, Missouri. She was twenty-nine, supporting herself as a milliner, and heading for spinsterhood when her cousin introduced her to Emil Ganz, a Phoenix hotel owner, banker, and mayor. They married in 1882 and had four children. Courtesy, Sylvia Ganz Houle, Phoenix, Arizona

disconsolate after ten long years in the Pacific Northwest, Nathan Cohen journeyed east in 1858 determined to bring back a wife. He set his sights on Fanny Hyman of Ohio, who was seeking an escort to the West Coast, where she planned to live with her two uncles, Portland tobacco merchants. Appointed as her guardian, Nathan took Fanny to New York City to book passage on a ship to the West Coast. Some time en route, Nathan delivered an ultimatum: either she marry him or he would leave her to starve on the city streets. Aided by one of Fanny's New York rel-

atives, Cohen held her captive for four months until in despair she submitted to his demands. They married and set sail for Portland in July. The moment she set foot on Oregon soil, Fanny fled to her uncles; with their help she obtained a divorce from Cohen by the end of the year. Apparently, Nathan's townspeople were compassionate about his desperation for a bride—no stigma attached itself to him in Portland. He became a prominent member of the town's Jewish community and married again in the 1870s. The fate of poor Fanny remains unknown.

Lacking time or money for an eastern journey, settlers sometimes counted on helpful friends and relatives to find suitable mates for them. Merchant Abraham Mooser was lonely in Elko, Nevada, until a relative told him of Henrietta Koshland, a young Jewish orphan living with relatives in New York. Mooser began a correspondence with Henrietta, and within a year she traveled west to marry him. They met face to face for the first time only when Henrietta stepped off the train at Salt Lake City. Without a word Abraham walked up to her and kissed her. "I was sure she was the right one," he liked to remark in later years.

Finding a suitable Jewish girl, though never easy, was relatively simple compared to convincing the girl to make the move west and persuading her family to allow her to do so. In 1869, Ichel Watters left Salt Lake City for Europe to look for a wife. His choice was Augusta Graupe, who lived with her parents in Ichel's hometown of Rogassen, Prussia. He met the family and showered them with enthusiastic tales of American life; Augusta's parents, however, swiftly shot down Ichel's hopes. Under no circumstances would they send their daughter to the American West, to them a frightening, Indian-infested wilderness. Thoroughly dejected, Ichel sailed back to the United States. He continued to write to Augusta, but the situation seemed hopeless until late that year, when Watters fell victim to the exploding hostilities between Utah's Mormons and non-Mormons. After speaking out publicly against the violence and intolerance raging through Salt Lake City, Ichel was severely beaten twice, the second time with brass knuckles, so

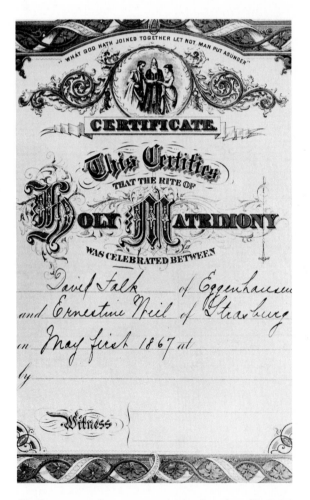

Finding no marriage prospects in rough-and-tumble Boise, Idaho, David Falk went to Strassburg, Germany, in 1867 and persuaded nineteen-year-old Ernestine Weil to come with him to Idaho. They would become leading citizens of Boise. Courtesy, Bessie Falk, Boise, Idaho

Annie Stargarth of Stockton, California, married Levi Mitchell of Visalia, California, in 1866. Her home for the next forty years was the mining town of Tailholt, Tulare County, where Annie, an excellent cook, never turned a hungry person away. Nineteen years after her marriage, Levi died and Annie continued to run their business, the White River Hotel, and raise their four children. Courtesy, Annie Mitchell, Visalia, California

that he nearly lost an arm. This nightmarish episode had one good result. Augusta, in anguish over her suitor's plight, overcame her parents' objections and traveled west to nurse Ichel back to health. A remarkable, determined young woman, she journeyed as far as Wyoming, where her betrothed met her and took her to Utah. The pair were married in 1871. Augusta thrived on the challenge of frontier life, becoming a hardy pioneer and, eventually, a mainstay of the Salt Lake City Jewish community.

Augusta's parents' objections were hardly unreasonable. The West was genuinely raw, crude, and quite often dangerous. Leaving family and friends behind for an unfamiliar land with different customs and language was a frightening, wrenching experience for a young woman. Why, then, did so many agree to come?

Beyond the obvious bonds of love, young women undertaking the arduous trip often had other motivations. Some, like Hannah Greenebaum, who married Lewis Gerstle, a California merchant, in 1858, had family in the West. She looked forward to the company of her three brothers and a sister already living on the frontier when she left Philadelphia for California with her husband. Others sought not to join relatives but to escape them: Twenty-year-old Matilda Lesinsky was eager to move to New Mexico with her new husband, Henry, in 1867; poor and miserable, she had been living with her sister and widowed mother in New York City, and, as her husband wrote years later to their son, "I had not a very severe task to induce your mother to accompany me." Still others, like Bertha Roman of East Prussia, who married Mark Levison in the California mining town of Placerville in 1862, came seeking equality. Free from pogroms and oppressive anti-Semitic restrictions, the Far West for Bertha and others like her was a place

where, seizing infinite opportunities, a husband and wife could begin their lives anew.

While prompted by promises of a better future, most young brides making their way west felt not elation but sadness, even dread. Dime-store novels and the sensationalist press of the period instilled fears of Indian attack in nervous brides crossing the prairies. Many had read of Olive Oatman and Fanny Kelly, captured and held by natives, or had heard the legend of a young Jewish woman named Rebecca who while en route to her fiancé Isaac Goldstein and her ailing brother was captured by Colorado Indians and killed as a sacrifice. (Goldstein, the legend continues, became a Colorado peddler and searched endlessly for his betrothed throughout the Indian camps until he himself died at their hands in the Mill River Massacre that occurred on September 29, 1879.)

Some of these women lived for years in the far western wilds in primitive surroundings and extreme climates, with Indian attack still a legitimate fear. Singlehandedly they ran their households—cleaning, baking, sewing, and raising vegetables, poultry, and cows—on a meager budget in a land where goods were scarce and prices high. Those fortunate enough to afford servants still had to carry a major portion of the work themselves. They gave birth alone or with the help of husbands or friends—rarely with that of a doctor. Once the children were born, Jewish frontier women struggled to raise them properly, often being forced to send them away for their education. Finally, should their husbands' nascent businesses flounder or need additional hands, they would put in hours in the store or on the ranch to keep the fledgling enterprise from going under.

All of this describes the life of Anna (Freudenthal) Solomon, born in Posen in 1843. Anna

This Solomon family photograph was taken on June 14, 1907, following the marriage of Jacob Weinberger to Blanche Solomon (standing third and fourth from the left). The Arizona Bulletin *reported: "By reason of the bride having lived here all her life, the event was of more than ordinary interest to the townspeople and the company which witnessed the ceremony included practically all of the American families in the vicinity." Courtesy, Arizona Historical Society, Tucson*

married Isadore Elkan Solomon in Inowroclaw, Prussia, in 1872, and left the next day for Towanda, Pennsylvania, where I. E., as he was called, ran a livery business. Four years and three children later, with business slow, Anna persuaded her husband to move to the Southwest, where members of the Freudenthal family had been living for two decades. An assertive, quick-minded, hard-working woman (she had managed the Freudenthal store when her father was in the New Mexico Territory and had helped her ailing mother rear her five brothers and sisters), Anna was sure she and I. E. would fare better on the booming western frontier.

The young couple scraped together the money for the overland journey west, selling, Anna noted wryly, "everything we possessed except our three children." Boarding a train, they rode as far as La Junta, Colorado, then switched to a stagecoach. Anna would later remark, in understatement: "We had a very hard time." "Packed in like sardines," the family raced across the plains and desert for six days and nights, stopping only to change horses and for occasional brief meals of chili or frijoles. They arrived in Las Cruces in the New Mexico Territory thoroughly exhausted. Leaving Anna and the children in the care of her two brothers, I. E. set out on his own into the countryside in search of a new business.

Within four months he had found one—manufacturing charcoal for the Longfellow Copper Mines, owned by the Lesinsky brothers and Julius Freudenthal, all Anna's cousins. As his manufacturing site, he chose a dense growth of mesquite along the Gila River in the Gila Valley, an Apache stronghold in the Arizona Territory, where the only other nonaborigines were soldiers from Fort Thomas, a handful of Mexican families, and a tiny Anglo group in Safford. I. E. rented a trading post and a house and returned to Las Cruces to get his family.

For Anna this second journey was worse than the first. With tents, bedding, food, and children piled behind her in a two-seat wagon, she rode alongside her husband for several days and nights, imagining Apaches in every shadow. "I did not expect to get here alive with our children," she confessed. When they finally arrived, she saw for the first time, in the soft moonlight of a beautiful August night, what was to be her and her children's new home—an empty, crumbling adobe isolated in the desert. Anna stretched out on the mud floor of her new house and cried herself to sleep.

The future looked no brighter in the morning. Anna had to begin housekeeping with "no furniture, no cooking stove, and not anything else that belongs to the comfort of the human race." A stove, furniture, and other provisions had been sent from Las Cruces by ox team, but the wagon dropped everything in the road; it was three months before they finally arrived. In the meantime, Anna baked bread from cornmeal, cooked food out of doors, and ate her meals seated on the ground.

A far worse burden was the laundry. Lacking any household help, she did the washing

Israel and Adele Maas Katz; courtesy, Jefferson County Historical Society Museum, Port Townsend, Washington

alone, something to which she was unaccustomed, and with dire consequences:

After my second washing I took sick with chills and fever. My baby Rose also took sick. My husband sent for the doctor to Fort Grant, but the Mexican came back after three days and said he could not get the doctor to come. . . . The chills and fever are dreadful in our place. There were pools of green standing water all over the place.

Anna would suffer from chills and fever for two years.

In addition to cooking, cleaning, and caring for the children (who grew to six in number with the birth of twins in 1879 and of a daughter in 1884), Anna ran the family store while I. E., aided by Mexican crews, was busy day and night manufacturing charcoal. The couple's exhausting work load continued unabated for over a year, until other workers slowly began to arrive.

Despite its dismal beginnings, Anna soon began to accept and ultimately relish her life in the West and played a major role in building Solomonville, which became the Graham County seat in 1883. Around 1880, Anna, faced with caring for a large family and an endless parade of visiting relatives, friends, and wayfarers, did what many women in similar situations threaten to do—she opened a hotel. The two-story Solomon Hotel was situated on the northwest corner of Bowie and Main streets, opposite the Solomon store, which she continued to operate. The territorial-style adobe, banded with a porch, accommodated the Solomon family, local unmarried lawyers, judges, the schoolteacher, Graham County people in Solomonville on court business, and travelers journeying between Tucson and El Paso.

Run by Anna with the help of a Chinese cook, Gin Awah Quang, Mexican chambermaids, and gardeners, the hotel became famous throughout the territory for homelike hospitality, keyless rooms (some guests were slower than others to accept the omission), and excellent meals. Fruits and vegetables came from Anna's own orchard across the road; meats were carted from the Solomon ranch, and Continental pastries were prepared in the kitchen under Anna's supervision. Graham County historian William R. Ridgeway wrote of the hotel: "Here centered the social life of the Gila Valley, with fashion-conscious women and mustached men serenaded by the music of a Fort Grant band of local musicians."

Life in the grinding heat and primitive, isolated surroundings of the Southwest damaged a fair share of marriages, but conditions elsewhere on the frontier were often no more conducive to marital harmony. One dazzling and cultivated young European bride, Adele Maas, went to great lengths to adapt to the planks-over-mud life in

Port Townsend, Washington, on the Olympic Peninsula. Her husband, eighteen years her senior, Israel Katz, a prominent businessman, spared no expense to help her. The ups and downs of their ill-matched union intrigued their fellow citizens at the time and for years after.

Katz, a native of Germany, came to Port Townsend in 1868, when he was sixteen, to work for Waterman and Katz, a firm owned in part by members of his family. For nearly twenty years he helped build the business, which dealt in general merchandise and shipping supplies. When

Adele Maas Katz founded a posh beauty salon in San Francisco in 1906. Courtesy, Jefferson County Historical Society Museum, Port Townsend, Washington

his brother William died in 1887, Israel succeeded him as a partner in the firm—by then a complex the townspeople called Solomon's Temple—a three-story emporium, three warehouses and a deep-water wharf. Thirty-six and able to keep a wife in style, Israel decided to marry.

His search for a bride ended in Wiesbaden, Germany, where, by previous arrangement, he was betrothed to Adele, the eighteen-year-old daughter of architect Adolf Maas and his wife, Cecilia. Adele's lively green eyes, translucent skin, titian curls, and quick-witted intelligence had attracted numerous suitors. Why her parents chose as her husband a middle-aged businessman residing in a small seaport at the northwest tip of the United States is not known. But they did, and Adele, with considerable trepidation, accepted their decision.

Israel and Adele met for the first time the day before their wedding. The bridegroom was instantly enchanted; the bride, somewhat less so. Adele insisted that her seventeen-year-old brother Louis and her personal maid accompany her when, after the wedding, she embarked with Israel for Port Townsend.

Adele hated the place from the start. Decked out in an elaborate dress and high-button shoes, she clambered unsteadily down a rope ladder from the ship into a waiting canoe, when salt spray dashed her from head to toe. On shore, an obliging gentleman carried her across the sand to a crude wooden sidewalk; her heels stuck in the cracks between the boards. Her first home was a small cottage, too tiny to accommodate Louis, the maid, or even Adele's belongings.

After his extended bachelorhood, Israel was delighted to have a wife, particularly one as enthralling as Adele, and he did his best to please her. Sending for an architect and craftsmen from Seattle, he built Adele an ornate house that became the showplace of Port Townsend. Thus indulged, for more than a decade, Adele used her abundant resources to create a pleasant life in Port Townsend. She bore Israel four children, three sons and a daughter. And she staged a whirlwind of parties that made their home the small town's social center.

That relatively harmonious period ended when first one of her sons and then her only daughter died. In her sorrow, Adele again found Port Townsend oppressive. Hoping travel would abate her grief, Israel allowed his wife to visit her brother William, the German consul to Mexico City. For two years she diverted herself in Mexico, playing hostess for her single brother. When she returned to Port Townsend, she resumed her social whirl, this time with more serious consequences. Around 1906, she met a handsome young army officer named Herbert Millar at a party. They fell in love, and Adele asked Israel for a divorce. He agreed, and Adele departed, leaving her two remaining sons, William and Edwin, with their father.

Adele and her new husband moved to San Francisco, where her vibrant personality, stifled to a large extent in Port Townsend, revived. With Herbert's help, she opened the city's first beauty salon, an elaborate operation that was highly successful. However, Herbert eventually ran off with one of their beautiful employees and Adele's assets. On her own and without funds, Adele suffered a nervous breakdown, then a stay in a rest home. When she had regained her strength and resiliency, she returned to the beauty business. In the ensuing years, she had a brush with the law over impurities in one of the cosmetics she manufactured; went through two more marriages and divorces; and suffered a leg amputation, all without losing her remarkable zest.

Both before and after Adele's departure, Israel had his own troubles. Once expected to become the leading coastal city in the Northwest, Port Townsend began to decline in the late nineteenth century. To stimulate his waning business, Israel overextended credit to his customers, then had to apply pressure to collect. Nonetheless, he remained popular in town, and in 1915 was elected mayor. During the next two years, though his financial problems worsened, Israel's sons and his circle of friends failed to notice any change in his quiet though genial demeanor.

On the morning of January 13, 1917, however, Israel vanished. He was last seen at 3:30 A.M., when his son came to his room to say good-

bye before departing for the nearby San Juan Islands. At 7:00 A.M. a servant discovered that her employer was gone but that the watch, spectacles, and overcoat he usually wore were where he had left them the night before. He had been in a jovial mood on the previous day, said his son, and, reported the local newspaper, his business affairs were in "excellent shape considering the long siege of financial depression in the Northwest." Artillerymen stationed nearby combed the woods adjacent to the city, and search parties scoured the beach along the harbor, but no trace of the missing man was ever found.

Separations and divorces like the Katzes' occurred but were uncommon. Most Jewish frontier brides learned to cope, though slowly and sometimes grudgingly, and their marriages, happy or not, lasted. Doretta Hartung Rothschild, an earlier bride from Germany who settled in Port Townsend in 1860, survived a shipwreck en route from San Francisco, a horrifying event that might have dampened any young wife's enthusiasm. Yet she learned to accept the perils of life in that raw fishing and shipping village, and her marriage (to merchant David Rothschild) remained solid.

Others among these pioneer wives did more than simply adjust. Finding their new homelands receptive to women of talent and ambition, a number of Jewish brides gloried in western life. Occasionally boldly and rebelliously, more often shyly, slowly, and nearly accidentally, these early Jewish women eluded the conventional "separate spheres" and developed strong identities independent of their husbands.

The perils of frontier life sometimes figured prominently in these women's development. When some mishap—a mining accident, an Indian attack—befell her husband, a young bride far from any family help often became the sole support of herself and her children. If she didn't already possess moneymaking skills—and some Jewish women did, particularly those from Eastern Europe, where a woman often provided a portion, or at times all, of the family income—she developed them in a hurry out of sheer desperation. Such was the case of thirty-four-year-

Hannah Marks Solomons; courtesy, The Bancroft Library, University of California, Berkeley

old Mary Prag, born Mary Goldsmith in 1845. As a seven-year-old, Mary had crossed the Isthmus of Panama with her father, a *schochet* (ritual slaughterer), and had grown up in San Francisco. At the age of nineteen she married fortyniner Conrad Prag; the pair settled in Utah, where Prag worked as a merchant. When he died fifteen years later, leaving Mary to support their ten-year-old daughter Florence, she drew on her long-neglected teaching skills, becoming one of San Francisco's first Jewish schoolteachers and vice-principal of San Francisco Girls' High. After her retirement at eighty-two, Mary was appointed to the San Francisco Board of Education. By then nicknamed "Little Gibraltar," she became a strident advocate of women's rights.

Another important factor in the West's openness to women lay in the relative fluidity of western society. Many Jewish women found that

they were freer to do as they pleased in these nascent settlements where everyone was a newcomer and no rigid social structure had yet taken hold. Sometimes their moves toward independence meant opening a store. Other times they could be as simple as that of Hannah Marks Solomons, who in 1853 broke her engagement to a man her family had chosen and vowed to choose her own mate according to her own standards.

Hannah Marks was the child of Polish parents who had emigrated to America in 1835 and settled in New Bedford, Massachusetts. Orphaned during her girlhood, Hannah grew up in the home of her Orthodox uncle in Philadelphia. One senses from Hannah's letters to her brother Bernhard in California that her experiences in that household further inflamed her already rebellious nature. As soon as she was able, Hannah found work in a store and made plans to leave her relatives' home. At her pious uncle's insistence, she moved into a kosher boardinghouse, an establishment located miles from her job and charging what was for her meager income an exorbitant rate. She was barely able to make ends meet. When a lonely western suitor sent her passage money to California in 1853, she hastily accepted.

After meeting with her betrothed, she refused to go through with the marriage. Her family in the East was outraged—at the time, an engagement was considered nearly as binding as the wedding itself. Only Bernhard came to her defense. He refused to say anything about "that cattle matching project," except that it was "not exactly consistent with the spirit of an American education in the 1850s."

Her mind made up, Hannah went to work as a schoolteacher. In time she found her man, Gershom Mendes Seixas Solomons, a leader of the San Francisco Jewish community who had come west during the gold rush. They were wed in the early 1860s.

Although Hannah took a major step toward independence in choosing her own husband, her judgment was not necessarily flawless. As one biographer has noted, she "did not get a great bargain, proving the time-worn maxim that love is indeed blind." Publicly, Solomons was an impressive figure—a founder of San Francisco's Temple Emanu-El who could trace his Sephardic ancestors to colonial America and fifteenth-century Spain. Privately, however, he became a heavy drinker, and Hannah's strength was tested as she was left to raise a family virtually alone. Nonetheless, her children did her great credit—sons Theodore, a journalist; Leon, a doctor of philosophy at twenty-three and a professor of psychology at the University of Nebraska; and Lucius, an attorney; and two extraordinary daughters, Adele and Selina.

A bolder, more far-reaching rebellion marked the life of Anna Rich, who was born in Russian Poland in 1847 and who journeyed to the Utah Territory around 1870. Raised in poverty and haunted by the constant fear of pogroms, Anna had fled her native land as a young girl, vowing never again to be poor or powerless. She married Wolff Marks of London in 1862; they settled in New York but after a time headed west to Salt Lake City.

In the freewheeling West Anna found opportunities that would have been closed to a woman elsewhere. After a few years in business in Salt Lake City, she moved to Eureka City in the Tintic mining district of Utah. She hoped to make her fortune in land and mining ventures, and make it she did. With Wolff decidedly in the background (a pleasant, rather innocuous type, he ran the family store and treated local kids to candy), Anna speculated in land in Salt Lake City and Eureka; invested money in diamonds; and owned controlling interests in two mines, the Anna Rich and the White Cloud, near Eureka. A tough, at times vicious, businesswoman renowned for her foul language, Anna wasn't averse to carrying on negotiations from behind a rifle. At one time she held up the building of the Denver and Rio Grande at gunpoint until the railroad met her price to cross her land; frequently she would threaten and fire upon neighbors in disputes over boundary lines. Anna had acquired a vast fortune by the time she died of a heart attack, in 1912.

Many other early Jewish wives found the

West a challenging environment and grappled successfully with it. Therese Ferrin worked as a nurse for an Arizona doctor and became known as "the Angel of Tucson" for her knowledge of herbal and other natural remedies. Fanny Brooks with her husband, Julius, lived the life of western gypsies—traveling by covered wagon to Utah in 1854, on to San Francisco and the California

Elizabeth "Lizzie" Levy (daughter of Esther and Aaron Levy) and Isaac Cooper were married on October 25, 1886, in Genesee, Idaho. She was born in the California gold mining town of French Gulch in the early 1860s. She spent part of her childhood in Sitka, Alaska, where her father ran a general merchandise store and brewery, and the rest in San Francisco where she attended Girls' High. In the 1880s the family moved to the new community of Genesee, Idaho, where Aaron opened the first store. After her marriage to Cooper, a Washington merchant, Lizzie lived in Farmington. Six years later, the Coopers moved to Seattle where Lizzie's father and husband established the highly successful grocery company Cooper & Levy. Courtesy, Seattle Jewish Archives Project, Suzzallo Library, University of Washington, Seattle

Los Angeles native Sarah Harris married Portland, Oregon, native Herman Frank on November 14, 1888. (Frank was an employee of his bride's father, Leopold Harris, and the two subsequently became partners in the men's clothing store chain Harris & Frank.) One hundred and fifty guests attended the ceremony and champagne wedding dinner. The sumptuous feast was prepared by a master caterer and served by uniformed waiters. "For years afterwards," according to Frank, "when traveling to and from San Francisco, railroad porters informed us they had attended our wedding." From Scrapbook of a Western Pioneer, *Herman Frank, Times Mirror Press (Los Angeles, 1934)*

mining camps, back east to New York, across the isthmus to California, then to Portland and Boise—before ultimately settling in Salt Lake City in 1864 and opening a millinery business. Delia Stern Fleishhacker loved every minute of her 1857 journey across the isthmus, an unusual experience in itself, and traveled with her husband, Aaron, back to Virginia City, Nevada, where she became a midwife to the miners' wives. In the 1850s, San Francisco entrepreneur Amelia Dannenberg manufactured children's clothing and in 1867 received an award for excellence in the production of infants' apparel at the Mechanics'

Fair. Ernestine Greenebaum, one of the earliest Jewish women in Los Angeles, opened the White House Hotel there in the 1870s, catering to unmarried immigrants. Hannah Schiller Mannasse of San Diego speculated in property and cattle in the 1860s and even had her own cattle brand. A tough-minded businesswoman, in later years she took her husband, Joseph, to court to ensure that he would keep his hands off her property. (Not coincidentally, Hannah had divorced Joseph's brother Hyman in 1866 when he deserted her to work in the Arizona Territory; lacking shelter, clothing, or food, she had been forced to turn to relatives for support. That experience had undoubtedly ground into her the value of self-reliance.)

As the years passed and settlers poured into the Far West, life in raw western villages gave way for many to an easier, more "civilized" existence. As early as the 1860s in some areas, rickety frontier outposts expanded into permanent and fast-growing towns with solid Jewish communities. Jewish men desiring to marry within their faith no longer had to cross the Atlantic for wives; their brides, often native westerners, no longer faced an agonizing adjustment to primitive life.

But new obstacles arose to plague mate seekers. As urban Jewish communities grew, they developed rigid social stratifications difficult for an unestablished newcomer to crack. By 1890, an enterprising young man like San Francisco's J. B. Levison had a hard time winning the girl of his choice, Alice Gerstle, daughter of pioneer San Franciscan Lewis Gerstle. Alice loved J. B. for his spirit and determination, the same frontier-busting qualities that had raised her father from a lowly mining camp merchant to a wealthy urban businessman; Lewis, on the other hand, saw only a fellow with little money and an undistinguished family.

Harriet Lane Levy, who grew up in turn-of-the-century San Francisco, recorded in her delightful memoir, *920 O'Farrell Street,* the anxiety-ridden status scramble marriage had by then become. Born of Polish parents, Harriet and her sisters had grown resigned to their lesser status,

Early insurance executive J. B. Levison married Alice Gerstle, daughter of San Francisco entrepreneur Lewis Gerstle, on July 29, 1896, then honeymooned aboard the steamer Queen *bound for Alaska. Courtesy, Robert M. Levison*

taking their place below German Jewish girls in the social scale, "as the denominator takes its stand under the horizontal line." On marriage alone rested their hopes of elevation. An advantageous betrothal—to a promising city dweller of even vaguely German descent—could raise their entire family in San Francisco's rigid social hierarchy, giving them a distinct edge over less fortunate neighbors and friends. Harriet's mother, tensely peering at the hopeful young men who pursued other women's daughters, was no less anxious:

Any advantageous betrothal was greeted by Mother with resentment and with reproach of Father for his social shortcomings. No sooner had an engagement been announced, a younger brother or sister bringing the glad tidings, then a shadow fell upon the house for the day. Often the prospective groom would be a stranger, perhaps the older bachelor brother of a friend of the family who, after years of seclusion, had been persuaded that the last bell had been rung for marriage; or he might be a rising merchant from Nevada. In either case conjecture was in the air and the blow softened by thought of the suitor's age, or the separation from the family and city, entailed by an out-of-town marriage. On the other hand, he might be a young city merchant already enjoying good credit; or, worse, the son and heir of a member of an old firm; or, worst of all, an attorney with high degrees at the Odd Fellows, equipped at any moment with an eloquent speech for a wedding dinner, or B'nai B'rith banquet. Beneath the blow of such a betrothal Mother sat still, her hands folded.

Once the betrothal was made, anxiety could be set aside and grandiose preparations begun. Weddings in late-nineteenth-century upper- and aspiring middle-class western society were elaborate, at times gaudy, affairs rivaling anything held in the East. A man like San Francisco's Louis Sloss, who by rising from small-town merchant to millionaire not only retained faith in the American dream but was himself its personification, would naturally stage an extravagant display of wealth, splendor, and romantic fancy for the wedding of his daughter Bella to Ernest R. Lilienthal in 1876. For this occasion an elaborate pavilion was built on the lawn, wherein the couple took their vows. Afterward their guests sat down to an eight-course French dinner, its gold-lettered menu printed on white silk, followed by

Above: *Jessica Blanche Peixotto (1864–1941); courtesy, Norton Stern, Santa Monica, California*

Bottom left: *Adele Solomons Jaffa; courtesy, Adele Solomons Jaffa Collection, Western Jewish History Center, Judah L. Magnes Museum, Berkeley, California*

an evening of dancing perfumed by the scent of the "choicest California flowers" strewn across the Slosses' home. Even the modestly well-off but aspiring Levys, Harriet's family, had spared no expense when their daughter Addie married Oakland merchant August Friedlander; they transformed their bottom floor into an ornate banquet hall cloaked in vines and white cloth and served an elaborate dinner topped off with pyramids of macaroons, nougat, and ice cream.

These extravaganzas were hardly limited to cosmopolitan San Francisco. The 1890 wedding of Jennie Oppenheimer, daughter of a prominent Spokane banking family, and Samuel Hanauer, then a rising young merchant, rivaled even the excesses of Louis Sloss. The ceremony took place in the bride's father's massive home, strewn with flowers, ferns, and palms for the occasion and decorated with a marriage bell of chrysanthemums and roses suspended from a large bay

Congresswoman Florence Prag Kahn (1869–1948) was the first Jewish woman to serve in the United States Congress. Courtesy, Western Jewish History Center, Judah L. Magnes Museum, Berkeley, California

window. The bride, decked out in silk and lace adorned with diamonds, descended the grand staircase into the parlor to the strains of Spokane Auditorium's string orchestra, somehow crammed into the house along with hordes of wedding guests. After the ceremony and the sumptuous wedding supper, the guests in their best evening attire danced to the orchestra throughout the house until the early hours of the morning. Such formal splendor was far removed from the rough, raw days of the frontier.

Second-generation Jewish women in the West received from their pioneering mothers a legacy of confidence, self-reliance, independence, and pride in achievement. Lacking trails to blaze or towns to build, some of these women became groundbreakers in new roles and occupations from which women had traditionally been barred. Adele Solomons Jaffa, Hannah Solomons's daughter, became a physician and child psychiatrist. Emma Sutro (daughter of Adolph), Amelia Levinson, Natalie Selling, Sarah Vasen, and Anna Reznikov also were doctors. Hannah Solomons's other daughter, Selina, a genuine eccentric, was a writer, a practicing astrologer, and an ardent campaigner for women's suffrage. Selina's childhood friend Jessica Peixotto, daughter of a prominent San Francisco Sephardic family, received a Ph.D. from the University of California, Berkeley, in 1900—the second woman to do so—and four years later became a teacher of social economics there. By 1918 she would become the first woman at the university to achieve the rank of full professor. In 1901 Bella Rosenbaum of Seattle became the first woman to practice law in Washington State; in 1911 Blanche Colman, a native of Deadwood in the Black Hills, became the first to practice law in South Dakota and later worked as an attorney for the Homestake Mining Company.

By World War I, throughout the West, Jewish daughters of the frontier were moving from home and hearth into radically untraditional lines of endeavor. Even the U.S. Congress felt their impact. Mary Prag's daughter Florence, married to California congressman Julius Kahn, served as his chief advisor during his twelve terms in office. After Kahn's death in 1924, she succeeded him for an additional six terms, becoming America's first Jewish congresswoman.

Blanche Colman began clerking for the Homestake Mining Company in Deadwood, Colorado, in 1902. Studying on her own—she never attended law school—she passed the bar in 1911 and became one of the first woman attorneys in the country. Courtesy, Al Alschuler, Miami, Florida

Chapter Five
DYNASTIES

Jews settled wherever opportunity beckoned: in shanties on sandlots in booming ports; in sloping, one-street mining towns; at dusty crossroads in agricultural and trade centers; in splintery settlements flanking new railroad tracks, or in adobe huts in lonely deserts. As these communities shot up into towns and cities, the most ambitious and energetic of their Jewish inhabitants rose to prominence, attained leading-family status, and passed it on to their offspring. These dynasties had much in common: They were newly affluent, they were pioneers in a mercurial region, they were Americans living through a highly transitional age, and they were Jews exercising leadership in a largely non-Jewish environment. At the same time, they were markedly dissimilar. Personality as well as luck—a force in every early far western life—uniquely tinted their destinies. Location also colored the lives of these families, in some cases more decisively than did any other factor. The population, resources, terrain, and prevailing customs varied dramatically from place to place in the Far West. Natives reflected these differences from birth, and newcomers frequently acquired them. With an ease born of long experience living in other people's cultures, Jews were often among the first pioneers to adapt to the customs in a new locality.

The Haas-Lilienthal House, at 2007 Franklin Street in San Francisco, was built in 1886 for merchant William Haas, his wife, Bertha (Greenebaum), and their children. Courtesy, Marilyn Blaisdell Collection

Nowhere was this more apparent than in the New Mexico Territory. Spared the obliterating effects of large-scale mineral strikes and attendant rushes, Indian and Hispanic New Mexicans retained their native cultures. Most Jewish families who settled there picked up Spanish and occasionally some Indian dialects and learned to accommodate to the semifeudal habits of both pueblo and rancho. As a consequence, their enterprises and households were often an amalgam of American drive, German *kultur* and *gemütlichkeit,* Jewish *tzedakah* (justice or charity), Hispanic conviviality, and Indian attachment to nature.

Such was the case in the lives of territory-wide merchant, sheep raiser, and landowner Charles Ilfeld—"Tio Carlos" or "Tio Charlie"—his wife, Adele (Nordhaus), and their five sons, Arthur, Herman, Louis, Willie, and Ernst, who lived and died (the last two boys in childhood) in Las Vegas, New Mexico, sixty-five miles north of Santa Fe. In 1865 Charles, then eighteen, left his home in Homburg, Germany, and traveled to Santa Fe, where his older brother Herman lived. He worked with Herman at Elsberg & Amberg, a busy new store on the Santa Fe plaza, until he could speak Spanish; he then went to Taos to clerk for merchant Adolph Letcher. Taos, a mule-train trade center, was headed downhill and Las Vegas was on the rise, so in 1867 Letcher and Ilfeld, partners by then, packed their merchandise on seventy-five burros and rode to Las Vegas. There on the burgeoning plaza they started Letcher and Ilfeld, General Merchandise.

Charles "Tio Carlos" Ilfeld was already a leading merchant and citizen of Las Vegas, New Mexico, when in 1897 his holdings soared with the sudden success of his wholesaling business. Courtesy, Museum of New Mexico, Santa Fe

Las Vegas commerce to a large extent depended on the barter system—local ranchers exchanged wools and hides for manufactured goods—or on supply contracts with nearby army posts. Although competition was brisk, the aggressive newcomers cleared $18,000 the first year and soon opened branches at nearby Montón de los Alamos and Tecolote. In 1873 Charles took a breather long enough to return to Germany to find a fiancée, nineteen-year-old Adele, daughter of Rabbi Jacob Nordhaus of Paderhorn. He also obtained store help, his fifteen-year-old brother, Louis. Shortly after his marriage in 1874, Charles bought out Letcher for $36,000 and formed the Charles Ilfeld Company.

Living on the Las Vegas plaza, the youthful German bride was forced to adjust to the sound of gunfire and the sight of violence. One morning soon after she arrived, Adele looked out her window to see three lynched killers hanging on the windmill tower, an image she would never forget. Despite this grisly introduction to Las Vegas, Adele quickly settled into her role of leading citizen's wife, mother, and hostess of parties that grew increasingly elaborate after the Ilfelds moved to a spacious Victorian house in the newer East Las Vegas.

In 1879 Charles faced two business problems with far-reaching consequences. The Atchison, Topeka and Santa Fe Railroad situated its depot in East Las Vegas, and a new business district sprang up around it. That same year Louis decided to join his brothers Noa and Herman in another dynamic New Mexico mercantile firm—Ilfeld Brothers, situated first in Albuquerque and then in Santa Fe. Luckily, Charles's business was strong enough to survive on the plaza, although few others were, and in 1883 Max Nordhaus, Adele's eighteen-year-old brother, arrived to provide Charles with much-

Ilfeld's on the Plaza, the pride of Las Vegas, New Mexico, was constructed with sandstone quarried two miles west of the plaza and had wooden beams from northwest of the city. The store also featured electric lights and a greatly expanded ladies' ready-to-wear department. Courtesy, Museum of New Mexico, Santa Fe

needed assistance. By the time Max was twenty-one, he was second in command and first in line as Charles's successor.

Through the years, a stream of European cousins and countrymen were indoctrinated into southwestern commerce in the company's three-story retail center called the Plaza, in country store branches, and in the wholesale and jobbing end of the business, which waxed as the retail trade began to wane. At the turn of the century the firm also entered sheep raising via the *partido* system (*partidarios* raised sheep for large ranchers and were paid in ewes and wool). Livestock ranches and other Ilfeld branch stores came later.

After Albuquerque overtook Las Vegas as the hub of commerce, Ilfeld acknowledged its commercial superiority by opening a branch, then transferring the company's headquarters there; he and Adele, however, remained loyal Las Vegans. Max Nordhaus and his wife, Bertha, the daughter of prominent merchant Abraham Staab (they married in 1907), relocated in Albuquerque to supervise the company headquarters.

In their later years Adele and Charles traveled extensively and even kept an apartment in New York City, but they continued to think of Las Vegas as home. He kept a hand in the business and in a variety of American, Jewish, and Hispanic community affairs. He was a director of the New Mexico Normal School (now New Mexico Highlands University); a member of the board of Temple Montefiore (founded in Las Vegas in 1886); and an honored guest at weddings, christenings, and funerals.

The Ilfeld sons were no less attached to their high-plateau hometown. They attended local schools and enjoyed an active out-of-doors boyhood before they entered their father's business. The eldest, Louis, graduated from Yale and earned a law degree from a New York law school, then returned to Las Vegas to serve as the firm's counsel. Arthur and Herman worked at the sales counter and on a drummer's route before they became Ilfeld Company executives in Las Vegas. After Charles's death in 1929, Max Nordhaus assumed the top post and was president of the firm until his death in 1936. He was succeeded by Arthur Ilfeld, who, sharing his executive duties with general manager Earl Moulton, continued to reside in Las Vegas. In 1941 when Arthur died, Moulton took his place and remained in the presidency until the Ilfeld and Nordhaus families decided to liquidate the business eighteen years later.

Far western Jewish families typically chased chance in and out of several towns before acquiring a permanent address. Utah pioneers the Auerbach brothers, Frederick, Samuel, and

Theodore, who were natives of Fordon, Prussia, lost stores in the California Mother Lode and Nevada mining towns before they turned east to Salt Lake City, where in 1864 they founded a commercial empire that remained in the family for 113 years.

"A peculiarly retiring man with a clear, cool business judgment and wonderful executive ability," Fred was the eldest, a lifelong bachelor and the family trailblazer. He arrived in the United States in 1854 and came to California in 1858, near the end of the California gold rush. Fred opened his first mining-town store in Rabbit Creek, Sierra County, where he was joined by his brothers Sam and Theodore. When mining waned in Rabbit Creek in the early 1860s, the Auerbach brothers tried enterprises in Bodie and Marysville in California and, after neither of those panned out, in Austin, Nevada. When boom went to bust in Austin in 1863, the broth-

This series of stores illustrates the rising fortunes of the Auerbach brothers in California and Utah. Fred Auerbach's first store, Rabbit Creek, California, 1857 (facing page, top); Ogden, Utah, circa 1869 (facing page, bottom); Salt Lake City, 1879 (top); Salt Lake City, 1912 (left). Courtesy, Marriot Library, Western Americana Section, University of Utah, Salt Lake City

ers, who were deeply in debt, decided to try Utah, where a minor mineral rush was under way. Fred went to Salt Lake City and met with Brigham Young, who took a liking to him and agreed to help the financially depleted brothers start their first Utah enterprise, the People's Store, F. Auerbach & Brothers. When the Union Pacific Railroad entered the territory in 1868, the Auerbachs opened tent stores in Bryan, Wyoming, and Promontory, Utah, as well as branch outlets in Ogden and Corrine. A full-scale mining boom commenced in 1870, further expanding opportunities for the Auerbachs in Utah.

During the next decade, one brother, Theodore, decided to move back to the East. Sam married Evaline Brooks, the daughter of Fanny and Julius Gerson Brooks, even earlier Utah Jewish pioneers, and started a family. As their business interests grew, so did the Auerbachs' involvement in the community. Possibly out of loyalty to Brigham Young, Fred and Sam avoided the Mormon-"Gentile" conflicts that had raged in the late 1860s and that plagued Utah politics thereafter. "We're merchants, not missionaries," asserted Fred. Instead, they focused their attention on nonpartisan and Jewish affairs. Both played key roles in forming Jewish organizations, including B'nai Israel Congregation in 1873. As congregation president in 1884, the year the group switched from Orthodox to Reform, Sam was largely responsible for quieting the turbulence that surrounded the change. Fred served as president of the chamber of commerce, regent of the University of Utah, and grand master of the Odd Fellows. When he died in 1896, a host of relatives, many of whom he himself had brought to the Far West, inherited his $1.5 million estate. Sam headed the business until his death in 1920, when his sons, Herbert, Fred, and (for a period) George, took over.

A number of heirs of Jewish pioneers built on their parents' accomplishments, but few rose to excellence in as many areas as Herbert S. Auerbach, longtime head of Auerbach's, energetic civic leader, and Utah state senator. Before assuming the presidency of the family business, Herbert had a brief career as a concert violinist and a somewhat longer one as a mining engineer. Working in western mining districts, Herbert developed a fascination for regional history and assembled the renowned Herbert S. Auerbach Collection of Western Americana, which was dispersed after his death in 1945.

Family enterprises, such as the Auerbachs', were popular among the pioneer Jews. Husbands and wives, fathers and sons (or sons-in-law), or uncles and nephews teamed up, but the majority of these partnerships were composed of brothers, up to five or six, united under the leadership of the oldest or the most capable. The advantages of working together were myriad and far-reaching. In the early days in a lonely outpost, relatives provided one another with the comfortable sociability of a common language, customs, and religion. Since the partners tended to be equally responsible, an effective division of labor often resulted. One, two, or three worked in the store, another went out to drum up new business, while still another went east or to San

Francisco to purchase merchandise. Occasionally a wastrel son or a wayward brother threatened the welfare of an undertaking, but "little beavers" were more often the rule than "little foxes," particularly in the founding generation. With trust in one another and in future success, many were willing to live modestly and to plow profits—even wages—into expansion until the business was well established.

Such was the approach of David, Nathan, and Sigmund Falk, natives of Egenhausen, Bavaria. David Falk arrived in Boise (then called Idaho City) with the wave of sixteen thousand gold seekers and suppliers who surged into the Boise Basin in 1863. Nathan followed a year later. The pair peddled goods and operated a trading post until 1868, when they started D. Falk and Brothers, a dry goods store and grocery business. Sigmund joined his brothers in 1873.

In the early, hard-pressed years, the brothers were at work at six in the morning to light fires and lamps and were often still waiting on customers or doing store chores until midnight. The business enjoyed a big boost in the mid-1880s, when a gold strike at Coeur d'Alene brought a new rush of settlers to Idaho. By 1897 the Falks were doing business in an elegant three-story building called Falk-Bloch Mercantile Company Ltd., at the corner of Eighth and Main. The "Bloch" was partner I. Bloch; when he withdrew a few years later, the name reverted to Falk Mercantile, and then became simply Falk's.

In 1867, when David was thirty, he journeyed to Strassburg and persuaded nineteen-year-old Ernestine Weil to share his modest lot in Boise, still a raucous mining supply town short on everything but hope. The pair had four children. By 1888, Leo F., the oldest, was a trusted executive in training at the store. Nathan, who was ten years younger than David, waited until 1878 to marry Rosa Steinmeier of Munich. Two of their six children—the oldest, Leo J., and the youngest, Theodore—also entered the business.

Like other successful mercantile families of the period, the Falks did their share to boost their community's social and civic life. Nathan served on the school board and the chamber of commerce and was active in the Odd Fellows. The brothers also took part in early Jewish ob-

This photograph of Nathan and Rosa Falk and their family was taken about 1890. When Nathan returned to Germany, where he wed Rosa in 1878, he was arrested by German military authorities for avoidance of military duty (Nathan had left Germany at the age of fifteen). Refusing to pay a fine, Nathan was vindicated in court as an American citizen. Left to right, back row: Anne Falk (Rothchild), Rosa S. Falk, Nathan Falk, Bella Falk (Smith), and Leo J. Falk; left to right, front row: Harry Falk and Ralph Falk. Courtesy, Idaho Historical Society, Boise, Idaho

servances. In 1895, when one hundred Boise Jews, spurred by the dynamic Moses Alexander (soon to be Boise mayor, and eventually Idaho governor), met to organize the Reform Congregation Beth Israel, both brothers were among the incorporators. David, called "the grand old man of Boise" (he was fifty-eight and had been in residence in the community for thirty years) was founding president.

Both David and Nathan Falk died in 1903. Their brother Sigmund took charge of Falk Mercantile Company, and David's son Leo F. presided over Falk's Wholesale Company, later Boise Wholesale and Dry Goods. After a dozen years as company president, Sigmund joined the United States Diplomatic Corps and was sent abroad to serve as American consul in several European cities. Leo J., Nathan's son, who had been serving as company treasurer, stepped into the post vacated by his uncle. During his long

tenure as president of what became known simply as Falk's, Leo J., an able and energetic entrepreneur, also organized early irrigation projects, helped establish the Boise-Winnemucca Railroad, developed mines, built the $400,000 Owyhee Hotel, and served as vice-president of the Star Orchard Company of Star, Idaho.

During the difficult Depression years, Falk's was partially acquired by Sears Roebuck and Company. In 1966, eleven years after Leo J.'s death, P. M. Hirsch Company, a division of Interco, Incorporated, purchased Falk's, lock, stock, and company name. So Falk's stores as well as the Falks themselves are still much in evidence in Boise. Falk's on Main Street remained in operation until 1982, when the new owners opened Falk's Idaho Department Store at two new locations. A tiny community outside Boise, the site of an early Falk trading post, is still called Falks. And the fourteen Falks listed in the Boise tele-

The David Falk family of Boise; left to right: *Mrs. David Falk, Lena (wife of Henry),*
Bertha, Henry, Leo F., Carolyne, and David Falk. Leo F. headed Falk's wholesale branch.
Courtesy, Bessie Falk, Boise, Idaho

phone book leave no doubt that those "peddlers"
were not just passing through.

"All the Schwabacher brothers married
women who were strong personalities and had
definite ideas of what they wanted," says Abraham Schwabacher's granddaughter Joanna Eckstein, "and what they wanted were great big Victorian houses in San Francisco." What they didn't
want was to live in Walla Walla, Washington Territory, where the Schwabachers initiated their
northwestern mercantile holdings.

The three brothers, Sigmund, Louis, and
Abraham, natives of Zindorf, Bavaria, were veterans of ventures in San Francisco and The Dalles

(near Portland, Oregon) when they struck out
for Walla Walla in 1860. The frontier Indian
village in the southeastern section of the Washington Territory was the jumping-off point for
the gold rush in progress in the Orofino Creek
area of northern Idaho. When they arrived, Walla
Walla was a raw settlement cut off from civilization during the five months of the year when
the swollen Columbia River was impassable. A
decade later, the town was still described as "a
jumble of buildings, hitching racks, livery stables, gambling houses, and saloons; its streets
choked with Indians, soldiers, Kanaka, Chinamen, hunters, deserting sailors, cattle rustlers,

The Schwabacher family, circa 1890; left to right: *Babette (Schwabacher) and Bailey Gatzert; Bella and Abraham Schwabacher; Sarah and Louis Schwabacher; and Sigmund and Rose Schwabacher. Courtesy, Seattle Jewish Archives Project, Suzzallo Library, University of Washington, Seattle*

mountaineers, settlers, and ox teams, pack trains, [and] covered freight wagons."

Sig Schwabacher, who was short and jovial and favored an I'm-on-your-side manner, was the resident partner in Walla Walla and one of the town's most energetic boosters. He served on the city council, helped raise funds to establish the Seattle–Walla Walla Railroad, and was a director of the First National Bank. In 1872 he married his first cousin Rosa Schwabacher, who endured the lonely isolation of Walla Walla for ten years. When Leo, the oldest of their six children, turned ten, Rosa convinced Sig it was time to move the family residence to San Francisco. Brother Louis married Bella Blum in 1877 and thereafter maintained a home base in San Francisco while managing branch stores in eastern Washington. Abraham headed the Schwabacher headquarters in San Francisco and never broached the possibility of a Walla Walla residence to his wife, Sara Lehrberger Schwabacher, also a first cousin.

The first woman in the family to establish a permanent home in a northwestern frontier town was Babette Schwabacher Gatzert, the Schwabachers' only sister. She went along when her husband, Bailey Gatzert, a key addition to the family partnership, went to Seattle in 1869 to open a new branch of Schwabacher Brothers. Seattle at the time was a village of 1,107 people with plank sidewalks flanking mud-puddled streets. Well-educated and energetic, Bailey Gatzert, a native of Darmstadt, Germany, turned out to be as good for Seattle as he was for the Schwabachers. Under his direction, Schwabacher Brothers built the town's first brick building and opened its first wholesale outlet, which sold groceries, clothing, hardware, and building materials. They also built a warehouse and a wharf. During the great fire of 1889, when most of Seattle burned, the Schwabachers lost their store, but their wharf was spared. The city's only pier to escape destruction, for some years it served as Seattle's main point of arrival and departure. In 1893 another fire destroyed the Schwabachers' hardware department. By the second rebuilding, the business had grown to such proportions that the partners decided to split the firm into two divisions: Schwabacher Brothers, for groceries, and Schwabacher Hardware Company, for a wide variety of goods. Gatzert headed the former; Sigmund, who divided his time between San Francisco and the Northwest, handled the latter.

The Gatzerts were also mainstays of Seattle's early civic and social life. Bailey, a popular civic leader, served on the city council, headed the chamber of commerce for many years, and in 1875 was elected mayor. Babette, in addition to her duties as wife of a ubiquitous city builder, was an early and active member of the Ladies Hebrew Benevolent Society.

By the time the second generation took over, around the turn of the century, Seattle had edged out all contenders to establish itself as the most promising trade center in the Northwest. After Sig's death in 1900, his son Leo, then twenty-eight, became headman in the hardware division. When in 1903 he married Edna Blum, a native San Franciscan and a University of California graduate, he had no trouble persuading her to join him in the budding metropolis.

Mina Schwabacher, Abraham's daughter, also willingly joined the family forces in Seattle when she married Nathan Eckstein, successor to the childless Bailey Gatzert. The two San Franciscans Mina and Edna added their vitality and intelligence to the social and philanthropic life of urbanizing Seattle and aided their husbands, both indefatigable civic leaders, in their various undertakings. Edna and Leo's son, third-generation Morton Schwabacher, was the first company president who was born and bred in Seattle.

The only heir apparent to the Schwabacher empire, Morton grew up taking for granted that he would eventually head the business. He prepared for the post by obtaining a first-rate education at Yale University, then by starting at the bottom in Schwabachers' hardware division and working his way up through the ranks. His father, Leo, died in 1931, when Morton was twenty-nine. With Nathan Eckstein's help, Morton completed two more years of on-the-job training before he assumed the presidency, a post he held for forty-four years. During his long and judicious reign, Morton, along with his wife, Emily (still another San Franciscan), accrued a distin-

guished record of community service. He served as a longtime board member at Temple de Hirsch, as vice-president of the ecumenical Camp Brotherhood, and as president of the Council on Aging. Emily was for many years a key board member of the Children's Orthopedic Hospital. When Morton, the father of one child, Eleanor (Mrs. Philip Boren), died in 1977, the dynastic rule of Schwabacher Brothers ended. Still intact is a record of the myriad ways the Schwabachers helped to transform a tiny, mud-splattered fishing village into a city worthy of being called the Queen of the Northwest.

The Badt family, of Wells in northeastern Nevada, was one of the many Jewish families that rooted early in remote sections of the far western hinterlands. Their decision to do so proved richly remunerative and communally gratifying. Yet, as did most Jewish parents, Morris and Lina (Posener) Badt soon grew concerned about the lack of educational, social, and religious facilities in their tiny town. Deficiencies of this kind prompted some families to sacrifice a prosperous business and move into a large city. Others sent their children off to boarding schools in San Francisco or New York. Still others, the Badts included, maintained two homes: one close to the store, the ranch, or the mine and a second, school-year residence in a city. This country-city way of life turned out to be replete with rewards as well as penalties.

Early in 1869 Morris Badt rode the Central Pacific Railroad, then still in construction, to the end of the line, which at the time was Elko, Nevada. There he met the Cohn brothers and with them added a tent store to the other businesses clustered around a lodging house, restaurant, and gambling saloon. By the time the Central Pacific and the Union Pacific had met in Promontory, Utah, to form the first transcontinental railroad—the Golden Spike ceremony was held on May 10, 1869—Badt had moved fifty miles down the line to the east to Wells, Nevada. Soon thereafter he bought out his partners and formed M. Badt & Company. Then he built a house and brought his bride, Lina Posener Badt, from San Francisco to live with him in the tiny town. Inhabited primarily by railroad workers, Wells boasted little more than a few frame buildings,

Left: *Morris Badt, an early settler, headed many enterprises in Nevada, including the mercantile store of M. Badt & Company in Elko and Wells, the Bank of Wells, cattle ranches, and a wagon train to Ely, Nevada. Courtesy,* Northeast Nevada Quarterly, *Elko, Nevada (Summer, 1978)*

Right: *After her eight children reached school age, Lina (Posener) Badt ran her San Francisco household during the school year, then joined her husband, Morris, in the summer months in Wells, Nevada. Courtesy,* Northeast Nevada Quarterly, *Elko, Nevada (Summer, 1978)*

a roundhouse, a repair shop, snowplows, and a water tank; four miles away were the celebrated natural springs Humboldt Wells. In typical pioneer style, Morris developed a retail and wholesale mercantile business and delivered freight into the surrounding mining camps by sixteen-horse wagon teams. He would later add to his enterprises the Bank of Wells and large cattle ranches. Lina was no less occupied raising little Badts—eight of them eventually.

Whistle-stop Wells—with a population of two hundred in 1884—had a one-room schoolhouse and not much else; so when the oldest child was ready for grammar school, the Badts bought a newly built house in San Francisco for Lina and the children to occupy during the school year. Morris remained in Wells and frequently hopped the train to San Francisco on buying trips and for holidays and special occasions. The family spent summers in Nevada, at least partly on the ranch, where, one of the offspring recalled, the boys became fairly accomplished cowpunchers.

In addition to attending good schools—secular and religious—in San Francisco, the children had German-speaking governesses and were trained in various sports, in music, and in other subjects as well. Each was encouraged by their mother to follow his or her bent. Herbert, for example, studied violin, Milton, foreign languages. Ultimately, when it came time to choose between the city and the country, four of the Badt children—Herbert, Melville, Selby, and Milton—opted for northeastern Nevada. Of these, the first three joined their father and expanded M. Badt & Company. In 1903 they bought the U-7 Ranch, which included ten thousand acres of land with all water rights, fifteen hundred head of cattle, and thirty thousand additional fenced acres. Within a year they added another ten thousand acres and fifteen hundred more head of cattle. Milton, a University of California graduate, earned a law degree at Hastings Law School. He practiced law in San Francisco for five years and then returned to Nevada. He opened an office

*Aaron Meier, founder of Meier & Frank department
store; courtesy, Oregon Historical Society, Portland*

in Elko and built a civil law practice handling,
among other matters, the Shoshoni Indians' suit
against the federal government and water rights
cases. He also served as Elko city attorney and
district judge. In 1947 Milton was appointed to
the Nevada State Supreme Court. He remained
on the bench until his death in 1966, serving a
portion of his years as chief justice.

The three Badt brothers who returned to
Nevada as bachelors had difficulty reconciling
their dual attachments to religion and birthplace. Unmarried Jewish women were as scarce
as water in that section of the Far West, and
persuading one to come there was more easily
considered than accomplished. Milton fell in love
with non-Jewish schoolteacher Gertrude Nizze
and eventually coaxed a maternal marriage
blessing from Lina. Herbert and Selby remained
for the rest of their lives Nevadans and bachelors.

It took a dynamo to lead a big family business and keep it on the move in the calamity-
prone Far West, and it took an autocrat to contain the intense rivalries that often erupted in a
prosperous family partnership. In Jeannette
Meier, the Meier-Frank family had both a dynamo and an autocrat.

When Aaron Meier returned to Ellerstadt,
Bavaria, to visit his family in 1863, he left behind
his general store, Meerholtz and Meier, the forty-
third such store to open in Portland. The town
of thirteen hundred residents, two bowling al-
leys, six saloons, and one photo studio was in a
slump following the waning of the gold rush of
1857. When Aaron returned to Portland with a
new bride, Jeannette Hirsch, and with $14,000
in inheritance money, he found his store had
gone under. His inheritance money went too as
merchants defaulted on payments for merchandise he had brought west for them. Meier had
to make a new start in a store he built by hand.

Nonetheless, Aaron came out ahead; as a
result of the journey he had obtained an invaluable asset: Jeannette. In the early years of their
married life, she was busy raising children Fannie, Abraham, Hattie (who died in childhood),
and Julius. She then began importing Hirsches
from Germany to help run the store. Her nephew
Max remembers the devotion required of family
employees. When he once asked for a few days
off, he was told, "What do you want a vacation
for? You just came." (The young man at the time
had already spent seven years in service at the
store.) Some of the Hirsch family later broke
away from the Meiers to form the well-known
sports clothing company, White Stag, which initially made canvas sails and tents for Alaskan
gold prospectors.

The *Frank* in Meier & Frank was Sigmund,
a music teacher who came from San Francisco
with his brother Emil to work for the Meiers; he
ended up marrying Fannie in 1885 and becoming his father-in-law's partner. Sons Abe and Julius Meier also took a large role in store business,
Abe as the figurehead president (known as the
store "greeter") and Julius as general manager
and behind-the-scenes decision maker.

Jeannette, however, was the real moving
force behind expansion of the business from

*Jeannette Meier never held an official title at Meier &
Frank, the store she led to prominence. Courtesy, Oregon
Historical Society, Portland*

idating—that when an eastern dressmaker attempted to bring a suit against her, no Portland lawyer would take on the plaintiff's case.

With the fire of 1873 and the flood of 1894 behind them (they took customers through the aisles in rowboats) Meier and Frank built a five-story edifice in the heart of the Portland business district. The next leap came in 1914, when the company completed a modern, fourteen-story structure, including the first escalator on the Pacific Coast. After Aaron died in 1889, Sigmund Frank headed the firm until his death in 1910. Then it was time for Sigmund and Fannie's son, the stern and forceful Aaron, to preside.

The most famous Meier, though, turned out to be tall, attractive, and witty Julius. A lawyer and an important civic booster in the early years of the twentieth century, he promoted the 1905 World's Fair in Portland and guided the development of the scenic Columbia River Highway from 1912 on. Julius was elected Oregon governor in 1930, winning by a record plurality.

Jeannette died in 1925 at the age of eighty-two, leaving a will requesting that "my children and their children and their children and their children's children and so on shall remain together and harmoniously carry on and continue such great enterprise commended by my husband and their father." Jeannette's "harmony wish" visibly prevailed for nearly forty years, mainly under the stern leadership of Aaron Frank. In 1965 rebellious shareholders, mostly angry widows and their daughters, resentful of Aaron's low dividends and tight control, forced a sale of Meier & Frank to the May Company.

As powerful as she was, Jeannette Meier was a traditional matriarch whose primary concerns were her family and its business. Other wives and daughters in these leading families were beginning to enter new spheres opening to women all over the nation, especially in the Far West. The new region took the lead in making universities coeducational and in granting women suffrage. In 1869 Wyoming became the first territory—and in 1890, the first state—to give the vote to women (Idaho, Utah, and Colorado soon followed suit). Many Wyoming women, Bertha Frank Myers of Cheyenne and her daughter Elsie among them, used this freer ambience to de-

country store to uptown establishment. A short and stout woman, eleven years Aaron's junior, she visited the store every day and oversaw the tiniest of matters, down to the use of dustcloths instead of feather dusters. She is purported to have had a hand in choosing the proper spouses for her children as well, particularly in the Sigmund Frank–Fannie Meier union. Jeannette, or Grandma Meier, as she was called in her later years, held court before Sunday family dinners, sumptuous affairs complete with roasted goose and oysters, homemade ice cream, and gaily decorated cakes. It is said that Jeannette was so well regarded in Portland—or perhaps was so intim-

Completed in 1914, a major addition to downtown Portland was the Meier & Frank building at Fifth and Morrison. Courtesy, Oregon Historical Society, Portland

velop their talents and to expend them in behalf of their communities.

Bertha, a native of New York, was twenty-one, handsome, and vivacious when she came to Cheyenne in 1873 as the bride of William Myers, a prosperous, forty-year-old merchant. The town, then in its fifth year, was but a hint of the rail, trade, and cattle center it would become, but Bertha wasted no time creating a tasteful setting for her future family. Within a few months she was installed in an eleven-room house at 114 East Nineteenth Street, purchased from Territorial Governor John A. Campbell, and was waiting for her newly selected furniture to be delivered from the East. Sixty years later Bertha remembered the walnut and mahogany items—a dining table to seat forty, a Wing piano, and marble-top dressers. The four Myers children were born in that house: Elsie in 1874, the first

Jewish native of Cheyenne, who lived most of her life there; Millie in 1876, who married and moved to Boise, Idaho; Evaline in 1880, who died during the 1918 influenza epidemic; and Arthur in 1884, the babe of the brood, who spent his adult years in Minneapolis.

While the children attended local schools, Bertha utilized her abundant talents to enhance her home and her community. She made a showplace of the Nineteenth Street house and, after 1891, of the family's larger and much grander home at 808 East Seventeenth Street. Her interest in horticulture spilled over into city beautification projects, including the planting of trees and lilac bushes in the Jewish Circle in Cheyenne's Holiday Park. Brimming with energy and high purpose, Bertha was a leader in the Eastern Star and Women's Relief Corps. In the 1890s she organized the Jewish Sewing Circle to raise funds

Bertha Myers, a native of New York, was a horsewoman, bicyclist, and the first motorist in Cheyenne, Wyoming. "I didn't know what to do," recalled Bertha. "When I waved from my motor car, they said I was a show-off and when I didn't, that I was stuck up." Courtesy, Lyman Spaulding, Cheyenne, Wyoming

to build a house of worship for Reform Congregation Emanuel, which she helped establish in 1888. Although that project failed, more successful was the Jewish religious school that first Bertha, then Elsie taught for a total of twenty years. Bertha was also long remembered as an avid horsewoman, bicyclist, and eventually as the first motorist in Cheyenne.

Elsie was something of a Cheyenne celebrity, too. She graduated from Vassar College in 1895, then returned home to teach English and German at Cheyenne High School for eight years, arriving daily in a buggy drawn by a matched

team. A talented musician and musical director, Elsie was for many years a key member of the Cheyenne Symphony and Chorus, the Morning Study Music Club, and the Cheyenne Cooperative Concert. In recognition of her long service to the American Association of University Women, after her death the Cheyenne chapter established the Elsie M. Spaulding Award.

In 1903 Elsie married Arthur Spaulding, a non-Jew, and with him had two sons, Lyman and Arthur, Jr. Throughout her long life (she lived to be 101) she retained an avid interest in Judaism. For some years she arranged the choral music for Congregation Emanuel's High Holy Days services, and she was long active in the Jewish circle and B'nai B'rith Women. After the Orthodox Mount Sinai Congregation replaced Emanuel as Cheyenne's only Jewish religious group in the 1920s, Elsie joined the Mount Sinai Sisterhood and was twice elected president.

Belle Fligelman of Helena, Montana, aimed her efforts directly at the issue of the day: women's suffrage. She campaigned with Montana's most determined suffragists to win the vote for women, first in her state and then across the nation. When that battle was won, Belle continued to work for good government and for legislation to improve the lot of women and children.

Her parents, Herman and Minnie Fligelman, natives of Rumania, moved to Helena in 1889 when Herman was appointed president of the newly incorporated New York Dry Goods Store. A year later Minnie gave birth to their first child, Frieda. Fifteen months later she delivered Belle, unfortunately succumbing shortly thereafter. Several years after his wife's death, Herman married German-born Getty Vogelbaum, a well-meaning but strict disciplinarian—particularly when contrasted with the girls' easygoing, broad-minded father.

During Belle's childhood, Helena was a miniature metropolis with regular train service, good schools, opera house, dancing academy, natatorium, and a progressive point of view. Jews of diverse national origins were plentiful, prominent, and well organized. Belle recalled attending religious school at the Reform Temple Emanu-El in the house of worship completed

The Bertha and William Myers family of Cheyenne at home; left to right: *William, Bertha, Arthur, Arthur, Jr. (Elsie's son), Evaline, Elsie, and Millie. Courtesy, Lyman Spaulding, Cheyenne, Wyoming*

the year of her birth, 1891. Also fixed in her mind were images of her father collecting money for Russian pogrom victims and of her stepmother buggying around town gathering food, clothing, and money for poor Jews who had drifted into town. The relationship between Helena's Jews and Gentiles was by and large amicable, and Belle remembered that she and her sister, who regularly played with Gentile children, endured only an occasional insulting "sheenie" or "kike"—an incident that was so rare as to be mortifying.

More frequent were the conflicts she and Frieda had with their letter-of-the-law stepmother, who was determined to give her young charges a traditional rearing. Herman encouraged his daughters' intellectual curiosity, but he sided with his wife on some issues—for example, that finishing school was more appropriate for young ladies than was college. Frieda issued her edict: her father would send her to college or she would work her own way. Unable to dissuade her, he reluctantly consented. Frieda earned a degree in sociology and did graduate work at a half dozen American and Continental univer-

sities, establishing herself as a pioneer in social linguistics. Belle attended the University of Wisconsin and graduated from the School of Journalism in 1913. Upon her return home, she took a job as a reporter on the *Helena Independent*.

"As it turned out," Belle wrote, "I was just in time to get involved in the state's suffrage campaign." In 1914 Belle joined in a new suffragist drive led by Montanan Jeannette Rankin. The diminutive campaigner (Belle measured slightly under five feet) spoke on street corners; drove a horse and buggy to gold-mining towns and ranching communities; wrote for the *Suffrage Daily News;* paraded down Helena's Last Chance Gulch; and celebrated on November 3, when the amendment passed. Two years later, when Rankin ran for Congress, Belle was a key member of her campaign, and when her candidate became the first American congresswoman, Belle went to Washington, D.C., to work in Rankin's congressional office.

In 1918 Belle married New York–born Norman Winestine, a Yale graduate who was working in the capital; soon thereafter they moved to New York, where he served on the staff of

Courtesy, Barbara Sherrod, Fort Collins, Colorado

Nation magazine. Several years later, after a stint in Paris, the pair returned to Helena, where Norman entered his father-in-law's business. Marriage and motherhood failed to slow Belle. While she was raising two daughters and a son, she was active in Jeannette Rankin's Good Government Clubs, a forerunner of the League of Women Voters; lobbied for women and child welfare legislation; and in 1932 made an unsuccessful bid for the state senate. She eventually recorded her experience as a suffragist in a memoir entitled *Mother Was Shocked.*

The forces assaulting the traditional Jewish home were minimal when compared with the revolution going on at the store, warehouse, or factory. By the late nineteenth century, fast-growing corporations—their chief objectives rapid gains and unlimited expansion—were edging out family enterprises. Most of those who preferred to limit their business to a family partnership and a single community were eventually acquired by mercantile chains. The more competitive enterprises, following the trend, incorporated and learned new methods of management, advertisement, and marketing. (A few managed to keep family members in policymaking positions.) An outstanding example of these adaptable firms was the one founded by the ebullient, change-oriented David May and his brothers-in-law, the Shoenbergs—first Moses, then Louis and Joseph.

David May, who was born in Kaiserslautern, Bavaria, in 1848, started his mercantile career in 1864 in Hartford, Indiana, clerking in a store for $25 per month plus room and board. A dozen years later, he sold his partnership in that store for $25,000 and moved to Colorado, hoping the salubrious Rocky Mountain air would help his asthma. May was in Manitou Springs when he heard of the silver strike in Leadville; he decided to give mining a try. He and an equally inexperienced partner, Jake Holcomb, staked a worthless claim. Dismayed with their loss, the pair swiftly shifted to May's forte, selling goods. Their first store was a muslin-covered shack, and their first wares were red woolen longies and Levi's. When his partners (a third man, named Dean, had joined the pair) balked at expansion, go-getter May bought out his cohorts and started the Great Western Auction & Clothing Store. Several months later he teamed up with Moses Shoenberg, whose father, Elias, ran Leadville's Shoenberg Opera House.

David's successful partnership with Moses, which was to last six years, led to a more enduring one with his brothers, Joseph and Louis, and to a lifelong marital union with their dark-eyed, dark-haired sister Rosa, who arrived in Leadville in the summer of 1880. The courtship was brief, the marriage long and fruitful. By the fall of 1881, Rosa had given birth to Morton J., the first of May's three sons and successors. Tom, the second son, was born two years later in Lead-

Left: *"Up to that time, no one in Montana, or anywhere else for that matter, had heard of a respectable young woman making a public street corner speech. . . . I was terrified as I took my place on what was supposed to be a busy Helena street corner. . . . Miraculously, someone stopped to listen, and then another came running, and soon I had a big audience, all listening attentively. . . . My mother was horrified." From Belle Fligelman Winestine, "Mother Was Shocked,"* Montana: The Magazine of Western History *(July, 1974); photo courtesy, Montana Historical Society, Helena*

Right: *On one of his many buying trips, David May discovered an overstocked dress shop in Chicago. A shrewd businessman, he bought up the velvet and brocade dresses and had them shipped to Leadville. The wives and daughters of miners bought the entire stock of dresses within a week for from two hundred to four hundred dollars each. Courtesy, The May Company, Denver, Colorado*

ville. Two younger May children, Wilbur (born in 1898) and Florene (born in 1903), arrived after the family moved to Denver.

In the late 1880s, May compared his prospects in declining Leadville to those in Denver, a new railroad hub that was fast growing into a metropolitan center; he decided to transfer his hopes there. He bought a bankrupt store on Larimer Street and renamed it May Shoe and Clothing Company. Hiring a brass band to signal the store's opening, he sold out his first stock in a few days. Before long, his brothers-in-law Jo-

seph and Louis joined him in the business. With three ambitious merchants drumming up business by day and dreaming up promotional ploys at night, sales surged. By June 1882 the company, occupying a block on Sixteenth Street between Lawrence and Larimer, ran a double-page ad in the *Rocky Mountain News* proclaiming its owners the "CLOTHING MONARCHS OF THE WEST." The same year, the partners acquired the Famous Department Store of St. Louis for $300,000; several years later, they added the William Barr Dry Goods of Cleveland to form Fa-

Four years after he arrived in Leadville, Colorado, David May was successful enough to open this branch store in the new Colorado mining camp of Irwin in 1881. Two years later when the silver boom collapsed, Irwin was a ghost camp, and May closed the store. Courtesy, The May Company, Denver, Colorado

mous Barr Department Store in St. Louis.

While her husband was occupied with business and communal affairs, involved in lengthy buying trips, or relaxing at cards, Rosa decorated houses. During their fourteen years in Denver, the Mays moved three times to accommodate their growing family and their rising social status. Their last house was a twenty-two-room red stone mansion, now Chappell House of the University of Denver.

Although comfortably ensconced and well regarded in Denver, the May family moved again. In 1903, when the company president Louis

Shoenberg retired, David assumed the post at the firm's headquarters in St. Louis. Fourteen years later, David was succeeded by his eldest son, Morton J. Capitalizing on the extensive holdings and dynamic policies of the founders, during Morton J.'s reign the firm became one of the nation's largest mercantile chains. Other second-generation family members who had grown in the business played course-setting supporting roles. Wilbur May and Sydney Melville Shoenberg (Moses's son) were vice-presidents and directors, as was Tom May, who went to southern California to head the proliferating May enter-

Harris Newmark offered a sample of the easygoing business practices of Los Angeles in 1868 (when this photograph was taken): "I was walking down Spring Street one day and saw a crowd at the City Hall. On a large box stood Mayor Joel H. Turner, and just as I arrived a man leaning against the adobe wall called out, 'Seven dollars!' The Mayor then announced the bid—for an auction was in progress—'Seven dollars once, seven dollars twice, seven dollars three times!' and as he raised his hand to conclude the sale, I called out, 'A half!' This I did in a spirit of fun; in fact, I did not even know what was being offered! 'Seven dollars fifty once . . . twice . . . three times, and sold—to Harris Newmark!' I then inquired what I had bought." Thus casually Harris had purchased twenty acres, at $7.50 an acre, in what would become the Wilshire district of Los Angeles. From Harris Newmark, Sixty Years in Los Angeles, *Zeitlin & Ver Brugge (Los Angeles, 1970)*

prises there. Alfred Triefus, David's nephew, guided the growth of the May store in Denver. The last family member to head the company was Morton J.'s son, Morton D. May, who was president from 1951 to 1967 and chairman of the board from 1967 to 1972. When Morton D., a director emeritus, died in 1983, May Department Stores Company owned 142 department stores, 47 discount stores, 1,205 shoe stores, and 26 shopping centers. Tom May, director emeritus, is the last of the line to hold an official title in the century-old firm.

When a far western town declined, its pioneering families were often stricken with an enduring sense of personal disappointment and defeat. Conversely, when a town boomed beyond all expectations, its early settlers, who felt personally responsible, were jubilant. Such was the case in Los Angeles, a sleepy little adobe village, which to everyone's surprise shot up and became the region's largest city. One group of early Angelenos who had earned the right to crow was the multibranched Newmark family. Harris Newmark, who was founder of H. Newmark & Company (a wholesale grocery business), an important real estate developer, and an indefatigable city builder, warmly and wittily recorded that growth. His memoirs, *Sixty Years in Southern California, 1853–1913,* recount his experiences including those of his hard-working and creative clan, as well as those of hundreds of other Los Angeles pioneers.

Harris, a native of Loebau, West Prussia, was nineteen when he joined his older brother, Joseph Philipp ("J. P.") Newmark in Los Angeles, then a pueblo of twenty-six hundred. Clerking at J. P.'s store, Harris learned to speak Spanish (not English) and to enjoy what he would later call "the fandango years." He swiftly developed a taste for tortillas, tamales, and pinole; for local fruits—quinces, pomegranates, prickly pears, watermelon; for beef and lamb from the surrounding ranches; and for fresh fish hawked by the *pescadores* from nearby San Pedro. Eden, of course, was not without afflictions, the worst of which was loneliness. That pain was permanently eliminated in 1854, when Harris's uncle Joseph Newmark, his family, and their Chinese servant settled in Los Angeles. Joseph had been in the United States since 1821, and his wife was a native of England. Five of their six children had been born and educated in New York. English-speaking and gregarious, the newcomers swiftly taught Harris English and made him a member of their congenial group. His tie to the family was double-knotted in 1858, when he and his first cousin Sarah were married. (They had eleven children, six of whom died in childhood.) Sarah's three sisters each married one of an able trio of related and soon-to-be-prominent French Jews. Matilda married Maurice Kremer; Caroline, Solomon Lazard; and Harriet, Eugene

A man with a foot in two worlds, Michel "Big Mike" Goldwater led a life of extraordinary diversity in the Far West. On the Arizona frontier Big Mike was engaged in such activities as shipping half a million pounds of corn to Army forts, fleeing Apache ambushes on horseback, relinquishing gold dust to masked desperadoes, and overseeing shipments of merchandise along desolate, forbidding desert roads. In San Francisco, Goldwater led a vastly different life as a wealthy member of elite Jewish society: He was a close friend of Rabbi Jacob Nieto, a president of Congregation Sherith Israel, and an articulate spokesman and officer for Jewish charitable organizations. Courtesy, Arizona Historical Society, Tucson

Meyer. Sarah's brother Myer J. added another French increment to this American-Polish-Prussian-French clan when he married French immigrant Sophia Cahen. In ensuing years, the circle continued to expand by birth and by the arrival of more relatives: Harris's brother Nathan Newmark; his nephews Max N. and Morris A. Newmark; and his nephews Kaspare, Samuel, and Max Cohn, all of whom were energetic Los Angeles builders.

The names of the clan's companies are prominent in the rolls of pioneer Los Angeles businesses: M. A. Newmark & Company (Harris's firm, expanded by his sons and nephews); City of Paris (owned by Eugene and Constant Meyer); Solomon Lazard & Company; Rich, Newmark & Company; Kremer & Company; J. P. Newmark & Company; Kaspare Cohn & Company; Kaspare Cohn Commercial and Savings Bank (renamed the Union Bank and Trust Company by Cohn's sons-in-law); and Brownstein, Newmark & Louis. The family was also active in area-shaping real estate transactions. H. Newmark and Company acquired, then sold Rancho Santa Anita to E. J. "Lucky" Baldwin in 1897; the company also sold the Temple Block to the City of Los Angeles in 1909. Harris and partners, including Kaspare Cohn and I. W. Hellman, in 1886 acquired and later developed Repetto Ranch, once known as the community of Newmark, now called Montebello.

Other family members were pioneer professionals. Myer J. Newmark was the first of the clan's many attorneys—most notable among them, Harris's grandsons Joseph and Edwin Loeb, founders of the historic law firm Loeb & Loeb, established in 1907. Nathan Newmark's son Philip and Solomon Lazard's son Edmund were both prominent Los Angeles physicians, and Solomon's daughter Jeannette Lazard was an early Los Angeles schoolteacher.

Harris's ubiquitous relatives were also active in Los Angeles's budding civic affairs. Myer J. served as city attorney (1862); Solomon Lazard was on the city council (1853 and 1861); and Maurice Kremer was county treasurer (1859–1865), county supervisor (1865–1866), member of the school board (1866–1875), and city clerk (1869–1880). Myer J. founded the first Los Angeles Chamber of Commerce, and Solomon Lazard was its first president. Other family members worked with the chamber to hasten the construction of San Pedro Harbor and to promote the railroads that precipitated Los Angeles's first large-scale boom in 1887.

This lively bunch was no less involved in religious, social, and fraternal affairs. Joseph Newmark was from his arrival until his death

Sarah Nathan Goldwater (1825–1905) was a native of London. She lived in Sonora, Los Angeles, and San Francisco, California—but never in the Arizona Territory. Photo from the Historic Collection of Herb and Betty McLaughlin, Phoenix, Arizona

the patriarch of the Los Angeles Jewish community. His mantle passed to Harris, who was president of the B'nai B'rith Congregation in 1887. In 1869 Solomon Lazard, Eugene Meyer, Harris Newmark, and Leon Loeb—who would become Harris's son-in-law—helped start the Los Angeles Social Club. Newmark and clan were also leaders in the Odd Fellows and Masons, and in 1868 Eugene Meyer organized a branch of the Alliance Israélite Universelle. In the late 1880s, when a wave of anti-Jewish exclusion cut an arroyo between the prominent Jews and non-Jews in town, the Newmark crowd soon reacted. In 1891 Harris's son Maurice H. and his brother-in-law Leon Loeb founded a posh Jewish preserve, the Concordia Club. Years later, J. P.'s son Samuel was the founding president of the Concordia's present-day counterpart, the Hillcrest Country Club.

Harris ended his account in 1913, when the population of Los Angeles County, to the amazement and delight of its inhabitants, had passed the half-million mark. Concluding with a forecast, the proud pioneer noted:

As nineteen hundred years ago the humblest Roman, wherever he might find himself, would glow with pride when he said, "I am a Roman!," so in years to come will the son of the metropolis on these shores, wheresoever his travels may take him, be proud to declare: "I AM A CITIZEN OF LOS ANGELES."

Of these far western families, the only name to achieve national household familiarity—besides Strauss and his "Levi's"—was Goldwater, an early political as well as a mercantile dynasty. Although the best known of this clan are no longer Jews, these third- and fourth-generation far westerners have warm memories of their Jewish antecedents. When campaigning for the

United States presidency in 1964, Senator Barry Goldwater, a first-generation Episcopalian, regaled the American public with stories of his Polish Jewish grandfather, Michel ("Big Mike") Goldwater, his granduncle Joseph ("Little Joe") Goldwater, and their sons, all of whom were frontier merchants, freighters, and politicos in the roughhouse days of the Arizona Territory.

Big Mike (he was six-foot-three) was born in 1825, the son of an impoverished innkeeper and his wife, Hirsch and Elizabeth Goldwasser of Konin, the parents of twenty-two children. At fifteen he went to Paris, where he worked as a tailor until the 1848 revolution, when he fled to London. There he met and in 1850 married Sarah Nathan. The next year his brother Joseph Goldwater, nine years Mike's junior, turned up with a contagious case of gold fever. The two men set off alone for California, leaving Sarah to follow with their two children.

The family reassembled in July 1854 in Sonora, Tuolumne County. Mike started a fruit store there, went bankrupt, began a second business in his wife's name, and lost that one, too. In 1858 the Goldwaters decided to try their luck in Los Angeles, where the brothers failed in several more undertakings. In 1862 Los Angeles businessman Bernard Cohn asked Mike and Joe to open a store for him in La Paz, a new mining camp on the east bank of the Colorado River. The outpost was hot, mosquito ridden, and chaotic, and its inhabitants, as described by the *New York Herald*, were "greasers, Indians, Jews, outlawed white men, and desperadoes." The merchandise had to be hauled across a long distance by mule train and steamer, the length of the boom was uncertain, and La Paz was clearly no place for Sarah and the children. Mike and Joe, however, had run out of capital, credit, and choices. Four years later, the Goldwaters bought out their employer and renamed their thriving retail, wholesale, freighting, and forwarding partnership J. Goldwater and Brother. In the late 1860s, when floods separated the town from the river, the brothers moved their business six miles downstream. There they founded a riverside settlement they called Ehrenberg, in honor of their late friend Herman Ehrenberg.

Sarah and the children (there were eventually eight) remained in Los Angeles for a few more years. In 1868, at last able to afford the advantages of the region's largest city, she moved her family to San Francisco and established a permanent residence. Legend has it that Sarah

The children of Joseph and Rosa Newmark, Los Angeles, 1883. Standing, left to right: *Abraham J. Newmark, Sarah (Mrs. Harris Newmark), Meyer J. Newmark.* Seated, left to right: *Matilda (Mrs. Maurice Kremer), Harriet (Mrs. Eugene Meyer), and Caroline (Mrs. Solomon Lazard). Courtesy, Norton Stern, Santa Monica, California*

A Community of Dynasties

Writing about the Jews of San Francisco in 1860, I. J. Benjamin observed: "Nowhere else are they accorded as much esteem by their non-Jewish brothers and nowhere else are they so highly valued in social and political circles." Twenty-eight years later, in the view of Hubert Howe Bancroft, their position was still uniquely favorable. Wrote the San Francisco–based historian, "Never since the great Egyptian exodus have the Hebrew race found a soil and society better suited to their character and taste." Acceptance, along with what Bancroft called "gold and golden opportunities, moneymaking and freedom of thought, speech and action," attracted Jews in numbers. Between twenty and thirty thousand were living in San Francisco when the foregoing words were penned. By that time, the more successful families had formed their own clique— an exclusive Gilded Circle, forged of interrelated clans linked by blood, marriage, and business. Before long, a code of behavior evolved much like those that governed the newly affluent entrepreneurial circles emerging in other large American and European cities.

The first rule was to make money. Without it, circle members plummeted as swiftly as they had risen. Occasionally an unusual opportunity

The Alaska Commercial Company was formed in January 1868 by president Louis Sloss, vice-president Lewis Gerstle, Simon Greenewald, Hayward M. Hutchison, Albert Boscowitz, William Kohl, A. Wasserman, Gustave Niebaum, and John F. Miller. The San Francisco headquarters (310 Sansome Street) of this fishing, canning, shipping, and trading empire exuded Far North atmosphere and enterprise. As described by Samuel Johnston in the Alaska Commercial Company, *the odor of seal skins stored on the third and fourth floors permeated the building, blending with the spicy scent of China tea stored in chests on the second floor. Dropping in for a smoke and a chat were notables such as James Jackay, James Flood, Charles Crocker, Claus Spreckels, Senator George Hearst, David Starr Jordan, and Eugene Meyer. Army and Navy men, visiting explorers, reporters, and politicians also stopped by, as did ne'er-do-well oldtimers in need of a handout. Courtesy, The Bancroft Library, University of California, Berkeley*

M.J.B.—the widely-recognized trademark—are the initials of the founder of the company Max J. Brandenstein. Son of a gold rush prospector turned tobacco merchant, Brandenstein and his brothers Mannie and Edward formed M.J. Brandenstein and company in 1894. Courtesy, M.J.B. Coffee Company, San Francisco, California

paved the way. One such windfall was the twenty-year (1872–1892) federal contract that permitted Louis Sloss, Lewis Gerstle, Simon Greenewald, and other partners in the Alaska Commercial Company to build a vast sealskin, salmon canning, trade, and shipping empire. The majority of these early prominent families, however, such as the (Levi) Strauss-Stern-Sahlein and the Seligman-Lilienthal-Steinhart clans, started in retail trade, then switched to more profitable wholesale distribution, manufacture, real estate, stockbroking, and banking. In some cases offspring boosted a pioneer family into the Gilded Circle. Aaron and Delia Fleishhacker's sons began their careers in their father's modestly successful San Francisco box factory. By 1907 they had spearheaded the acquisition of the Seligman family's Anglo-Californian Bank and the Lazard Frères London, Paris, and American Bank, which they then reorganized as the Anglo & London, Paris National Bank of San Francisco, the Anglo California Trust, and other banking concerns. Anthony and Theresa (Mohr) Zellerbach's son Isadore turned his father's stationery, wrappings, and bag company into the multi-million-dollar Crown Zellerbach Corporation. Manfred and Max Joseph Brandenstein, sons of Joseph (who started as a prospector, then became a tobacco merchant), founded M. J. Brandenstein Company, importers of tea and coffee, the manufacturers of a variety of MJB products. And Abe and Fanny Haas's son Walter and their nephew and son-in-law Daniel Koshland hoisted Levi Strauss and Company into the manufacture of Levi's for a multi-million-dollar world market.

In 1870 Anthony Zeller-bach started a tiny business selling paper goods—stationery, bags, and wrappings—to support his wife Theresa (Mohr) and their nine children. By 1887 he had developed a moderately successful concern. His oldest son Isadore built the company into a paper kingdom, the Crown Zellerbach Corporation. Courtesy, Crown Zellerbach Corporation, San Francisco, California

A second Gilded Circle rule was to marry one's own kind. In the early years, "one's own kind" meant someone who was Jewish, of the same national origin—most of the circle were of German or French stock—ambitious, and of good character. By the second generation, with fortunes at stake, these basic prerequisites were merely openers with regard to matchmaking. Suitors who found favor were such men as the Lilienthals—seven brothers and cousins, the sons of the noted German-born Reform rabbi Dr. Max Lilienthal of Cincinnati and of his brother Dr. Samuel Lilienthal of New York, a renowned physician. Of prestigious lineage, excellent secular and religious education, and outstanding business and professional skills (several were also unusually handsome), the Lilienthals had no trouble finding brides in the Gilded Circle. Philip N. married Bella Seligman (Joseph's daughter); Ernest R., Bella Sloss; J. Leo, Bertha Gerstle; and Theodore, Sophie Gerstle. (Jesse Lilienthal, who brought a wife, Lillie Bernheimer, from New York, and Dr. James Lilienthal, a bachelor, were also highly valued in that set.)

A vital trio of women, the two Hecht sisters and their Boston cousin, were equally welcomed. The sisters were the daughters of Marcus Hecht of Buckingham & Hecht, San Francisco shoe manufacturers; he later became the president of the Emporium. Quiet Mark Gerstle became enamored of vivacious Hilda Hecht. Five years after they were married, his younger brother Will married Hilda's eye-catching sister Saidie. When their cousin Marcus (Max) Sloss was attending Harvard Law School, he fell in love with the Hecht girls' Boston cousin Hattie Hecht, a small dynamo who would for years reign as a *grande dame* in the cultural and civic life of San Francisco.

A romanticized drawing of the Levi Strauss overall factory; courtesy, Levi Strauss & Company, San Francisco, California

Disadvantageous marriages were shunned as energetically as good marriages were sought. Eugene Meyer's stunning daughter Rosalie was pressured out of her engagement to Simon Greenebaum, whose prospects were poor, and nudged into a marriage with Sigmund Stern, a Levi Strauss heir, who could promise her both love *and* luxury. ("I can't afford to keep you *and* a husband," Eugene bluntly informed his daughter.) Bella Gerstle carried on a secret romance with Dr. Charles Levison (her brother-in-law J. B. Levinson's brother), who for some reason was not a welcome suitor. When Bella was twenty-nine, her mother, Hannah, and Delia Fleishhacker convinced her she was duty bound to marry Delia's son Morti, then thirty-eight, thereby making both families happy. She complied, but by the time Bella's third-generation son Morti Fleishhacker, Jr., was old enough for love, Victorian parental authority was no longer ironclad. The younger Morti fell for Janet Choynski, whose San Francisco Jewish pioneer forebears were Polish-English firebrands—her grandfather Isadore, a journalist, regularly sprayed the German Jewish elite with verbal buckshot. "That Polish girl" was clearly not "their kind," but Bella failed to dissuade Morti, who believed (rightly, it turned out) that he and Janet had a bright future together.

The Gilded Circle also made it a rule to belong to the Reform Temple Emanu-El or to no congregation, and provided much of that congregation's dynamic leadership. Some circle members who were given to spiritual intensities or to severe physical and emotional anguish found the rational and decorous form of Judaism at Emanu-El wanting. Stricken with unremitting depressions, as was her mother, Harriet (Newmark) Meyer, Rosalie (Meyer) Stern sought solace in Christian Science. Her mother's brother, J. Myer Newmark, also nervous and high-strung, turned to Christian Science as well. To ease her emotional afflictions, Bella Gerstle Fleishhacker experimented with Christian Science, Hindu cults, a German psychiatrist, and eventually, creative activity. After a summer at Carl Gustav Jung's institute in Zurich, Bella became a dedicated and accomplished painter.

Circle members were also expected to acquire the tastes and appurtenances of people of rank. By the early 1870s, San Francisco's Gentile "nobles of new money" were covering the crests and slopes of Nob Hill and other fashionable neighborhoods with monumental mansions stuffed to the rafters with European furnishings and objets d'art. The Jewish rich were equally avid home builders and decorators.

A Gilded Circle soiree, sirca 1890; left to right, standing: *Florence Guggenheim Colman, May Lilienthal Levy, Vera Colman Goss, and name unknown;* seated: *name unknown, Edith Mack Bransten, and Amy Sussman Steinhart. Courtesy, Sophie Gerstle Lilienthal Collection, Western Jewish History Center, Judah L. Magnes Museum, Berkeley, California*

Whether it was parvenu insecurity or strong attachment to family, Gilded Circle clans frequently built houses on the same street and often in the same summer retreat. Sprawling estates merited manorial names. The Gerstle's summer place in San Rafael, adjoining the Slosses', was the much-loved Violet Terrace. Marcus and Corrine Koshland's thirty-room mansion on Pacific Avenue was called Le Petit Trianon—it was modeled after the original at Versailles. The Isaiah W. Hellman, Jr., family lived in Oakland in the Dunsmuir House, set in a parklike setting, now owned by the city of Oakland. Later-day architectural heritage buffs would lovingly preserve Victorian beauties built by the Gilded Circle, designating them by such names as the Haas-Lilienthal House and the Lilienthal-

Lewis Gerstle and family on a visit to Frankfurt, Germany, in 1875; left to right: *William, Bertha, Sophie, Lewis, Alice, Hannah, Bella, Clara, and Mark. Courtesy, Western Jewish History Center, Judah L. Magnes Museum, Berkeley, California*

Pratt House. Early modern architects shaping a gracious, California style also found attuned appreciators in this well-heeled crowd. Willis Polk designed a home for the Walter Haases, and Charles Sumner Greene came from Pasadena to do a home for the Sigmund Sterns.

Large families living in commodious homes staffed by a minimum of six servants entertained frequently and lavishly, hosting coming-out parties, weddings, anniversaries, musicales, and dinner parties. Until the early 1900s, their lengthy guest lists were largely confined to the Gilded Circle, other socially acceptable Jews, and a smattering of affluent Gentiles. During her girlhood in the 1880s and 1890s, recalled Amy Steinhart Braden, daughter of William Steinhart, socializing was confined to a select Jewish set. Young women who accepted more than an occasional invitation to non-Jewish parties (actually, very few were issued) were roundly criticized.

To prepare them for a life of privilege, the young received disciplined training. Nurses and governesses instructed them in proper manners and in the French and German languages, and tutors gave them art and music lessons. Most of the boys were permitted to attend public schools before the more academically inclined were sent either east, to Harvard or Yale, or closer to home, to Stanford or the University of California. The less studious were rushed directly into business. Most of the girls attended private schools—Miss West's, Miss Burke's, Mme Ziska's (later called Miss Lake's)—schools described as long on the social graces and short on learning. Rosalie Meyer was one of the few to attend San Francisco's Girls' High in the early days. Later, girls, Ruth Brandenstein among them, fought to go to public school. "I'm sick to death of refinement," Ruth wailed to her father, Manny Brandenstein. Higher education was considered *coarsening* for women, and only a few persuaded their fathers otherwise. Among those who did was Amy Steinhart, who enrolled at the University of California in 1896, aspiring to become a professional social worker. (She eventually became the executive secretary of the State Department of Social Welfare.)

Although occupied as they were with fortune and family building, circle members nevertheless always gave high priority to good works and civic duty. Members supported the Fruit and Flower Mission, the Occidental Kindergarten, the Women's Exchange, the Ladies' Protection and Relief Society, the San Francisco Free Public Library, the San Francisco Protestant Orphan Asylum, the Mission Street free dispensary (Dr. James Lilienthal organized it), and numerous other city charities. Circle members were also much in evidence in a variety of Jewish undertakings. By 1880 thirty organizations—charitable, mutual aid, and educational—served San Francisco Jews. Ten more were organized over the next decade. To strengthen the network, in 1910 Jewish leaders founded the Federation of Jewish Charities. Judge Marcus C. Sloss was the first president, and J. B. Levison and Henry Sinsheimer (a Koshland son-in-law) were vice-presidents. Other Gilded Circle members were on the forty-six-man board of governors. Outstanding among the many who were patrons of the arts, civic leaders, and philanthropists was Rosalie (Meyer) Stern, who headed the Parks and Recreation Commission for nineteen years. One of her gifts to the city is the sixty-five-acre outdoor theater, Sigmund Stern Grove. Energetic Hattie Sloss, who kept a half dozen groups humming, and Corrine Koshland were best known for their work on behalf of the opera and the symphony, and their aid to young musicians. Insurance executive Albert Bender collected artworks, including those of young San Francisco artists, and donated a number of works to Bay Area museums. Public facilities funded by Gilded Circle families dot San Francisco and its environs: Fleishhacker Pool, Playground, and Zoo; Steinhart Aquarium; Daniel E. Koshland Park; and Gerstle Park are just a sampling.

In times of the city's tribulation or glory, the Gilded Circle was often at the forefront. "My experiences during and following the San Francisco disaster [earthquake and fire] in April 1906 were among the most momentous in my life," wrote J. B. Levison, a Fireman's Fund Insurance Company executive who was active in both relief and rehabilitation work, as were many other circle members. The Abe Ruef investigation and graft trials of 1906 to 1912, which one author called San Francisco's second earthquake, also commanded the circle's attention. Some members, J. B. Levison among them, pressed vigorously for a conviction. Others staunchly held that the political boss Ruef was no more to blame than the vindicated "captains" of industry, officials of the telephone, trolley, and other large San Francisco enterprises who bribed him. Either way, all were eager to erase the blemish on their city, and—by reason of Ruef's religion—on San Francisco Jewry.

When the rebuilt San Francisco was ready to flutter her fan and trill high notes to the world, circle members helped lay the groundwork. In 1911 Congressman Julius Kahn successfully led through Congress the city's bid to host the Panama Pacific Exposition, a celebration to mark the completion of the Panama Canal. Vice-presidents on the planning committee included the senior Leon Sloss, Michael H. de Young, and Isaiah W. Hellman, Jr.; Hattie (Hecht) Sloss was the chairman of the Women's Board. J. B. Levison administered the $665,000 music program, which included, among other highlights, a performance of *Hail California*, composed by Camille Saint-Saëns for the event.

By the early twentieth century, when the third generation was coming of age, the circle's code of behavior had solidified into a tradition to be conformed to or, with increasing frequency, rebelled against. Circle members had by then begun to mingle freely with non-Jews at social, cultural, and charitable events, and intermarriage was clearly on the rise. Vicissitudes in the outer society had also demanded some adjustments. Mainstream acceptance, noted so often in the early years, had diminished—not greatly, but enough to curtail the circle's field of activity. The erosion was largely the result of a nationwide epidemic of anti-Semitism that reached San Francisco in the 1880s. (Even while describing unprecedented hospitality toward Jews, Bancroft concomitantly noted some degree of antipathy as well.) Most apparent were the barriers raised at San Francisco's elite social clubs: the Bohemian Club, the Olympic Club, the Pacific Union Club, and similar organizations that had previously been open to Jews. Some sociologists explain the outbreak as an age-old ideological disease; others interpret it as a new drive to limit economic competition. Whatever the cause, in San Francisco, Jewish exclusion at the top dented the dream but failed to destroy it. Pained but philosophical, members of the Gilded Circle made their adjustments and continued their vital exchange with the city their forebears had helped build, and to which they felt a deep attachment.

M. Goldwater & Brothers, Prescott, Arizona Territory, was founded in 1876. The "M."
stood for Morris, the oldest of Michel and Sarah Goldwater's eight children. The brothers
were Henry and Baron, who was the father of Senator Barry Goldwater. The man leaning
against the column is Morris, who, in addition to running a successful business, was
mayor of Prescott (for ten terms), territorial legislator, Democratic party county chairman,
vice-president of the Prescott National Bank, and a Grand Master of Arizona Masonry. For
years Masonic lodge meetings were held on the second floor of the Goldwater store. Cour-
tesy, Arizona Historical Foundation, Hayden Library, Arizona State University, Tempe

never ventured into Arizona Territory throughout the twenty-three years her husband operated in the Arizona wilds. During those years,
Mike visited his family frequently, and when he
retired in 1885, he joined Sarah in San Francisco. For much of the remaining eighteen years
of his long life (he died in 1903) Mike acted as
San Francisco buyer for the Arizona Goldwater

enterprises. He also became an influential and
often innovative leader at Sherith Israel Synagogue and the First Hebrew Benevolent Society.

The Ehrenberg operation—run by Mike and
Joe, assisted in time by Mike's sons Morris and
Henry—for a decade was the chief supplier of
the miners, merchants, farmers, and soldiers
Americanizing the territory. In 1880, when the

railroad demolished steamer and wagon train transport, the Goldwaters sold the Ehrenberg forwarding business. Mike joined Morris in the Prescott store, established in 1876, and Joe moved to Bisbee, where he went into business with Miguel Jose Castaneda.

By that time members of the family had already established a record of public service. Joe was appointed postmaster of Ehrenberg in 1869 and was on the school board. During his brief stay in Phoenix, Morris served as recorder. When he moved to Prescott, he organized a defense group, called the Prescott Rifles, and a volunteer fire-fighting association; in 1879 he was elected to his first term as mayor of Prescott. His father, Mike, succeeded him in that office. More contentious than his amiable and diplomatic son, Mike fought with the council and his constituents over board sidewalks, dog fees, and other such matters. Nine months into his one-year term, he resigned in a huff. Thereafter he left local politics to Morris, who served as the mayor of Prescott for a total of twenty-two years between 1879 and 1927. When not filling that office, Morris did stints as territorial legislator and as state senator. He also organized and for a period headed the Yavapai County Democratic Committee. An intensely loyal son, Morris courted a non-Jewish widow, Sarah Shivers Fisher, for years, but did not marry her until after his mother died; by then he was fifty-five. When brother Baron became a Bar Mitzvah in 1879, Morris wrote him a congratulatory letter and urged him to obey his parents and select proper friends. Family grief undoubtedly prompted Morris's cautionary: Brothers Ben and Sam were itinerant gamblers; compounding their problems, Ben contracted tuberculosis, Sam caught it from him, and both of them died before their parents.

The Bar Mitzvah boy of '79 came to Prescott in 1882, where he conscientiously learned the business from the broom up. By the time the firm was ready to branch out to burgeoning Phoenix (for a second try—Morris had a store there in 1874), Baron was placed in charge. In a decade M. Goldwater and Brothers (the other brother was Henry, who left the firm after a while) was on the way to becoming a big department store in downtown Phoenix.

In 1907 Baron married outdoorsy Episcopalian Josephine Williams, who came to Arizona suffering from supposedly terminal tuberculosis, but who recovered and lived an unusually long and active life. Barry was born in 1909, Bob in 1911, and Carolyn in 1912. All were baptized and raised in their mother's faith. Sportsman, photographer, and pilot, Barry eventually got around to assuming the presidency of Goldwater's, but only until he attained public office. He started out in the Phoenix City Council in 1949. An admirer of his Uncle Morris, but not of his political party, Republican Barry was elected to the United States Senate in 1952 and was reelected four times. His son Barry Goldwater, Jr., a California Republican, became a United States congressman in 1969.

The Goldwaters were but a few of the many pioneer Jews who took an interest in and then an active role in public life in the Far West. None can match this clan for length of service. What others lacked in years, however, they made up for in the number and variety of offices—from postmaster to governor—that they filled.

Chapter Six

ELECTED, APPOINTED, SELF-APPOINTED

After suffering for centuries from oppressive government, on the far western frontier Jews faced a new menace: little or no government at all. A fragile thread of federal authority backed by a small military force held the region together—but just barely. In remote and scruffy capitals, new and inexperienced officials spent their time and paltry public funds creating statewide or territorywide codes and facilities. Local governments in slapdash mining towns and rickety supply centers lacked the wherewithal and the organization to adequately protect their citizens' lives or property. When destructive forces—fires, floods, or widespread crime—became too massive for an every-man-for-himself defense, self-interested pioneers banded together against the common enemy.

Membership, at times leadership, in a volunteer fire-fighting or crime-fighting association was often a pioneer Jew's introduction to public service. Participation in these organizations, later regarded as a mark of social distinction, during pioneer days was a brute necessity. The first volunteer crime-fighting organization and the model for subsequent groups throughout the Far West formed in San Francisco in 1851. San Francisco was then in its fifth year as

Charles Strauss, shown here with an unidentified boy, was elected mayor of Tucson in 1883. During his term of office, Strauss created Tucson's first building and loan association; initiated the building of a city hall, a fire station, and a library; and began a program of street grading. Courtesy, Arizona Historical Society, Tucson

an American city. The population had reached thirty-five thousand, and the public coffers were nearly empty. Criminals from around the world had converged on the booming port city, and organized gangs called Sydney Ducks roamed the city, robbing, assaulting, and murdering at will. Outraged by the inability of the local authorities to deter them, a few San Franciscans issued a call for a citizens' army. Some two hundred men responded, including Jesse Seligman, William Langermann, Samuel Marx, and other Jewish merchants. The assembled drew up a constitution protesting the city administration's failures and pledging to "allow no theft, burglary, arson, or murder to go unpunished, either by the quibbles of the law, the insecurities of prison, or the laxity of those who pretend to administer justice."

For the next three months the vigilantes heard complaints, made arrests, conducted trials, and executed three burglars and one murderer. They also imposed fines, forced felons to leave the city, and inspected incoming ships to prevent new criminals from debarking. Angered at the usurpation of their power and fearing mob rule, city officials sought to curb the committee. When a grand jury failed to indict the leaders, local authorities appealed to the governor.

A large segment of the public, including some Jews, enthusiastically supported the committee during the chaotic summer of 1851. On August 24 a young immigrant named Alexander Mayer wrote to his friend in Philadelphia lauding what turned out to be the 1851 committee's last formal action:

Tombstone Fire Department, circa 1881; left to right, standing: *G. Brandalaw, G. Noddin, C. Thomas, C. Crupp, P. Corpstein, L. Aaron,* and *J. Coyle;* seated: *W. Barow, J. Nash, H. Lee, E. Lang,* and *E. Marks. Courtesy, Arizona Historical Society, Tucson*

Ed, Some time ago I wrote You about the Vigilence Committee This two men McKinzy, & Whiteker [Robert McKenzie and Samuel Whittaker] they were Sentenced to be Hung by the Com, at Once. This two Men were stolen away Midnight from their Rooms. The Governor of Cal the sheriff & Police Men took them. the Vigilence Committee they were bound to have this two Men back again 24th of August at ½ past 2 o'clock they entered the Prison and got this two Men out. and put them in a Carriage and Pursued to thier Head Quarters. and I followed them. I tell all this what they have done it did not take more than fifteen Minutes. I have seen them Hong I was very Glad of it too. I tell you Ed. that is a great Country. The Governor must be quiet or Else they Hang him.

From the outset, however, as many Jews opposed the ad hoc law enforcers as backed them. The most vocal and effective opponents were knowledgeable upholders of American civil liberties, including the right to a fair trial. Outstanding among them was Solomon Heydenfeldt, who was just starting a long and brilliant legal career in California. A native of Charleston, South Carolina (he was born in 1816) Heydenfeldt practiced law in Alabama from 1837 to early 1850. He also served a term in 1840 as county judge in Tallapoosa County and in 1842 was a losing candidate in a race for Mobile County judge. In 1849 Heydenfeldt vented his antislavery views in a pamphlet addressed to the Alabama governor, thereby snuffing all hope of public office in that state. He sailed for San Francisco in the spring of 1850. Experienced, able, and ambitious, he swiftly established a civil law practice, joined the Democratic party, and was almost immediately nominated to run for United States senator. His candidacy was blocked by Northerners, but he retained his high standing in the party.

Two weeks after the Vigilance Committee began administering its swift and arbitrary justice, Heydenfeldt undertook the only criminal case he ever handled in California. The crime—

the murder of Lewis Polock (described in chapter one)—occurred on the night of June 22, when San Franciscans were still reeling from the city's sixth fire. The conflagration had raged all day and had gutted fifteen blocks before finally being contained. Throughout the day the Vigilance Committee had been out in full force making arrests, primarily for arson and theft. After the fire one of the vigilantes, Charles Norris, went to Mary St. Clair's house, a local brothel, and was on the premises when Captain Samuel Gallagher was witnessed shooting Lewis Polock in a quarrel over one of the residents, Jane Hurley. City officials, learning where Gallagher was being held, rescued him. Heydenfeldt, along with his associate, Colonel John B. Weller (later elected California governor and United States senator), agreed to defend Gallagher.

Several days later a large crowd attended Gallagher's hearing in the recorder's court. After five witnesses were cross-examined, Gallagher was charged with murder and jailed to await trial. Weller and Heydenfeldt waived their client's right to be released on bail, fearing that he would not be safe on the streets as long as the public was in a feverish state of mind.

Gallagher's first trial (he was tried twice) took place on August 12 in San Francisco's Fourth District Court, Judge Delos Lake presiding. District Attorney Harry Byrne had a strong case against the accused murderer, but Gallagher had an unusually able trio defending him. Heydenfeldt, who was in charge, was assisted by Weller and by a Colonel Barton, an eloquent trial lawyer who argued the case. The jury deadlocked; a new trial was set for November 14. This time Heydenfeldt presented the closing argument. After the jury had been out for three hours, they sent the bailiff to advise Heydenfeldt they were split, seven favoring a conviction of murder in the first degree, and five concluding that Gallagher was not guilty. If it was agreeable to him, the bailiff told Heydenfeldt, the jurors would settle on a manslaughter verdict. "I concur," was Heydenfeldt's spare response. Judge Lake sentenced Gallagher to three years and fined him $500. The legal historian recording the case noted that had the judge learned of that conversation before he had sentenced the prisoner, "there would have been a signal exhibition of judicial wrath." As further evidence that official frontier justice was different but only a little more exacting than that of the vigilantes is the fact that Gallagher was pardoned six months later. Crude as these early efforts at government were, they represented a determined first step toward

As one of its final acts, the Vigilance Committee of 1851 executed Robert Whittaker and Samuel McKenzie, who were suspected of burglary. Soon after, the group, which had formed to clean up San Francisco's streets, disbanded and law enforcement was left to elected officials. Courtesy, California Historical Society, San Francisco

as a justice on the Supreme Court of California from 1849 to 1852. And Joseph Shannon, a Sephardic Jew despite his Irish name, was elected treasurer of the county of San Francisco in September of 1851.

The pay was small, the tenure uncertain, and the tasks facing these early officeholders were burdensome. Yet the political welcome accorded Jews in the Far West—unmatched anywhere else—made these posts highly attractive to Jewish office seekers who could not get elected at home. As late as the mid-nineteenth century, some barriers to Jewish participation in politics still existed in the East. Discrimination was sometimes covert—an unspoken refusal to consider a Jew for a position of public trust. At other times

the orderly and democratic administration of the Far West.

From the earliest days forward, pioneer Jews helped to advance that end as appointed or elected officials. Solomon Heydenfeldt was nominated at the Democratic convention held in December 1851 for the office of justice of the Supreme Court of California. He was subsequently elected and served in the state's highest court for six years. The forty-five opinions he wrote were later hailed as "fine examples of cogent legal reasoning and condensation"; they addressed such pressing issues as Mexican land grants, mining laws, and vigilance committees.

Heydenfeldt was one of a small group of Jews who held high office during the infancy of far western government. The majority of these men were Americans and usually from Sephardic families that had lived in the United States for generations. (Heydenfeldt's mother, Esther, was a member of the well-known Sephardic DePass family.) They were ambitious, articulate in English, grounded in American customs and ideas, and well educated. Among them were Elcan Heydenfeldt, Solomon's brother, who was elected to represent San Francisco in the state assembly in 1852, as was Isaac N. Cardozo, of Richmond (uncle of the renowned United States Supreme Court Justice Benjamin N. Cardozo). Henry A. Lyons of New Orleans served

Adolph Solomon (1853–1905) followed his brother, I. E. Solomon, to the Arizona Territory and was associated with him and others in a number of commercial enterprises. In 1882 he represented Cochise County in the Arizona territorial legislature. Later, when he moved to El Paso, Texas, he was elected to the city council and appointed acting mayor. Courtesy, El Paso Public Library Photo Archives, El Paso, Texas

Top left: *Solomon Heydenfeldt; courtesy, American Jewish Archives, Cincinnati, Ohio*

it took the form of a local or a state law barring non-Christians from voting or holding public office. (The last of these laws was lifted from New Hampshire statutes in 1876.) Once widespread, these restrictions began falling away with the first drive west. In struggling far western settlements beset by seemingly endless frontier problems, able and enthusiastic (white) settlers, willing to forego more direct forms of fortune hunting to seek county, state, or territorial office, found no religious restrictions to impede them.

Many Jews participated in politics on a local level. As merchants—with a direct stake in a calm, well-ordered community—Jews were usually quick to accept civic responsibilities. Moreover, they were often best prepared to do so. The majority were literate and sober where others were neither. Few had the formal education or the political experience of an American-born Heydenfeldt or Cardozo, but the traditional Jewish communities from which many came were well structured and democratically administered. A calm, intelligent Jewish voice was often among the first to urge the establishment or the improvement of basic community services.

In Los Angeles one of those early voices belonged to Morris Goodman. A native of Bavaria, Goodman came to Los Angeles in 1849 when Angelenos were prospering as major suppliers of the gold seekers in the north. The prosperity, however, also attracted gamblers and ruffians who settled in the *Calle de los Negros*, a seedy back alley of saloons, brothels, and gambling dens close to the center of town. Goodman reproved the lawlessness as dangerous to residents as well as bad for the business they depended on for survival. He resolved to do something about it. When Los Angeles was incorporated as an American city in 1850, he was elected to its first city council. As one of his early official acts, Goodman urged the council to establish a police department; but the tiny town—population 1,600—was not yet able to underwrite full-time law enforcement. Some years passed before it was. Until that time, a series of vigilance committees imposed the little order that Los Angeles knew. Having no other recourse, Goodman, Solomon Lazard, and other early Los Angeles Jew-

ish merchants served with the vigilantes. Even after a police force was established, Los Angeles's reputation as "the most lawless city west of Santa Fe" continued unabated.

Lawlessness reached its peak in 1871 with a brutal race riot in Calle de los Negros in which more than twenty Chinese were massacred. This tragic event was portrayed by contemporary media as the result of the murder of a white by warring Chinese factions. In truth the riot began when a white Angeleno attempted to steal $7,000 from a Chinese merchant. The storekeeper shot the man in self-defense; the mob, however, demanded blood. Among the feverish crowd, one of the few sane voices belonged to newly ap-

Emil Harris was a Los Angeles police chief and later a private detective. It was said he knew of every criminal among the 10,000 people of Los Angeles in the 1870s, and he ranged over the entire Los Angeles basin, pursuing bandits in the canyons of what would be Hollywood, wading across the Los Angeles River chasing gunwielding desperadoes, or arriving at the pueblo from San Buenaventura with a captured Three-Fingered Jack. Courtesy, Western States Jewish Historical Quarterly *(July, 1979)*

Nathan B. Appel was bailiff of the Los Angeles police court from 1890 to 1901. Courtesy, Arizona Historical Society, Tucson

pointed Los Angeles police officer Emil Harris, who shrewdly laid the blame where it belonged. He would later tell a coroner's inquest:

Between five and six o'clock, yesterday evening, while on duty in Commercial Street . . . I heard some shots fired and ran in front of Negro Alley. . . . [The sheriff] requested me and all citizens willing to obey the laws to stand alongside of him; a great number volunteered and others, more excited, wanted to force their way into the houses. . . . The excited multitude got the upper hand. . . . One Chinaman came running out [and I] heard a cry by some white persons, "Here is one!" and I succeeded in capturing him. . . . Then some parties unbeknown to me, about 100 or more took him from me [and] that was the last I saw

of him. . . . They cried "Hang him." . . . [Later] a Chinaman called me by name; I told him to come out and I would protect him if I could. I suppose the one taken from me was the first one hung.

Emil Harris had arrived in Los Angeles in 1869, when the population was approximately fifty-seven hundred. He worked briefly as a bartender and served as an urgently needed volunteer fire fighter before he was appointed to the police department in 1870. First as a patrolman and then as chief of police in 1878, Harris brought a marked improvement to the quality of law enforcement in the still-troubled town. Harris became a highly skilled detective and was well acquainted with the city's underground. He captured bank robbers, solved murders and larcenies, controlled the flourishing opium dens and brothels, and cracked down on juvenile delinquency. After an upheaval in local politics in 1879, Harris was turned out of office. Subsequently he continued his law enforcement work as one of the first of Los Angeles's legendary private eyes.

Other Jews took an active role in shaping local law enforcement in the early days. Mark Strouse, a native of Germany who came to the mining camp of Mokelumne Hill with his parents when he was fifteen, resettled in the booming Comstock Lode town of Virginia City, Nevada, in 1863 and was elected chief of police in 1868. Strouse later served two terms as city treasurer and was for seven years foreman of Company No. 1 of the Virginia City Volunteer Fire Department. Sol Levy kept the jailhouse secure in early Butte, Montana, and in 1878 Louis Wartenberg served the young town of Anaheim, California, as marshal and later as tax collector, jailer, and city health officer. Nathan Benjamin Appel was Tucson's chief of police in the early 1880s, and on settling in Los Angeles in 1887, he served as interpreter and bailiff in the Los Angeles police court.

Mail service was another necessity in isolated far western communities filled with lonely pioneers far from friends and relatives. A number of pioneer Jews held the important but tedious job of running a post office, partly because they could do the work and partly because having the post office in their store was good for

Left: *Mark Strouse was made Virginia City, Nevada, chief of police in 1868, when he was twenty-three years old. Strouse had come to Virginia City five years before by purchasing 5,500 sheep and driving them over the Sierra Nevada to the boomtown, where he opened a meat market and hog ranch. From* Western States Jewish Historical Quarterly *(October, 1979)*

Right: *Max Stein, mounted policeman, Pueblo, Colorado, circa 1900; courtesy, Rocky Mountain Jewish Historical Society, Denver, Colorado*

business. Letters arrived slowly, lines in many locations were long (many communities stipulated that people had to pick up their mail in person, thus bringing them into town—much to the satisfaction of local merchants), and stamps were rarely available. To make matters worse, employees were often inexperienced, at times incompetent, and occasionally openly corrupt.

In Deadwood, Dakota Territory, for example, where letters of complaint about mail service could fill entire columns of the local press, the first postmaster had been tossed out of office for absconding with funds. His successor was Solomon Star, a local flour merchant who had moved to Deadwood from Montana. Star helped to initiate government in the booming Black Hills mining settlement. He served on the first town

council, organized the first fire department, and later served as mayor of the town for twenty-one years. As postmaster, however, Star fell short of his usual success. He occupied the post from 1878 to 1881, when he went the way of his predecessor, accused, probably unjustly, of having participated in a mail fraud scheme that vastly inflated the cost of local mail carrying.

Another crucial frontier community service—especially in mining districts, where major fortunes could depend on the titles to specific plots of land—was that provided by the recorder, a functionary who verified and kept track of land and mining claims. In the earliest and most frantic days on the frontier, this service was often the first—and occasionally the only—semblance of government in a settlement. Accuracy

J. M. CASTNER,
Mayor of Virginia City,

A N D

JUSTICE OF THE PEACE.

Will Attend to all Claims and Collections,

And also to the preparation of

Legal Papers, Affidavits, Conveyancing,

ACKNOWLEDGMENT OF DEEDS, &c.,

And generally to all business entrusted to him by persons
out of the City.

Office—Over the Idaho Restaurant, two doors from the office of the
Montana Post, Virginia City.

Virginia City, Montana, October 23, 1866.

IDAHO

RESTAURANT!

Two doors from office of Montana Post,

VIRGINIA CITY,   -   -   -   MONTANA.

TABLE ACCOMMODATIONS EQUAL TO BEST IN THE CITY,

And best of Liquors dispensed at the bar by Jos. McGee.

ALSO, ACCOMMODATIONS FOR A FEW NIGHT LODGERS

Good Clean Beds.   Charges Moderate.

Oct. 23, 1866.   **J. M. CASTNER, Proprietor.**

During the years 1868, 1869, and 1870, in my opinion we suffered most from the cruelties of the Apaches. . . . Business was almost at a standstill, and very little if any mining was done, as no one dared to risk going into the mountains unless well armed, and the supply of weapons was limited.

Beleaguered pioneers pressured an often unsympathetic national government for weapons and federal troops. Instead, they received Indian agents—federal appointees sent to mediate between the Indians and the white set-

Deputy Sheriff Louis Ezekiels, Pima County, Arizona Territory; courtesy, Arizona Historical Society, Tucson

Top left: *Courtesy, William Andrews Clark Memorial Library, University of California, Los Angeles*

was essential, and for that reason during a copper mining boom in the late 1870s, the men of Clifton, Arizona Territory, chose Samuel Freudenthal as their recorder. He had already proven his skills as clerk and bookkeeper for the Longfellow Mining Company and had served as Clifton's unofficial postmaster, filling in for an appointee who knew nothing of the job. As recorder, Freudenthal logged in a vast string of mining claims. While occasionally offered an interest in some of them as payment, he was sensible enough to insist on cash.

From the late 1850s to the late 1880s, in sparsely inhabited areas beyond California, inadequately protected American settlers were compelled to resolve by various means their differences with the Indians. Samuel Drachman, who followed the rush of gold seekers to the Arizona Territory in 1867, remembered:

A pow-wow at Canyon de los Embudos, near the Mexican border, took place in March 1886 between General George Crook and his staff, and Geronimo and some of his Apache tribe. Charles Strauss, the mayor of Tucson, is on the far right side of the second row. Courtesy, Arizona Historical Society, Tucson

tlers—who though at times conscientious, proved understandably incapable of controlling such an explosive cultural clash.

Without effective aid from the federal government, some Jewish merchants and miners on the frontier, seeing their lives and property in jeopardy, joined their fellow settlers in defense groups. Moses Solomon, a fur trader on the Marias River near Ft. Benton, Montana, fought in at least one battle with neighboring Sioux tribes in 1868; Arthur Morrison, a New Mexico merchant who would later serve as justice of the peace and a member of the territorial legislature, joined with Kit Carson to subdue Navajo uprisings during the Civil War. New Mexican Louis Kahn battled marauding Indians throughout his career as an overland trader. When Bernard Goldsmith lived in Crescent City, California, in the mid-1850s, he volunteered his services in several campaigns against the local hostile tribes.

On one occasion, when the Indians threatened renewed uprisings after mistreatment by their Indian agent, Goldsmith persuaded them to hold off, and he personally argued their case for them before the superintendent of Indian Affairs in San Francisco. As Goldsmith's efforts indicate, not all Jews took a hard line toward neighboring Indians. Some Jewish traders in remote districts befriended their fascinating customers and learned to speak their language and appreciate their customs. Other Jews also served the common good not by fighting the "red devils" but by working on their behalf. Moses Baruh, a Pendleton, Oregon, druggist, gained the friendship of local Umatilla Indians when they came in droves to stare at his brass soda fountain, the first in the entire cattle country. As intrigued by the visitors as they were by his fountain, Baruh learned their language and became the tribe's trusted adviser and their court interpreter.

Another champion of Indian causes was Wolf Kalisher, an early Los Angeles merchant. Incensed by the injustice done Manuel Olegario, a deposed Temecula Indian chief, Kalisher assisted him in his struggle to regain his hereditary leadership. A local Indian agent had ousted Olegario and put in his office a man the agent had appointed and could control. In 1859 Olegario moved to Los Angeles, where for nearly a decade he was employed by Kalisher and his partner, Louis Wartenberg. During the Los Angeles smallpox epidemic of 1869, Olegario sought refuge in Temecula. There he found his people up in arms against their puppet chief. He took his problem to Kalisher, who encouraged the Indian leader to appeal to government authorities, advised him how to proceed, and gave him lodging, moral support, and probably financial help as

Edward J. Lackner (on the far right), Denver Police Force, circa 1910; courtesy, Rocky Mountain Jewish Historical Society, Denver, Colorado

well. In 1875 Olegario was granted an interview with President Ulysses S. Grant in Washington, D.C. Six weeks later the government reinstated Olegario as chief of the Temecula and nearby Pala Indian reservations.

In matters other than handling mail, recording claims, dealing with the Indians, and curbing dangerous criminals, the administration of these nascent towns was, in the style of the frontier, casual. Sam Drachman recalled with amusement a trial in Yuma (then Arizona City) in which he, newly arrived from the East, served as temporary court clerk:

Just think! but one day in Arizona, and already occupying such an exalted position as Clerk of a Justice's Court! I soon reached the court and was duly installed. Proceedings commenced and lasted several hours. Prisoner was found guilty and a fine of $100 was imposed and he was ordered to jail until the amount was paid. There being no jail in the place, he was chained to a log, and kept for half a day, when a committee of citizens took pity on the poor fellow, called in a body on his honor to intercede in his behalf,

and succeeded in having the prisoner released, after paying the Judge ten dollars, on the condition that the Judge treat all hands, to which he agreed. All hands took a drink, and thus ended the greatest trial on record. As regards my pay for services rendered, I am sorry to say I have never received anything, and doubt if I ever will.

Such slapdash law enforcement, however, was not always as good-natured as Drachman remembered. Most judges and administrators, though largely inexperienced, relied on common sense to make fair and balanced decisions. Yet since they lacked comprehensive knowledge of legal codes and of the framework of county, state, and national authority, these men at times fell victim to community or personal passions. Nonetheless, such initial attempts at organized government served an important purpose. In the words of Wayne Gard, an authority on frontier justice, "they showed that disputes could be settled without the use of the six-shooters and that crime could be punished without resort to the vigilante hanging ropes."

Numerous far western communities stumbled along for years with no more than rudimentary civic order. This was particularly true in towns born of mining enthusiasm, where miners stayed as long as the diggings remained profitable, and the merchants left with their customers. One town, Havre, Montana, successfully made the transition from lawless outpost to orderly community with the help of a Jewish resident. In 1900 Havre was a fading mining supply center east of the mining country. Its population of one thousand, while mainly miners and ordinary businessmen, included a large concentration of gamblers and prostitutes. A typical stroll down the main street was likely to include glimpses of a knife fight, a gun duel, and a drunk being booted out of a saloon into a nearby gutter.

In the early 1900s, railroad magnate James

A. H. Emanuel was mayor of Tombstone for three terms from 1896 to 1900. Courtesy, Bisbee Mining & Historical Museum, Bisbee, Arizona

J. Hill visited Havre to check on the progress of his Great Northern Railroad. Havre was a vital stopping point on that line, which extended across the Northwest. Shocked and angered at the lawlessness there, he issued town residents an ultimatum—either they improve their community or he would move the railroad station and division headquarters to another town. Louis Newman, a Jewish restaurant owner who had moved to Havre in 1900, heeded Hill's threat. Newman ran for mayor on a cleanup platform and won. With the aid of a new police force, the five-foot-two mayor drove out ruffians, closed a few saloons, constructed a city hall, and brought water and building ordinances in line with state standards. Under Newman, Havre gained a new stability. Grateful town members pronounced their mayor "the Little Giant."

From the 1880s on, numerous frontier towns like Havre either disappeared or developed into bustling little communities with sound small business economies. Many Jews who had settled temporarily discovered they liked where they were and, since their businesses were flourishing, had no reason to leave. As permanent citizens they began to think of government as a tool for community growth and so became ardent boosters. They organized chambers of commerce, expanded the school systems, and pushed for roads, railroads, and federal subsidies to advance their towns' interests. Jews also ran for public office at all levels and were often elected. Unlike most of the American Sephardic officeholders, these new politicos were not formally educated intellectuals but successful and respected local entrepreneurs. As such, complex national or international political and social issues figured little in their platforms and programs. Much like their fellow citizens, they were primarily concerned with hastening and expanding the growth of their towns. They assiduously separated their religious from their civic faith, and in general neither won nor lost support because they were Jews. Their constituents judged candidates on other criteria. First, they wanted a local man acquainted with the problems of the area, as a Deadwood newspaper made clear when Jewish merchant Nathan Colman ran for reelection as justice of the peace against a Christian newcomer in 1879:

If you want a man to settle your little difficulties in an honest and comprehensive manner, elect Judge Colman [who] . . . is familiar with the practice of this territory. In fact he is no slouch of a lawyer himself. . . . Mr. Hall, the old gentleman running [as Colman's opponent] . . . is comparatively a stranger to the frontier, and on account of his extreme age, his fogy notions . . . would make a good justice down east where puritanical and blue laws are still in vogue. Mr. Colman is a western man and consequently better fitted . . . out here.

Second, constituents insisted that a candidate be a businessman, a man with a concrete financial interest in the town's progress and prosperity. Wrote a Tucson editor of the mayoralty race between Charles Strauss and Hiram S. Stevens in 1882:

Mr. Strauss is even more largely interested in the real estate of the city than his opponent. It is no exaggeration to say that for every dollar Mr. Stevens owns in lands and properties Mr. Strauss controls two. He is a much larger taxpayer and is identified to an infinitely greater degree in the social and business interests of the city. A gentleman of culture—of wide experience in politics and trade—taking a just and pardonable pride in the growth and development of the material interests of the territory, his election to the office of mayor would honor the constituency which honors him. As charged by Mr. Stevens' friends, he is a Jew. In this country it is not a criminal offense. There are people here who even go so far as to tolerate religious convictions and the classes of race and condition.

Such matter-of-fact acceptance in politics created a heady atmosphere for Jews, and they responded with enthusiasm. Assured of their community standing, they demanded in public life to be seen as any other citizen and fought back quickly and with confidence against anti-Semitic legislation and disparaging statements by public officials. When in 1855 Speaker of the California Assembly William Stow attacked Jews from the floor of the legislature and advocated a special tax "as would act as a prohibition to their residence among us," groups of Jews in Sacramento, San Francisco, and Los Angeles exploded with indignation. Henry Labatt, a San Francisco lawyer and American native of Sephardic ancestry, wrote in an open letter to Stow:

Mr. Speaker: you would prohibit their residence here. How have they harmed you at all and in what respect? Pray on whom will you commence? In the [California] Supreme Court, where sits on the bench of three Judges, one Jew? [Solomon Heydenfeldt] What tax will you place on that bench to exclude the Jew? What will you do in the Halls of Legislature, our public offices, the bar and medical fraternity? Surely Jews fill, or have filled these positions in our State, and without the like disgrace and profound ignorance that hovers over yourself.

Although the door was open for Jewish political participation, not all Jews sought it. Some avoided politics out of a strong distaste for public life. The necessity of glad-handing, manipulating, and catering to special interests disenchanted Samuel Freudenthal in his term as an El Paso, Texas, alderman in 1887–1889; led a disgusted Michel Goldwater to resign as mayor of Prescott, Arizona, in 1886; and drove Ben Ezekiels out of the political arena. A Virginia City, Montana, resident with a long record of public service, Ezekiels endured one disastrous term as the town's representative in the territorial legislature when community wrath descended upon him for supposedly endangering Virginia City's position as capital of the territory. When Ezekiels attempted to explain his actions, the local press raged:

That charlatan and mountebank, Ben. Ezekiels, writhing under the charges of fraud and guilt proven against him by this paper, snaps and snarls like a belabored cur beneath his master's lash, and . . . seeks to clear himself of the glaring guilt resting upon him by pronouncing the charges against him to be lies. His established reputation in this community as a fraud and parasite on the public prevents our taking further notice of the moral leper than to condescend to spit in his face should he cross our path.

Two years later Ben Ezekiels moved to Helena, Montana, and never again entered politics.

Of those Jews who did respond to the unprecedented opportunity available to them, a number developed a pronounced political fever. They bounced from office to office, loving the political arena and willing to campaign with all the color and energy of Utah's Harry Joseph, who made his bid for the lower house of the

state legislature by leading a marching band through the streets of Salt Lake City, complete with "Princess Alice," an elephant borrowed from the local zoo. (He was elected.)

The number of offices they filled and the wide variety of people who filled them contradict the notion advanced by some, Mark Twain included, that Jews were profit-oriented shirkers of public duties. Moreover, a review of their pet causes reveals little evidence of a "Jewish vested interest." Harry Epstein of Nevada, for example, in his term in the state legislature of 1865 pushed for a railroad to connect his constituents with California. In addition, he introduced the Sole Trader Bill, authorizing married women to conduct business in their own names.

During his long years as mayor of Deadwood, Solomon Star crusaded for prohibition and improved mores. His was, however, a rather

Solomon Star; courtesy, William Andrews Clark Memorial Library, University of California, Los Angeles

Julius Durkheimer was elected mayor of Burns, Oregon, in 1895. Courtesy, Oregon Historical Society, Portland

selective campaign. Finding his election as mayor disputed by a local saloon owner named Romeo Dwyer, Star vindictively closed down Dwyer's establishment and raided the local brothel of which Dwyer's mother was madam. However grateful they may have been for this step toward propriety, Deadwood citizens disapproved of Star's motives. Under pressure, he finally reopened Dwyer's saloon.

Henry Altman, who was a pioneer merchant in Cheyenne, Wyoming, was called "Father of Cheyenne's Parks" for the role he played in the construction of that city's park system. A member of the city council in the 1880s, Altman was appointed chairman of the park committee. A hilly area near the state capitol was chosen as the site of the city's first park, and Altman went to work. At his own expense, he purchased a nursery in Nebraska and then persuaded the Union Pacific Railroad to transport the trees to Cheyenne free of charge. The tree planting began in 1888, when the country was suffering a depression and indigents filled the local jails. Altman offered the prisoners meals and a silver dollar to work on the park. On Arbor Day, 1888, Cheyenne schoolchildren planted trees in holes previously dug by the prisoners. Altman also planned and directed the improvement of Cheyenne's Lake Minnehaha, Sloan's Lake, and Country Club Lake.

In 1887 Julius Durkheimer brought his young wife, Delia, to the eastern Oregon town of Burns to open a trading post. Situated in the center of Oregon's sheep and cattle country, Burns was 165 miles from a railroad and isolated by surrounding mountains. The tiny five-year-old community was little more than a dusty road lined by rickety wooden shacks. Schooling and law enforcement were rudimentary, and the nearest doctor was 150 miles away. In this tough setting, the local ranchers didn't hesitate to use violence to achieve their ends. On one occasion, two feuding sheep raisers met by chance in Durkheimer's store and within seconds had shot each other to death. In a vain attempt to quell the unruliness of his fellow citizens by improving their attire, Durkheimer ordered one hundred men's formal dress suits from San Francisco. The outfits, however, only gathered dust until the exasperated storekeeper sold them to the local undertaker. Durkheimer also served his community as a volunteer fire fighter, as a member of the school board, and in 1895, as mayor.

Bernard Goldsmith pushed to beautify and to improve transportation in Oregon. As mayor of Portland from 1869 to 1871 he muscled into law unpopular measures providing for city parks and landscaping. Later, as a private citizen, he performed what he considered his greatest public service, financing the canal and lock system

Bernard Goldsmith, mayor of Portland, Oregon, 1869-1871; courtesy, Oregon Historical Society, Portland

serving Portland and the Willamette Valley. The system lowered the cost of transporting goods by half, to the benefit of the entire state—with the exception of Goldsmith. Dedicated to his project, he financed its completion when backers and contractors fell through and lost well over $400,000 in the process.

The pioneer Jews who made these determined stands were motivated by more than just a love of political hoopla or by self-interest. They also wanted to express their gratitude to a region that had allowed them the opportunity to participate fully as citizens. The sentiments of Morris Goldwater—longtime Prescott, Arizona Territory, business and civic leader—were typical. Goldwater was mayor of Prescott for twenty-two years and performed a host of other municipal and territorial duties. His interest in civic activity was derived in part from his belief that a stable community made for a healthy business envi-

ronment. In addition, wrote one biographer, he held that it was the moral duty of the successful to repay the communities that had made their success possible.

Of course, not all Jews approached public service with the high purpose of Morris Goldwater. The political careers of some far western Jews could be described at best as unfortunate, at worst as openly corrupt. In their defense, though it by no means exonerates them, the quality of the society at the time should be taken into account. The post–Civil War period has been described as the most debased in American politics. Leading off with Ulysses S. Grant's infamously unprincipled administrations of 1868 and 1872 and moving on to the "Corrupt Bargain of 1876," in which Republican Rutherford B. Hayes received the presidency in return for an end to Reconstruction—and with it black civil rights—in the South, the concluding decades of the nineteenth century saw an array of undistinguished officeholders coming to prominence.

Morris Sachs clearly saw his term of office as a game—faro, to be exact. A resident of Port Townsend, Washington, who had come west from Kentucky in 1883 and entered a law partnership, Sachs in 1890 was elected superior court judge of an area encompassing Jefferson, Clallam, Island, San Juan, and Kitsap counties. His nomination hinged on a promise he made to Republican party leaders and prominent local politicians that he would do away entirely with his passion for faro, a game of chance run at local gambling halls. Once safely ensconced on the bench, however, Sachs abandoned his vow. He even took part in games while on duty: One attorney swore he had had to seek out the judge in a faro parlor during court hours to have a legal document signed. Other, equally dark suspicions surfaced—principally that Sachs had prejudged cases in which either he or a relative held a material interest. Several incensed Port Townsend citizens held that Sachs had refused to press claims for collection against a particular local bank—where, not coincidentally, his father-in-law served as bank manager.

The game ended, however, in 1891, when the newly constituted Port Townsend Bar Association (which Sachs had helped form a month earlier) brought charges against him before the state house of representatives. A special investigating committee upheld the charges, and the judge found himself the subject of impeachment proceedings before both houses of the state legislature on grounds of misbehavior, malfeasance, and delinquency in office.

To the dismay of his supporters, Sachs did not entirely refute the charges. He maintained instead that his gambling did not interfere with the discharge of his duties and, moreover, that the vice was widespread among his constituents. Those constituents responded with outrage. At a mass meeting, Port Townsend citizens (including the future mayor, Israel Katz) denounced Sachs's slur on their good name; the local press, in its turn, scorned "the Faro Judge" as a "common gambler." When the legislature's votes were in, Sachs found himself soundly condemned by the lower house; the vote was 62 to 14 in favor of removing him from office. The senate, however, was less decisive—16 for, 16 against. Since only 8 senate votes were required to vindicate, Sachs was returned to his bench. Furious demands for his resignation followed, but apparently Sachs gave them no notice and finished out his term to retire from politics and enter the lumber business.

Less fortunate was Missouri-born Charles de Young, a self-appointed political crusader who slung the mud too vigorously for his own health. As the founder and editor of the *San Francisco Chronicle,* the city's most influential newspaper, de Young took the stance of an unrelenting reformer. His inordinately vicious attacks ultimately led to his assassination in the newspaper's offices in 1880.

Charles de Young arrived in San Francisco as a child of nine in 1854 with his mother and seven siblings. His father, Michael, a Dutch Jew who had been a merchant in Baltimore before embarking for California, had died en route. Early in his teens, Charles and his younger brother Michael worked as compositors at Rabbi Julius Eckman's *Weekly Gleaner.* Charles continued his apprenticeship in 1864 as a compositor for the *Alta California.*

In 1865, with the help of his brothers Michael and Gustavus, Charles rented printing equipment and desk space; on January 16 he published the first edition of the *Daily Dramatic Chronicle.* It was a free journal of theatrical advertisements enlivened by brief news items—as Michael described them, "criticisms of public men, crisp references to important events, shots at conspicuous people, and other such information." This spicy material soon gained the *Chronicle* a devoted reading public. By 1868, with its circulation well over ten thousand, the paper abandoned the theatrical emphasis and, under the new title *Daily Morning Chronicle,* concentrated on exposing to public scrutiny San Francisco's seamy underside.

With the energetic Charles at the helm, the *Chronicle* exposed stock market manipulations and municipal corruption and railed against emerging railroad, water, land, telegraph, and

gas monopolies. Also boosting its reputation—
and no doubt its circulation—were venomous
diatribes and spiteful gossip directed against
public officials and against any others who made
good copy. On one occasion, Charles slipped un-
invited into the plush wedding reception for the
socially prominent (and non-Jewish) Augustus J.
Bowie, Jr., and Elizabeth Friedlander, the
daughter of Jewish agribusinessman Isaac Friedlander. The ensuing *Chronicle* report speculated
on the pair's religious differences and detailed
the value of the wedding gifts. Ten months later,
on October 17, 1869, a follow-up entitled "The
Course of True Love" revealed the young husband as an adulterer, wife beater, and gamester
and gleefully reported the new Mrs. Bowie's
tearful flight from her Paris honeymoon back to
her father's San Francisco home. This penchant
for scandal brought Charles libel suits and even
resulted in physical attacks on his person.

The mudslinging session that would cost him
his life concerned a power play involving the
Workingman's Party of California (WPC), which
was founded in 1878 in reaction to widespread
unemployment. The party platform, in essence,
was antimillionaire and anti-Chinese—the rich
took the money, and the Chinese took the jobs,
raved its supporters. The WPC, armed with a
prolabor state constitution, won over the constitutional convention in 1878 in Sacramento, and
its document became law in 1879. The *Chronicle*
had been the only major newspaper to support
the WPC constitution, and de Young pushed for
his reward—the election to state and local offices
of his hand-picked candidates. When the WPC
refused to endorse his choices, de Young vowed
retribution. He aimed his deadly vitriol at the
Reverend Isaac Smith Kalloch, WPC candidate
for mayor and pastor of San Francisco's Baptist
Metropolitan Temple. Thundered the *Chronicle*
on August 20, 1879:

Kalloch. The Record of a Misspent Life. Infamous
Career of the Candidate for Mayor. Driven Forth from
Boston Like an Unclean Leper. His Trial for the Crime
of Adultery. The Evidence that Fully Established His
Guilt. Ten of the Jurors vote for Conviction. His Es-
capade with One of the Tremont-Temple Choristers.

Kalloch responded in kind. In a public address he plausibly refuted de Young's charges
and further characterized Charles and Michael
as "the infamous hybrid whelps of sin and
shame." To this apparent slur on his mother's
character Charles responded in a fury. On August 23 he rode to the front of Kalloch's church
and, calling him to the carriage on a pretext,
shot the minister twice in the chest and side.

Kalloch lived and was elected mayor in a
landslide. De Young, barely saved from a lynch-
ing, spent a week in the city prison before his
release on bail. Undeterred, Charles struck again,
producing this time a pamphlet giving a "complete history" of the mayor's gruesome mis-
deeds. Kalloch's son, the Reverend Isaac Kalloch, Jr., had had enough. On the night of April
23, 1880, he entered de Young's office and fired
four shots. Within minutes de Young was dead.
His murderer was acquitted after a witness's per-
jured testimony that de Young had fired first.
The *Chronicle* passed into the hands of the far
more sedate Michael de Young, who became one
of San Francisco's major civic leaders and
philanthropists.

From this vast array of characters, one fact
emerges. Jews played a prominent role in nineteenth-century far western politics—astound-
ingly so, when one considers they represented
only a small percentage of the population. Not
a post existed on a local, county, territorial, or
state level that they did not fill; nor, it would
seem, did a town exist where they did not fill
it—not as representatives of a religious or ethnic
minority, but as members of the mainstream.
The most thoroughgoing evidence of their acceptance in politics was exhibited on home
ground where they were best known. The citizens of dozens of far western towns and cities
chose Jews to head their municipalities as mayor.
A number of lodestar personalities—including
Morris Goldwater, Prescott, Arizona Territory;
Solomon Star, Deadwood, Dakota Territory; and
Emil Ganz, Phoenix, Arizona Territory—were
kept in office so long that they became, in the
fullest sense, city fathers.

As the new century loomed, however, the
wide range of political opportunities for Jews
began to diminish. In the cities the broad com-

Far Western Jewish Mayors

*Henry L. Jacobs, Butte,
Montana,
1879–1880*

*H. L. Frank, Butte,
Montana, 1885–1886*

*Charles Himrod, Boise,
Idaho, 1869–1870 and
1878–1880*

*Solomon Star, Deadwood,
South Dakota, 1884–
1893*

*Oscar Newburg, San
Bernardino, California,
1889–1891*

*Julius Durkenheimer,
Burns, Oregon,
1895–1896*

*Charles M. Strauss, Tuc-
son, Arizona, 1883–
1884*

*J. M. Sampliner, Grand
Junction, Colorado,
1901–1904*

*Bailey Gatzert, Seattle,
Washington, circa 1875*

*William Wurzweiler,
Prineville, Oregon,
1904–1906*

*Phillip Wasserman, Port-
land, Oregon, 1871–
1873*

*Adolph Sutro, San Fran-
cisco, California, 1895–
1897*

*Ben U. Steinman, Sacra-
mento, California, circa
1890*

*Abraham H. Emanuel,
Tombstone, Arizona,
1896–1900*

*Israel Katz, Port Town-
shend, Washington,
1915–1917*

*Willi Spiegelberg, Santa
Fe, New Mexico, 1884–
1886*

Samuel Jaffa, Trinadad, Colorado, 1876–1880

Moses Alexander, Boise, Idaho, 1888–1892

Abe Frank; Yuma, Arizona, circa 1890

Emil Ganz, Phoenix, Arizona, 1895–1900

Emil Marks, Bisbee, Arizona, circa 1900

Wolfe Londoner, Denver, Colorado, 1889–1891

Samuel Friendly, Eugene, Oregon, 1893–1895

Nathan Jaffa, Roswell, New Mexico, April–December 1903

Morris Goldwater, Prescott, Arizona, 1897–1919

Henry Jaffa, Albuquerque, New Mexico, 1885–1895

Adolph Solomon, El Paso, Texas, circa 1893

petitive business economy that had boosted Jewish merchants into the political limelight contracted as new corporations gobbled up increasingly large sections of far western commerce and industry. Many a small business-centered town that had provided a political field for a Jewish merchant lost its base as a transportation, military, or government center or ran out of its primary natural resource. Displaced by these events, many Jewish families moved to growing urban centers.

The big cities that dotted the west by the twentieth century were an entirely different story politically. Stratifications of class and nationality and extremes of wealth and poverty were more overt than in smaller towns. Controversies between the emerging labor unions and industrialists, old and new political parties, reformers and those they would reform, as well as the earlier pioneers and the new immigrants split cities into warring factions. No longer able to muster a following from the community at large, can-

didates sought support from a group or a coalition of groups. Once the commercial class lost its dominance, the established Jewish merchant who had previously entered politics as a town booster had difficulty gaining a foothold. Eastern European immigrants, who were arriving in increasing numbers, in some cases aligned themselves with one of the new factions, but the majority were too poor or too unacculturated to run for public office. As a consequence, in the early 1900s the Jewish population was rising, but the number of Jews in public office was dwindling in the Far West.

Jews who remained an integral part of city, state and federal politics were usually members of early and by-then-affluent pioneer families who were entrenched in entrepreneurial circles

Joseph Simon, senator from Oregon; courtesy, Oregon Jewish Historical Society, Portland

Top left: *Simon Guggenheim oversaw his family's western and Mexican mining operations before winning a Colorado seat in the United States Senate in 1906. Courtesy, Colorado Historical Society, Denver*

Julius Kahn (1861–1924) and his mother left Baden, Germany, when he was seven and joined Julius's father in Calaveras County, California. Julius attended high school in San Francisco and then began clerking but quit to pursue acting. He performed across America, playing with such famous partners as Edwin Booth. In 1890 he abruptly shifted to the study of law and two years later was elected to the state assembly. In 1898 he was elected to the first of twelve consecutive terms as a United States Congressman from San Francisco. Courtesy, California Historical Society, San Francisco

and had already accrued long political records. Although proportionally fewer were elected, those who were installed in office attained new heights. For example, Joseph Simon of Oregon and Simon Guggenheim of Colorado went to the United States Senate, Simon in 1898 and Guggenheim in 1906.

Neither Guggenheim nor Simon served more than one term. Guggenheim obtained his Senate seat by purchasing the votes of state legislators in a campaign "so bare-facedly corrupt that there is almost something refreshing about it." His senatorial career from 1907 to 1913 was generally undistinguished. Best remembered was his deciding vote in favor of a constitutional amendment mandating the election of senators by public vote rather than by the state legislatures, an amendment that his own dubious election had spurred to passage.

Lawyer and real estate speculator Joseph Simon of Oregon came to the United States Senate with considerably more political experience. He had been elected to the Portland City Council in 1877 and became the city's mayor in 1881. He had also served several terms in the Oregon State Senate and was chairman of the Multnomah County Republican party for nearly a decade before he became a United States senator. Preferring home waters to Washington, D.C., politics, Simon returned to Portland in 1904 and in 1909 served a second term as mayor.

One Jew in high office during this period who was neither wealthy nor a member of a socially prominent family was Julius Kahn, the honest and popular Republican who San Franciscans elected to twelve terms in the United States House of Representatives. Born in Baden, Germany, in 1861, Kahn's first home in California was in Calaveras County, where his father was a farmer. The Kahns later moved to San Francisco where they operated a restaurant and bakery. When he completed high school Julius became a professional actor and toured with leading theatrical companies. During a run in Washington, D.C., he became intrigued with politics. In 1890 he enrolled in law school and two years later was elected to the state assembly. After one term he returned to his law practice until 1898 when he was invited to run for Congress on the Republican ticket.

Kahn's lengthy voting record shows him to have been an effective defender of California

Edward Salomon was a Civil War hero and a controversial governor of the Washington Territory. Courtesy, Seattle Jewish Archives Project, Suzzallo Library, University of Washington, Seattle

and Republican party interests. He also developed a personal stake in some programs and spent years shepherding supporting legislation through Congress.

Among the most controversial of his activities was his interest in military preparedness. For much of his tenure in Congress, Kahn was a member of the Military Affairs Committee. He was for an extended period its ranking member, and when his party was in power, its chairman. Shortly after the outbreak of World War I, Kahn helped to found the National Defense League, which worked toward enlarging the Navy and improving the Army and the National Guard. In 1914, with his able support, the league won passage of a bill providing funds to supply civilian rifle clubs with free rifles and ammunition.

Two years later, he led to passage the National Defense Act increasing the standing army to 175,000 and the National Guard to 450,000. When the United States entered the war in 1917, Kahn advocated conscription and in May of that year pushed through Congress the Selective Service Act, called the "Kahn Amendment." His next and final effort was in behalf of universal military training, the National Defense Act of 1920. Kahn assured pacifists who fought its passage that defense was a better war deterrent than was the League of Nations. He died while still in office in 1924.

A somewhat larger number of Jews were elected to high office at the state level in the late nineteenth and early twentieth centuries. Two men of Jewish ancestry served as far western

Abe Ruef; courtesy, The Bancroft Library, University of California, Berkeley

governors before 1900. Edward Salomon, a practicing Jew, was appointed governor of the Washington Territory in 1869 by President Ulysses S. Grant. He resigned, possibly under pres-

sure, before his term of office was completed. Salomon relocated in San Francisco and was later elected to the California State Assembly in 1884. The other, Washington Bartlett, who had served two terms as San Francisco mayor in 1882 and 1884, was elected governor of California in 1886. Bartlett did not identify himself as a Jew, but his mother, Sarah Melhado, was a member of an American Sephardic Jewish family. During the early years of the twentieth century, some affluent and politically entrenched pioneer Jews—or the sons of these pioneers—were wending their way toward far western governorships. By 1931 four had acceded to the highest state office. Moses Alexander won the governorship of Idaho in 1915, becoming the first professed Jew in the nation to be elected governor. Two years later, early Utah citizen Simon Bamberger became the first non-Mormon elected governor of Utah. Arthur Seligman became governor of New Mexico in 1930; Julius Meier became governor of Oregon in 1931. Both Seligman and Meier were sons of successful pioneer Jewish merchants.

As these long-established and powerful members of pioneer families were moving toward new political heights, the turbulent early twentieth century produced a ground swell of new political activists, many of whom wielded wide influence without ever standing for public office. The most powerful figure of this type was the city boss, a vendor of favors. Administrative gaps in outmoded municipal government opened the way for "bossism," and most American metropolises entered the twentieth century in the hands of one. Shortly after the turn of the century, the "boss" in San Francisco, then the fifth largest city in the nation, was the calculatedly inconspicuous Abraham Ruef.

The only son of Alsatian Meyer Ruef, one-time Market Street merchant, "Abe" was born in San Francisco on September 2, 1864. Bright and gregarious, he graduated with honors from the University of California in 1882, then studied law at Hastings Law School. Over the next fifteen years, Ruef simultaneously built a law practice and a political base, first with the Republicans, then with the new Union Labor Party (ULP), which claimed to represent organized labor. In 1901 Ruef manuevered a victory for his ULP slate headed by mayoral candidate Eugene Schmitz, a bassoonist who became president of the Musicians' Union. He repeated the coup in 1903 and 1905, each time winning by a wider margin. Working out of a small office in North Beach, Ruef supplied—at a price—everything from police protection for gamblers and prostitutes to all kinds of licenses, franchises, and contracts. His mode of operation was to bill his "clients" for legal services, then split the take with cooperative public officials, primarily the mayor and members of the board of supervisors.

In May 1906 muckraking reformers mounted a cleanup campaign. When that proved impractical—everyone from the corner cop to the power elite was either giving or getting bribes— the reformers trained their sights on kingpin Abe Ruef. For nearly a decade he was the most talked about man in San Francisco.

Millionaire Rudolph Spreckels underwrote an investigation spearheaded by Fremont Older, the editor of the San Francisco *Evening Bulletin*, along with former mayor James Phelan. Special prosecutor Francis Heney and federal investigator J. Burns were brought in to collect evidence for a grand jury hearing. An initial indictment arose out of $8,500 in bribes paid to Schmitz and Ruef for licenses to operate houses of prostitution, known euphemistically as "French restaurants." As the investigation continued, three supervisors confessed to receiving numerous other bribes via Ruef from legal businesses and powerful public service corporations. When the lengthy "graft trials" began, the reformers vowed to see those at both ends of the bribe punished. Ruef was guaranteed leniency if he cooperated, so he pleaded guilty and was convicted December 1908. Instead of a light sentence, he was given a stiff fourteen years. Ruef spent a year in the county jail while a 2.5-million-word appeal was being prepared, all to no avail, as it turned out: The state supreme court resorted to a technicality to deny him a rehearing. Shortly after he was sent to San Quentin prison, Ruef began to press for parole. Surprisingly, among those supporting his release was Fremont Older. According to one Ruef biographer, the

Bulletin editor had come to believe Ruef had been made the scapegoat for crimes for which the whole people of San Francisco were responsible. To help Ruef muster public sympathy, Older encouraged him to write, for publication in the *Bulletin,* "The Road I Traveled: An Autobiography Account of my Career from University to Prison, with an Intimate Recital of the Corrupt Alliance between Big Business and Politics in San Francisco." The articles ran for three months. Even though they contained little that the public did not already know, they were entertainingly written and widely read. Just as Ruef was about to delve into unexplored material, someone convinced the political boss his chances for release would be greatly enhanced if he divulged no more. The articles ended abruptly.

Ruef was granted a parole in 1915. Soon after, the undaunted disbarred attorney opened a real estate office in downtown San Francisco. The sign on his door read, "A. Ruef, Ideas, Investments and Real Estate."

Other far western Jews, angered by the numerous public blights on newly urban and industrial America, sought to ameliorate those social and political wrongs. Prominent among them were women just stepping out into the world and eager to have a hand in setting it in order.

Seraphine Pisko succeeded Frances Jacobs, after Jacobs's death in 1891, as the leading lady of Denver philanthropy. Pisko was active in Denver charity work and also served as executive secretary of the Jewish National Hospital for many years. She had a special fondness for the settlement work in progress among the eastern European Jews of the West Colfax section. Pisko often commented on the immigrants' spiritual passion and noted that "young men and women who had come to scoff remained to pray."

Women in other far western cities were similarly engaged in aiding needy eastern European immigrants. Among the most effective was San Francisco's Temple Emanu-El Sisterhood, led by Bella Seligman Lilienthal, Bertha Haas, Matilda Esberg, and others. The group established a settlement house on Folsom Street that offered Americanization classes and vocational training. They also ran a kindergarten, a gymnasium, a ucation and organized recreational activities at the settlement house.

A highly influential figure in Portland in the early 1900s was attorney, merchant, lecturer, and civic leader David Solis-Cohen, who was a descendant of a prominent colonial American Jewish family. Among other activities, Cohen was dedicated to eliminating corruption in municipal government. He campaigned to have candidates nominated by ballot instead of by party caucus.

David Solis-Cohen, Portland businessman and city commissioner, was renowned in Jewish and secular circles as a gifted orator, writer, and dedicated civic booster. An ardent Zionist and organizer of the Zionist Society in Portland, he believed in the equal importance of Jewish integration into American society and preservation of Jewish culture and Orthodox practice. Courtesy, Oregon Jewish Historical Society, Portland

Dr. Charles Spivak; courtesy, Rocky Mountain Jewish Historical Society, Denver, Colorado

clinic, and eventually they established a dormitory for single women.

During those years, the Portland, Oregon, chapter of the National Council of Jewish Women raised funds, with the help of other organizations and individuals, to construct Neighborhood House in South Portland, that city's Jewish quarter. With a large membership (298 by 1907) that was young and progressive, the chapter, led by women such as Blanche Blumauer and sisters Ida and Zerlinda Lowenberg, provided adult ed-

*Labor organizer
Sigismund Danielewicz;
courtesy, The Bancroft
Library, University of
California, Berkeley*

With equal vigor, he sought to reform the police commission (of which he was a member) and with it the entire department. Cohen also advocated civil service reforms, women's suffrage, and union organization. An American Zionist of a sort, he championed the establishment of a secular Jewish homeland, possibly in Palestine, as a refuge for Europe's persecuted Jews.

Eastern European immigrants had their own ideas about political and social action. In 1904 Russian Jew Dr. Charles Spivak became the founding secretary of the Jewish Consumptives Relief Society in Denver. He also served as its

publicist, fund raiser, policymaker, physician, and counselor with no pay for the first eight years of his twenty-three-year reign. The organization proved an ideal vehicle for Spivak's political, religious, and ethnic stance. His appeals in Yiddish and in English, in print and on the podium, won him backing from eastern European immigrants who viewed the JCRS as an expression of their growing ability to help themselves. Within eight years the society, drawing on national support, was operating a facility for tuberculars on a twenty-acre site in the Denver foothills.

Much in demand as a public speaker, Spivak

rarely missed a chance to express esteem for "his people," preferably in Yiddish. "The real aristocrats of Denver are the Jews of West Colfax," Spivak used to say, citing as evidence their devotion to Jewish learning, their attachment to Jewish community, and their heartfelt wish to help the needy.

In San Francisco, Sigismund Danielewicz battled as a Socialist labor organizer and founded the Sailors' Union before he was ousted for his outspoken defense of Chinese civil rights. Near Glendale, Oregon, a group of young Russian Jewish intellectuals, mostly survivors of czarist pogroms, established the New Odessa Colony as a Marxist experiment in social values. The colony lasted from 1882 to 1886, when it collapsed as a result of inner conflicts. Alexander Horr, a lively, red-haired publisher, anarchist, and friend of Emma Goldman, took a major part in Equality Colony, a socialist/anarchist agricultural collective in Washington State in 1905. After the colony dissolved in 1906, Horr left for San Francisco, where he continued his political activities.

By 1912 far western Jews had accrued a political record of a height and a breadth undreamed of in the ghettos of Europe or in a younger America. They had come west seeking liberty and had found varying degrees of lawlessness. Some responded by joining with those who would make their own law, while others contributed to more and better government. In their scrappy frontier settlements, when they saw things that needed doing, they did them and, in the process, became valued citizens. Finding acceptance as candidates, they ran and were chosen by their fellows to fill a variety of public posts. Like officeholders everywhere, some were dedicated public servants, some were self-seeking opportunists. When the complexities of the twentieth century split the political spectrum into increasingly diverse vested interests, some Jews accepted a factional position and organized, especially after anti-immigrant and anti-Red activity increased sentiments against Jews. Others stubbornly fought to keep Jewish interests from becoming public issues.

Chapter Seven
HUMDINGERS

In European ghettos and *shtetlach* or in older, more convention-bound American Jewish enclaves, communal security took precedence over self-expression. On the far western frontier, where innovation was a necessity, self-sufficiency was a practicality, and a zestful, progressive outlook constituted a pragmatic approach to a new way of life, Jewish individuality blossomed. A number of remarkable characters—*humdingers*, in the vernacular of the period—of all kinds surfaced: eccentrics, renegades, expeditionaries, stage personalities, community luminaries, crusaders, reformers, artists, and scientists. Cultivating their personal inclinations, obsessions, and talents, these one-of-a-kind personalities tested modes of behavior and endeavors few Jews could have or possibly would have tried before. Some earned notoriety, others acclaim—a few on a worldwide scale. Whether reprehensible or praiseworthy, their pursuits widened the range of Jewish experience.

In an atmosphere where ventures spiraled or plummeted on luck, or so people believed, the proverbial bearer of good fortune, the "beloved madman," was tolerated and in some cases indulged. A few eccentric Jews earned fame ensuring their communities the favor of the gods and providing a few belly laughs.

Emperor Norton (1819–1880) was called "the wisest and shrewdest of madmen," living off the generosity of merchants, banks, and restaurant owners who honored his worthless "Imperial Currency." At his death his estate was found to be "a two dollar gold-piece, three dollars in silver, and an 1823 franc." Courtesy, California Historical Society, San Francisco

Colonel Morris Pinshower (Pinschower or Pinschauer) first drew public attention in Virginia City, Nevada, in 1868, when he stood as an independent candidate for sheriff of Story County. For two months Pinshower toured the county ("neither he nor his raw-boned horse stopped to eat") addressing voters as often as a dozen times a day. In heavily accented English he orated at length on the "shteam shvindlers" (the railroaders) and other enemies of the common good. Even though rewarded with only a dozen votes, the colonel was undaunted.

He appointed himself the chief engineer of Nevada and set out to find new sources of water for Virginia City, unfortunately without any luck. In 1870 he resumed his candidacy for sheriff. On October 22, 1870, *Territorial Enterprise* noted:

M. Pinshower, the irrepressible independent candidate for Sheriff was out on South C. Street near Taylor last night speaking "wid der peoples." His eloquence attracted such a large noisy crowd that it was found necessary to suppress him as a nuisance. He could not but open his mouth but his audience cheered, and he was literally drowned in the flood of his popularity. Pulling from under him the box upon which he was mounted did not discourage him. He stuck his ground, spouting and shouting climbed again to his box.

On June 12, 1872, some local wags arranged a meeting in San Francisco between Colonel Pinshower and his more famous counterpart, Emperor Joshua Norton. According to Pinshower's hometown supporter writing in the *Territorial Enterprise*, the colonel was "too fast for the emperor. He can talk whole columns while Emperor Norton was still uttering a single sentence."

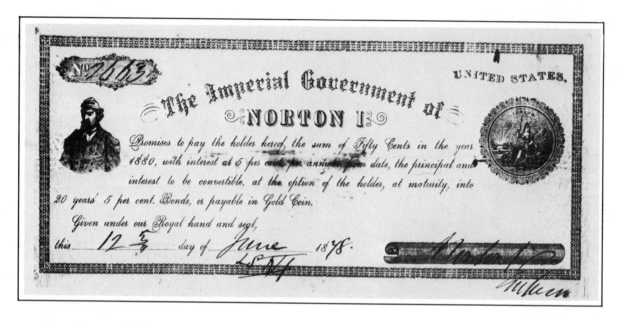

Courtesy, Wells Fargo Bank History Department, San Francisco, California

Not oratory but costume and a sweeping imperial manner won Joshua Norton a permanent place in the annals of San Francisco. According to one of his contemporaries, Nathan Peiser, Norton was the son of Sarah and John Norton, early settlers in Port Elizabeth, South Africa. Alone after his parents and his only brother died, in 1849 thirty-year-old Joshua boarded the *Franzika* and sailed to gold-crazed San Francisco. Norton arrived with $40,000, presumably his inheritance, which he quickly turned into a quarter of a million buying and selling real estate. In 1853 Norton risked and lost his entire fortune in an attempt to corner the rice market. Devastated by his losses, he vanished. When he reappeared, he had renamed himself Norton I, Emperor of the United States and Protector of Mexico. He later dropped the second half of the appellation, having ruefully decided that it was impossible to protect a nation as unsettled as Mexico. In line with his self-appointed post, Norton wore a blue uniform with gold epaulets, had a blue cap or a beaver hat ornamented with a feather and a rose, and carried a carved serpent-headed wooden cane. His two pet mongrel dogs, Bummer and Lazarus,

were his constant companions. Amused at his antics, restaurant, shop, and theater owners, stationmasters, and steamship officials all honored his personal scrip. His edicts and pronouncements were covered by the leading California newspapers, as were his letters to European royalty, Abraham Lincoln, Jefferson Davis, and other outstanding Americans. Shortly before his death, Norton decided to add "Emperor of the Jews" to his titles. He delivered the announcement to *The Hebrew,* but the editor refused to publish it.

When Norton died in 1880, thirty thousand San Franciscans attended his funeral, which was arranged by an early business associate. Rejected by the Jews—the emperor's coreligionists found him more embarrassing than amusing—Norton was laid to rest by the Episcopalians in the old Masonic cemetery. Fifty years later, when those burial grounds were abandoned, the citizens of San Francisco raised funds again for a full service featuring the Municipal Band of San Francisco, vocal music of the Olympic Club, and a salute by a United States Army infantry battalion.

Always outnumbered and intensely conscious of the attention they attracted, most pioneer Jews toed the line of good conduct. To the distress of these exemplary citizens, Jewish reprobates would occasionally turn up. Some of these renegades took pains to conceal their Judaic origins, but others flaunted their Jewishness like a distinctive feather in the band of their black hats.

Jew Ida (Levy) operated as a madam in the red-light district of Butte, Montana, from the turn of the century until World War I, an era in Montana when the leading female occupation after housewife was fancy lady or madam. Those who knew Ida remembered her as an able entrepreneur and an excellent Jewish cook.

One Jewish prostitute in Butte at that time earned her place in print by means of an avocation. Her name was Jew Jess (those of her colleagues were Mexican Maria, Hawaiian Hattie, Swedish Sue, Irish Eileen). Although a drug addict, Jess was a quick-witted and personable woman, as well as an astonishingly skillful pickpocket. She was frequently arrested but was usually able to stay out of jail. On one occasion in court, after talking her way out of a charge (rolling a client) Jess effusively embraced the judge, then departed quickly. The embarrassed magistrate was soon to discover that his watch, wallet, tie pin, and lodge emblem had left with her.

In some sections of the frontier, a man without a gun was not considered fully attired, and Jews learned to use firearms as proficiently as did their fellow pioneers. Even so, only a few engaged in gunfighting when they had other recourse. One who did, did so frequently and became widely known as a six-gun artist. His name was Jim Levy, and he was born in Ireland in 1842 of Jewish parents who brought him to the United States when he was a young boy. Levy's first shoot-out occurred in Pioche, Nevada, on May 30, 1871. Levy, who was working as a miner at the time, witnessed a street killing. The victor, Michael Casey, later maintained he had shot in self-defense, but Levy publicly contradicted him, asserting that Casey issued the first shot. Casey met Levy at a local store and chal-

Civic leader extraordinary, Ludwig Ilfeld (1874–1960), came to Las Vegas, New Mexico in 1892. He served as a major in the New Mexico Mounted National Guard, founded the Meadow City Polo Team, and also fostered fraternal, charitable, and cultural groups. For fifty-five years he was the chief of the volunteer E. Romero Fire Company of West Las Vegas. Courtesy, Dr. Fred Ilfeld, Beverly Hills, California

Josephine Sarah Marcus Earp (1861–1944), in her memoirs, I Married Wyatt Earp, *included a description of the shootout at the O.K. Corral: "I jumped up as I heard the firing start. . . . Without stopping for a bonnet I rushed outside. . . . A man in a wagon . . . yelled, 'Hop in, lady—I'll run you up to the excitement!' . . . I almost swooned when I saw Wyatt's tall figure very much alive. . . . He spotted me, and came across the street. Like a feather-brained girl, my only thought was, 'My God, I haven't got a bonnet on. What will they think?' But you can imagine my real relief at seeing my love alive. I was simply a little hysterical. Can you blame me?" Courtesy, J. Eduardo Robinson, Sonora, Mexico*

lenged the unarmed miner to a gunfight. Levy accepted the challenge, rushing off to obtain a weapon. He returned a short while later to confront Casey, gun in hand, in the alley behind the store. Levy called to his opponent, then opened fire; his bullet grazed Casey's skull. Casey dove at Levy, who shot him again, this time in the neck. When the wounded man keeled over, Levy struck him on the head with his revolver. Casey's companion, Dave Neagle, put one bullet into Levy's jaw, then turned and ran. Casey died some days later. Levy was arrested, tried, and acquitted.

Soon after this incident, Levy gave up mining to earn his living as a professional regulator, a gambler, and, on occasion, a merchant in mining and cattle towns all over the Far West—Virginia City (Nevada), Cheyenne, Deadwood, Leadville, Tombstone, and Tucson. He survived an estimated sixteen shoot-outs before he was gunned down himself.

On June 5, 1882, Levy was gambling and drinking at the Fashion Saloon in Tucson when he and John Murphy, the faro dealer, began to argue. They exchanged a barrage of insults, which culminated in talk of a shoot-out. Levy had no gun, nor would friends who were trying to keep him out of trouble loan him one. Murphy's friends, on the other hand, urged the faro dealer not to engage in a gun battle with a skilled gunfighter like Levy, but rather to catch him unawares. Later that night, as the still-unarmed Levy was leaving the Palace Hotel, Murphy and his friends sprang at him and without warning shot him dead.

The same year, 1882, some sixty miles southeast of Tucson in the mining town of Tombstone, eighteen-year-old Josephine Sarah ("Josie") Marcus, daughter of Sophie and Henry Marcus of San Francisco, was carrying on a love affair with Wyatt Earp, who was thirty-three and still married to his second wife, Mattie. It was not romance, however, that prompted the lovers' flight late one spring night. Wyatt had just killed Frank Stilwell and was on the run from his victim's cohorts and the sheriff. The murder was one of many reprisals triggered by the most publicized shoot-out in the Far West, the gunfight at O.K. Corral on October 26, 1881, which began as a showdown between the ranching and rustling Clanton family and the high-handed lawmen and businessmen, the Earp brothers.

Josie, who claimed to be an eyewitness, wrote her version in *I Married Wyatt Earp*. More to the point here is her own story, which she modestly supplied as background. Josie ran away to the Arizona Territory in 1879 as a (very) minor member of the cast of the Pauline Markham Troupe's production of Gilbert and Sullivan's *H.M.S. Pinafore*. By the time the actors reached Prescott, her family had alerted Jake Marks, a Jewish merchant, whose wife apprehended the runaway and escorted her back to San Francisco. Josie, however, had already acquired an ardent suitor, Johnny Behan, a perennial office seeker who followed her home to ask for her hand.

Josie claimed that she overcame the objections of her parents, who were by her description "models of conformity." That is hard to believe when you consider that Behan was forty-two,

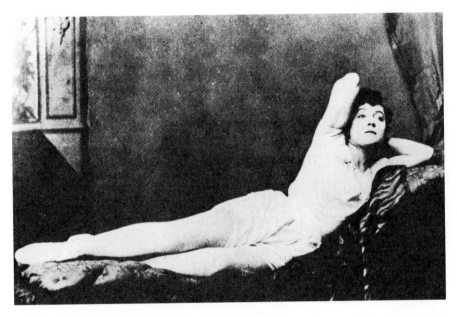

*Adah Isaacs Menken;
courtesy, Harvard The-
atre Collection, Harvard
University, Cambridge,
Massachusetts*

non-Jewish, a divorced father of two, and just entering a new business. On the other hand, she had run away before, had developed Saint Vitus's dance when she was returned home, and had never found it difficult to express her opinions, so she may have been telling the truth!

Shortly after Behan's visit, Josie followed her suitor to Tombstone. Several months after she arrived, her romance with the wily, ambitious Behan soured. Unwilling "to go home like a beaten dog," Josie sought employment. She found instead Wyatt Earp, deputy sheriff and proprietor of the Oriental Saloon, a gambling establishment. Earp at the time was involved in a pitched battle for the sheriff's job, which ultimately went to Behan.

Life after Tombstone was only slightly calmer for this common-law couple. (Despite Josie's protestations, no record has been found of their alleged wedding aboard Lucky Baldwin's yacht.) They spent nearly fifty years together mingling with a fast crowd of celebrities, gamblers, prospectors, and promoters in a number of boom towns throughout the Far West, and in Nome, Alaska, where they operated a saloon during the Klondike Rush. They finally settled in Los Angeles near the movie studios, where Wyatt hoped to turn his experiences into cash. He never succeeded in doing so, although others did.

The magnetic Far West attracted a host of visitors—sightseers, adventure seekers, actors, chroniclers, scientists, and government officials. The most dynamic and colorful among them left so deep an imprint that they were thereafter identified with the region and its lore. Prominent in that category was poet and stage personality Adah Isaacs Menken. She embarked on her dramatic career in 1859 at the age of twenty-three. With minimal training Menken undertook a variety of leading roles: *Cleopatra, The Jewess, The Lady of Lyons, The French Spy.* (She even tried Lady Macbeth once, to the despair of her costar tragedian James E. Murdoch—she came on stage not knowing a single line.) The part that established her as a star was the title role in *Mazeppa, or The Wild Horse of Tartary.* The widely publicized high point of the drama comes when, on the orders of a jealous rival, the nobleman Ivan Mazeppa, played by Adah, is stripped of his clothing and cinched to a wild steed. The sight of Menken, attired in flesh-colored tights and bound to a trained horse carrying her across the imaginary Russian steppes, invariably won a noisy ovation from the excited audience. The play opened in 1861, and for several years thereafter Menken toured the United States and Europe performing in *Mazeppa* and other plays. She swiftly became an international

"About this time a magnificent spectacle dazzled my vision—the whole constellation of the Great Menken came flaming out of the heavens like a vast spray of gas-jets, and shed a glory abroad over the universe as it fell!," wrote Mark Twain on March 8, 1864 in the Territorial Enterprise, *Virginia City, Nevada. Courtesy, Nevada Historical Society, Reno, Nevada*

celebrity and friend of such world-famed artists as Charles Dickens, George Sand, Alexandre Dumas, and Dante Gabriel Rossetti.

A sensation wherever she went, Menken found her most enthusiastic audiences in the entertainment-starved Far West in the early 1860s. During her stay in Virginia City, Nevada, miners threw bags of gold dust onto the stage as she made her closing bow, and mines and an entire mining district were named in her honor. Even the skeptical Mark Twain, a Virginia City newspaperman at the time, became an ardent and eloquent Menken fan.

San Franciscans were equally dazzled. Crowds lined the streets to watch the brilliantly attired performer ride through the city on horseback or pass by in an open carriage with other celebrities. California's "golden ambience," as Menken called it, moved her to uninhibited public displays of laughter, tears, poetic outpourings, and impromptu dances. Reporters followed her everywhere and recorded her every word and gesture.

Adah's conflicting statements about the

identity of her parents and the nature of her upbringing inspired speculations as wildly imaginative as the subject herself. Some facts appear to stand. She was born Adah Bertha Theodore in Milneburg, near New Orleans, in 1835. Her youthful essays and poetry reveal that she must have received a good education. In 1856 she married musician Alexander Isaac (later Isaacs) Menken in Texas. After the Panic of 1857, the couple went to live with Alexander's wealthy Jewish family in Cincinnati. During this period Adah became fascinated with Judaism, which was, she claimed, her native religion. Her prose and poetry on Jewish themes won the interest and admiration of American Reform leader Rabbi Isaac Mayer Wise, who published some of her poems in his newspaper, the *American Israelite*. When her poetic élan quieted, Adah obtained a divorce and traveled to New York in 1858 or 1859 to seek a career in the theater. She subsequently married California prizefighter John Heenan, satirist Robert Newell, and New York businessman James Barclay, but all three of these marriages failed.

Adah was preparing a new production of *Mazeppa* in Paris in 1868 when she fell seriously ill. As death approached she summoned a rabbi and left with him her request for a simple Jewish burial. She was interred in the Jewish section of the Cimetière Parisien on August 10, 1868. A week after Adah died, *Infelicia*, her second volume of poetry, was released. (*Memoirs* was published in 1856.) In one stanza of the poem entitled "Myself," Adah writes revealingly of her inner frustrations:

Still I trim my white bosom with crimson roses; for none shall see the thorns.
I bind my aching brow with a jeweled crown, that none shall see the iron one beneath.
My silver-sandaled feet keep impatient time to the music, because I cannot be calm.
I laugh at earth's passion-fever or Love; yet I know that God is near to the soul on the hill, and hears the ceaseless ebb and flow of a hopeless love, through all my laughter.
But if I can cheat my heart with the old comfort, that love can be forgotten, is it not better?
After all, living is but to play a part!
The poorest worm would be a jewel-headed snake if she could!

Another memorable sojourner was Solomon Nunes Carvalho, oil painter, photographer, and daguerreotyper, who spent one extraordinary year in the Far West. From September 1853 to September 1854 he participated in a historic and treacherous expedition, which he recorded in oil paintings, daguerreotypes—the first taken of the Far West—and a trip diary and letters, upon which he based *Incidents of Travel and Adventure in the Far West*. The book opens with a description of his first meeting with the organizer and leader of the journey, which occurred on August 22, 1853.

After a short interview with Col. J. C. Fremont, I accepted his invitation to accompany him as artist of an Exploring Expedition across the Rocky Mountains. A half hour previously, if anybody had suggested to me the probability of my undertaking an overland journey to California, even over the emigrant route, I should have replied there were no inducements sufficiently powerful to have tempted me. Yet in this instance, I impulsively, without even a consultation with my family, passed my word to join an exploring party, under command of Col. Fremont over a hitherto untrodden country in an elevated region, with the full expectation of being exposed to all the inclemencies of an arctic winter. . . . I know of no other man to whom I would have entrusted my life under similar circumstances.

Colonel John C. Fremont, celebrated American soldier, explorer, and politician, planned the arduous winter journey, his fifth and final expedition in the West, to demonstrate the feasibility of a year-round transcontinental rail route along the thirty-eighth parallel. Carvalho's task was to provide Fremont with daguerreotypes to illustrate the proposal.

Before this expedition Carvalho had led an artistically and intellectually productive yet supremely conventional life. He was born in Charleston, South Carolina, in 1815 into a family of Sephardic Jews that included rabbis, teachers, writers, and merchants. At twenty he became a professional portrait painter, and by the time Colonel Fremont approached him, he had attained mastery of photography and daguerreotypy. With these combined skills he earned a modest living for himself, his wife, Sarah (Solis), and their children.

Carvalho left Westport (Kansas City), Kansas Territory, in Fremont's twenty-two-man pack train on September 23, 1853. The train consisted of ten Anglo-Americans, two Mexicans, ten Delaware Indian guides, a few Indian women and children, and fifty pack animals loaded with food, clothing, blankets, scientific instruments, and artist's and daguerreotypy supplies. The open prairies, which he was seeing for the first time, deeply stirred the artist. Wrote Carvalho, "I could not master the nervous debility which seized me. . . . Was it fear? no; it was the conviction of my own insignificance in midst of the stupendous creation."

To make a daguerreotype view took him

Solomon Nunes Carvalho (1815–1897) was among the first daguerrotypists to accompany a Far West expedition—a task viewed with skepticism by his contemporaries. Courtesy, American Jewish Archives, Cincinnati, Ohio

from one to two hours—hours mainly spent un-
packing and carefully repacking the equipment.
In his journal he jotted down the various shots
he took and his impressions of the fine mild
climate, his first buffalo hunt, and prairie fires.
The party was high in the Rockies when Carvalho noted the first snow. The daguerreotyper,
accompanied by Fremont, took three hours to
scale a peak above camp one day to capture a
panoramic view. Exclaimed Carvalho, "Standing
as it were in this vestibule of God's holy temple,
I forgot I am of the mundane sphere."

By December and at ten thousand feet, Carvalho was no longer recording ecstatic moments.
The thermometer frequently dropped to thirty
below zero; their trail calculations often proved
wrong; the Delaware Indians had grown restive;
and the food supplies were dangerously low.
During the last fifty days of the five-month journey, the party survived by eating its pack animals. Deeply worried that his men might resort
to cannibalism, Colonel Fremont extracted a
pledge from them that they would not try to
survive at that cost.

The ordeal ended on February 7, 1854, when
the party straggled into Parowan, a Mormon settlement in Utah. Carvalho weighed one hundred
pounds, fifty pounds less than when he had
started. His feet and fingers were frostbitten, he
suffered from diarrhea and scurvy, and his
clothes were in tatters. Yet the daguerreotype
plates and equipment, which he had painstak-
ingly guarded, were intact and, as Mrs. Jessie
Fremont would attest in later years, admirable
and beautifully clear.

Cared for by the Mormons, Carvalho re-
cuperated, then continued on to Los Angeles.
He spent from June until September in the City
of the Angels, where on the invitation of Samuel
and Joseph Labatt he participated in the organization of the Hebrew Benevolent Society, the
first Jewish organization in Los Angeles. The
Labatts in turn helped Carvalho start a photographer's and artist's studio to earn money for his
trip home.

A year after Carvalho's return to Charleston, Colonel Fremont became the Republican
presidential nominee. Aware that the daguerreotyper had kept a journal during the expedition,
Fremont suggested via his campaign manager
that Carvalho publish his account of the journey,
which the Pathfinder hoped would win him
widespread public favor. Colonel Fremont had
had prints, drawings, and paintings made of the
Carvalho daguerreotypes, but he did not make
them available to Carvalho—he was saving them
to illustrate the book *he* was intending to write.
Even without his unprecedented visual record
of the Far West to depict the journey, Carvalho's
book was enthusiastically received and went into
four printings.

For thirty years Carvalho's daguerreotypes
lay untouched in a warehouse that, according to
the Fremonts, eventually burned down. Fortu-
nately, the artist retained some of the landscapes
and portraits he painted on the journey, and a
number have since become part of private and
institutional art collections.

Equally distinctive and far more numerous
were those Jewish individualists who came to the
Far West in their youth and spent the rest of
their lives cultivating a personal style that added
to the color and character of their communities.
One such city enhancer was matriarch Mary Ann
Magnin. Her offspring called her "Queen Victoria" behind her back, but face to face the doy-
enne of San Francisco fashion usually got what
she wanted. What she wanted was to build a
business selling high-quality attire to luxury-lov-
ing San Franciscans and to keep her five sons
working with her toward that end. Although the
family firm was named for her husband, Isaac—
a pamphlet-passing Socialist dubbed "Karl Marx"
by his children—from its inception Mary Ann
was in charge. She conceived of the elegant specialty shop, guided its growth into an important
chain, and trained her sons to carry on the enterprise in her footsteps. Only genteel notions
of the Victorian age prevented her from using
her own name over the door.

Born in Scheveningen, Holland, in 1848,
Mary Ann Cohen later moved with her family
to London, where at age fifteen she met Isaac
Magnin. The red-bearded young man from As-

Mary Ann Magnin; (1848–1943); courtesy I. Magnin Company, San Francisco, California

sen, Holland, was six years her senior and had already been to the United States, an adventure that included an unwilling stint in the Union Army and pushcart peddling in New Orleans. Unable to locate his father upon returning to Holland, Isaac was referred to the Cohens in London, and he soon had a bride.

Married at sixteen, Mary Ann started her family almost immediately. In 1875, when they set sail around Cape Horn for San Francisco, the entourage included young Samuel, Henrietta, Joseph, Emanuel John, Victor, Lucille, and Flora. All survived the rigorous sea journey, despite the lack of amenities in the ship's grubby steerage section.

It didn't take long for the Magnins to achieve a more comfortable economic standing. Skilled at wood carving and applying gold leaf—a trade much in demand in those days—Isaac soon went to work as a frame gilder for art and antique dealer Solomon Gump. Gump reportedly offered Isaac a substantial raise to work on the gilded ceiling of Saint Mary's Cathedral, but Mary Ann vetoed the idea, fearful that she would lose her husband in a fall off a scaffold. Having thus eliminated the family's source of income, Mary Ann went to work in a profession popular among Cohen women, that of making baby clothes for the gentry. In 1876 she and Isaac opened their first tiny business establishment, a Yankee Notions store in Oakland.

As Mary Ann's reputation for fine handiwork—which soon included lace-trimmed lingerie and bridal gowns—grew, so did her ambition and business acumen. She and Isaac established I. Magnin in San Francisco in 1877,

*Frances Wisebart Jacobs
(1843–1892) was the
only woman among six-
teen pioneers depicted in
stained glass in the Colorado state capitol building
built in 1899. The
"Queen of Charities" was
also made the namesake
of a Denver hospital she
helped found. Courtesy,
Western History Depart-
ment, Denver Public
Library, Denver, Colorado*

and by 1886 the store was doing business on
Market Street, in the heart of San Francisco's
business district. During that year, Mary Ann
also gave birth to her last child, Grover.

From the outset Mary Ann fashioned
I. Magnin into a lavish shopping establishment
adorned with Rose de Brignolles marble and expensive bronze fixtures. She was a "penny-
pinching, stubborn woman who never bought
unwisely," according to her grandson Cyril Magnin. She courted the upper crust of San Francisco society but had the common touch as well,
playing poker with her employees on Saturday
night and catering to the raunchy but rich clien-
tele of the Barbary Coast.

As the children grew, Mary Ann, still cling-
ing to her old-country ways despite her own considerable worldly achievements, taught them
along traditional gender lines: the girls learned

handiwork, the boys business. Grover later recalled that his mother trained him to identify
fabric by touch alone and that during his apprenticeship, he had worked in every department in the store.

In 1900 Mary Ann retired from the day-to-
day operations of the company and named son
John, then twenty-two, as president, passing over
her older sons Sam and Joseph. (This led to
some rancor, so that Joseph sold his stock in the
company in 1913, soon thereafter forming his
own self-named chain of department stores.) Five
years later Mary Ann sent John to New York to
establish and head East Coast and European
buying offices and made twenty-year-old Grover,
her favorite son, the general manager. He was
in that post in 1906, the year the great San Francisco earthquake leveled a six-story I. Magnin
Store under construction and nearly leveled the

company. But no matter—Mary Ann responded by setting up shop in her house while new commercial quarters were being completed.

Until almost her last breath, Mary Ann Magnin still visited her San Francisco store daily, arriving in a limousine from her luxurious Saint Francis Hotel suite two blocks away. When finally confined to a wheelchair, she took to rolling down the aisles, and it has even been said that she had herself wheeled around the store on a gurney shortly before her death in 1943 at the age of ninety-five.

No less a luminary was Frances Wisebart Jacobs, who dedicated the last twenty years of her life to brightening the prospects of Colorado's infirm and impoverished. Jacobs's hands-on, stops-out approach to good works made her a Colorado folk heroine as well as a pioneer philanthropist.

Born in Harrodsburg, Kentucky, and raised in Cincinnati, Jacobs came to Colorado in 1861 as the eighteen-year-old bride of Abraham Jacobs, the Central City, Colorado, business partner of her brother Ben Wisebart. For fifteen years she kept house in the mountaintop mining community and later in Denver; cared for her two sons and a daughter; and played a supporting role in her husband's and brother's numerous civic and social undertakings.

After the family moved to a chaotically burgeoning Denver—the city grew from approximately five thousand to about eighty thousand between 1870 and 1887—Frances made the needy her primary concern. The city at the time was overrun with "lungers," most of them indigent. Denver hospitals and clinics could not or would not accommodate them, particularly those too poor to pay, and many landlords refused to rent them quarters, forcing the ailing newcomers to camp out wherever they could. Jacobs's first response was personal and immediate. Unable to pass a tubercular collapsed or hemorrhaging in the street—a frequent sight—Jacobs summoned her doctor or placed the sufferer in a hospital at her own expense. It soon became apparent that the widespread problem could not be substantially ameliorated by an individual acting alone, so Jacobs enlisted the aid of the He-

brew Benevolent Ladies Society and then of the Denverwide Ladies Relief Society. Her passionate interest and outstanding ability swiftly brought her in contact with Denver's leading social workers and philanthropists. In 1887, to heighten the effectiveness of individual charity organizations, Jacobs, two Protestant ministers, and two Catholic priests formed the Charity Organization Society, a federation of twenty-four charity groups and the forerunner of the Denver Community Chest.

Jacobs worked to assist the impoverished in a variety of ways, but Denver's sick continued to occupy most of her time. To raise funds to build a much-needed hospital, she badgered businessmen for contributions, wrote letters to newspapers, and spoke at countless balls, luncheons, and meetings. Those activities were, however, only ancillary to her daily, often daylong, on-the-spot ministering. She visited the poor in their homes; brought them food, clothing, and medicine; changed the sheets on their sickbeds; cooked meals; chided the errant; and encouraged the disheartened. Her dress austere, her hair pulled back into a tight bun, and her capacious handbag full of Grandfather's tar soap to press on anyone who would use it, Jacobs became a familiar sight in the Denver slums. In contrast to her severe appearance, she had a ready wit and an unfailing sense of humor. More conventional practitioners of good works were often aghast at the merriment she inspired amid misery and degradation.

Her work ended abruptly in 1891 at the age of forty-nine: She went out in a rainstorm to bring medicine to an ailing baby, caught pneumonia, and succumbed. Two thousand people attended her funeral at Temple Emanuel, and a second memorial service was held a week later at Denver's First Congregational Church. In 1899, "the Queen of Charities," as Jacobs was dubbed, was awarded a permanent place of honor in Colorado history. She was one of sixteen pioneers (the only woman) selected for depiction in the stained-glass windows that were placed in the rotunda of the new Colorado state capitol building.

Combining the practical inventiveness he

David Lubin's (1849–1919) early plan to aid the farmer by shipping produce cheaply through the United States mail met with considerable scorn. One angry opponent was a state assemblyman who confronted Lubin: "Why, d'you mean to say you'd send a cabbage through the mails?" "Certainly," replied Lubin. "Would you send a pig?" asked the assemblyman. "Why, yes," said Lubin, "I would send anything; I would send you." From Olivia Rossetti Agresti, David Lubin, *University of California Press (Los Angeles, 1941); photo courtesy, David Lubin Collection, Western Jewish History Center, Judah L. Magnes Museum, Berkeley, California*

had learned in the Far West with the Zionist dream of the agricultural restoration of Palestine, merchant-turned-crusader David Lubin fashioned for himself a mammoth mission. His feet-on-the-ground, head-in-the-clouds goal was the amelioration of poverty through the worldwide institution of small, independently owned farms, cooperative marketing, and the exchange of agricultural information.

Lubin was born in 1849 in Klodowa, Poland. After a pogrom in 1853, his family fled to the United States and settled in New York's Lower East Side. He moved west as a young man, where he, in partnership with his half-brother Harris Weinstock, built the highly successful emporium Weinstock & Lubin in Sacramento, California. Lubin's dealings with the struggling farmers around Sacramento awakened him to the problems of the small farmer, and an 1884 visit to Palestine further confirmed his view of the small

farm as the cornerstone of democratic self-sufficiency. Returning to Sacramento in 1885, Lubin began to buy land and study agricultural problems. As a fruit grower, he was immediately confronted with the saturation of the local fruit market and the extremely high cost of shipping fruit to eastern markets. Lubin responded by organizing the California Fruit Growers' Exchange, a cooperative that radically changed the marketing of produce. He grew wheat as well, and swiftly learned that shipping costs put American wheat farmers at a great disadvantage in the international market. His answer was a government bounty to be paid the farmer in order to offset high shipping costs. He lobbied his plan, known as "Lubinism," and stirred national interest. Although never adopted, it aroused the first attention to the need for price supports for the farmer.

Further travels abroad drew the energetic

Lubin's attention to the international scope of the small farmer's predicament. After many failed attempts, Lubin succeeded in activating the International Institute of Agriculture. The first meeting took place in 1905 in Rome, with representatives of forty nations present. The institute effectively studied worldwide farm problems until it merged with the United Nations Food and Agricultural Organization in 1946. Lubin died in 1919 in Rome, where the institute maintained its headquarters. His dedication to his enormous and often fiercely opposed task had by then earned him international renown. Hardworking to the end, Lubin bore lightly the honors bestowed on him, preferring to think of himself as "an ordinary scrub with a mission."

A crusader of a different ilk, Rachel "Ray" Frank—teacher, journalist, and celebrated public speaker in the Far West in the 1880s and 1890s—beamed her evangelical light on the practice of an ethical and socially conscious Judaism. Her soft though unsparingly honest elocutionary style caused her to be called "the Prophetess," "the Lochinvar of the West," and "the Modern Day Deborah."

Frank was born in San Francisco in 1864 or 1865 to eastern European Jewish parents. After graduation from high school in 1879, she taught school for six years in Ruby Hill, Nevada, instructing the miners' children by day and their parents by night. In 1885, yearning for intellectual companionship, she moved to Oakland, California, where she gave private lessons in literature and elocution and began to write articles and short stories. During those years, vitriolic journalist Ambrose Bierce became her devoted friend, lively correspondent, and literary mentor. She also took a job as a Sabbath school teacher at the First Hebrew Congregation of Oakland. Her efforts to understand her faith and convey its meaning to her pupils won Frank a wide reputation as a Jewish educator. When the rabbi left in 1891, she was appointed superintendent of the Sabbath school.

Frank gave the first of her thought-provoking sermons in 1890, after only a few hours of preparation. While in Spokane Falls (Spokane), Washington, on a writing assignment, she inquired if a holiday service were being planned for the following day, Rosh Hashanah. Only if she consented to speak, her coreligionists replied. She was already well-known as a writer and a lecturer, and a swiftly placed announcement brought a huge crowd to the opera house to hear her speak. Frank was rousingly received

"I lived among trappers and Indians, but always as a Jew. Did I need grander temples to worship in? . . . In the murmurs of the pines I hear the psalms of David; the fragrance of the incense is as of old, the winds speak to me in His voice." From The Sounding of the Shofar *sermon, (Rachel) Ray Frank; courtesy, American Jewish Historical Society, Waltham, Massachusetts*

Judah L. Magnes; courtesy, Western Jewish History Center, Judah L. Magnes Museum, Berkeley, California

ganization and modern methods of education, and the role of the emerging American Jewish woman. Frank was also popular with general audiences, whom she addressed on aesthetic and intellectual topics: "Art and What It Means to Me," "The God Idea in Art," and "Thought and Its Origin and Development."

In 1898 she spent several months studying with Rabbi Isaac Mayer Wise in Cincinnati. Wise was an advocate of women's rights, but he did not think Frank or any other woman was suited to serve in the rabbinate. Frank apparently concurred—pulpits were offered to her, but she turned them down. Nor did she support the suffragists, believing that women were not yet strong enough for politics, a view born possibly of her own difficulty in dealing effectively with the opposition leveled at her as a woman in the public eye and a social critic. In a series of letters to Bierce—the first dated January 1897—she complained of an ailing throat and emotional distress. He lovingly chided her inability to accept even the "friendliest and gentlest of criticism" and urged her to adopt a more just and cheerful view. Wrote Bierce to Frank:

The hand of everybody is not against you. The things that rouse your anger are not always significant of unfriendliness. . . . I'm rather an expert in enmities and antagonisms, and I find that they have not so large and important a place in one's life as one has a tendency to think.

He challenged her disinclination to serve as a rabbi, suggesting she was afraid of incurring the hatred of the "colonels" of her own sex, and he urged her to reconsider her ideas about the rights of women.

In the spring of 1898 she accepted an assignment to cover a world Zionist meeting in London. When it concluded, Frank traveled in Europe, where in Munich she met a young Russian Jewish economics student, Simon Litman, who had been living in Paris. He was going to the University of Zurich for the winter semester, and she joined him there. They were married in London on August 14, 1901. Thereafter, she lectured occasionally and wrote articles but never fully resumed an active public life.

During his long years in the national, then

and invited to preach again on Yom Kippur Eve. Viewing the occasion as an auspicious first, Ray declaimed:

From time immemorial the Jewish woman has remained in the background . . . and it is well that it has been so; for while she has let the strong ones do battle for her throughout the centuries . . . she had gathered strength to come forward in an age of progressive enlightenment to battle for herself if necessary.

By 1892 she was much in demand as a lecturer and journalist throughout the Far West and Midwest. She declaimed to Jewish groups on such subjects as class and ethnic schisms among Jews, the pressing need for Jewish or-international religious and political arena, Rabbi Judah L. Magnes—born in San Francisco in 1877 and raised in Oakland—was labeled a rebel, a gadfly, and a firebrand. Magnes attributed his dissident stance to his western upbringing. That upbringing and his subsequent education reveal not one but a blend of portentous cultural and religious forces.

His father, David Magnes, was a Yiddish-speaking Russian Jew with a warm regard for his Hasidic background. His mother, Sophie, was a member of the Abrahamson family, observant Orthodox Jews who lived in Oakland close to the Magnes family. At Oakland High School, where Judah was a brilliant student, champion debater, and star pitcher, innovative thinking was praised and unpretentiousness respected. His first teachers, recalled Magnes, implanted in him an image of "the glories of the real America—no badges, no titles, no special uniforms." When Judah was in his early teens, Jacob Voorsanger, the prestigious Reform rabbi of San Francisco's Temple Emanu-El, took the gifted Oakland youth under his wing, exposing him to still another viewpoint. At sixteen and with Voorsanger's aid, in 1893 Judah enrolled at Reform Hebrew Union College (HUC) and seven years later emerged the first native Californian to, as the *Oakland Inquirer* put it, "enter the Jewish priesthood." While studying for a doctorate in Berlin and Heidelberg between 1900 and 1902, Magnes became involved with Zionist intellectuals who also influenced him.

Magnes's role as a dissenter was foreshadowed in his first published work, entitled *Palestine—or Death?* Written during his second year at HUC, the essay attacked anti-Zionist American Reform Judaism. According to historian Arthur Goren, "The *Death* in the title was the danger of assimilation."

Magnes launched his problematic career in New York. In 1904, at twenty-seven, he became the spiritual leader of the Reform Temple Israel in Brooklyn. During the two years he was there, he actively championed the causes of the eastern European Jewish immigrants in Lower Manhattan. He helped organize protest marches against the raging Russian pogroms, became head of the Jewish Defense Association, was the secretary of the Federation of American Zionists, and served on the board of the newly organized American Jewish Committee. By 1906 he was a national figure but an unemployed rabbi.

The next stop for the eloquent and charismatic young maverick was Manhattan's Temple Emanu-El, place of worship for the American Jewish power elite. With the partial blessing of his uptown "bosses," Magnes continued his work with the downtown Yiddish-speaking Zionists, Socialists, and labor unionists. In 1908, the same year he was judged "counter-Reform" and asked to resign at Temple Emanu-El, Magnes married Beatrice Lowenstein, member of a well-to-do German Jewish mercantile family. In her he found an invaluable partner and obtained a small regular (inherited) income and access to influential American Jewish circles. In 1909 Magnes formed and became the first chairman of the *Kehillah* (Hebrew "community"). The aim of the Kehillah was to institute in New York City a democratic, representative Jewish assembly. While only a minority of Jewish organizations joined, the group nonetheless made substantial progress in educational and cultural affairs during the eleven years Magnes served as its head. He was initially seen as an ideal unifier of the split community, but as Magnes became an increasingly vocal pacifist and civil libertarian, the Jewish establishment turned its back on him.

Magnes waged his longest and most controversial struggle in Palestine during his twenty-three years as the chancellor of Hebrew University. As a pacifist (until World War II) and an unswerving supporter of equal rights, Magnes strongly advocated an Arab-Jewish binational Palestine. He proclaimed that "it is one of the great civilizing tasks before the Jewish people to try to enter the promised land, not in the Joshua way, but bringing peace and culture, hard work and sacrifice and love."

Magnes died in October 1948. As the causes he backed gain support, appraisals of Magnes are changing. Some historians now view his career as oracular, prophetic, and trailblazing.

Countless Jewish youths found themselves in possession of talents their elders, who had

MAGUIRE'S OPERA HOUSE

Manager and Proprietor....... THOS. MAGUIRE.

FRIDAY EVENING, OCTOBER 13th,

Second Appearance

OF

DANIEL E. BANDMANN,

AS

SHYLOCK.

In the Shakespearian play

THE MERCHANT OF VENICE.

BANDMANN EVENINGS,

German Jewish actor Daniel E. Bandmann (1840–1905) was known as "the man who brought Shakespeare to the mining camps," touring the nation in the 1860s and 1870s. After circling the globe four times, Bandmann settled down outside of Missoula, Montana, to pursue farming, teaching, conservation work, and social reform. He also produced fundraising shows for the many causes he backed. From The Hebrew (*October 11, 1865*)

come west penniless, uneducated, and unencouraged, barely knew existed. Once a western wunderkind showed real artistic or intellectual promise, the lack of first-rate educational and cultural facilities in the Far West became sorely apparent. The most promising of far western youth were as a consequence obliged to go to the East or to Europe to train their exceptional minds in outstanding universities or academies in established centers. After their training was completed, the majority remained in these centers to carve out a niche and a name for themselves among their peers and patrons. Consequently, these gifted *émigrés* rarely returned to the Far West. Most, however, idealized their far western childhood and paid tribute to those influences that had stirred their calling and prompted them to develop it.

Actor, playwright, and producer David Belasco, who was the leading American theatrical personality of the late nineteenth and early twentieth century, was born, reared, and received his early theatrical training in the Far West. The hallmark of Belasco's dramatic style was naturalism, a movement aimed at accurately reflecting human life and nature in art. He was often commended for presenting characters and locales as vibrant and colorful, even when tragic. Belasco and others attributed his outlook and techniques to this early work in the unrestrained frontier theater and to the far western landscape. Once, when asked what had inspired some brilliant and innovative stage lighting he had devised, Belasco replied:

I gained my first ideas of lighting from the wonderful skies of Southern California. . . . There on the brightest days, I would sit among the hills and watch the lights and shadows as they came and went. After a time, I began to try to reproduce those lights and shadows.

Belasco could never allow the truth to go

unembellished, even (or maybe especially) when writing his autobiography. He maintained that his father, Humphrey Abraham Belasco—a Spanish-Portuguese Jew whose theatrical family had long resided in England—was a gifted harlequin and that his mother, Reina Martin Belasco, was a gypsy and a mistress of folk wisdom. His fine early education he attributed to an aging priest, a Father McGuire, who purportedly recognized the boy's astonishing abilities and persuaded his parents to allow him to tutor their son in a monastery. After a few years of exacting study, recounted "the Bishop of Broadway" (he later affected clerical garb and quasi-ecclesiastical manner), he ran off with a South American circus, in which he became Davido, the boy bareback rider. After achieving considerable fame—he said he had posters to prove it—he contracted a fever and would have died in Rio de Janeiro had his father not retrieved him.

Only partly true, wrote biographer Craig Timberlake. David was born on July 25, 1853, shortly after his parents arrived in San Francisco. They lived in a shabby little house South of Market, where Humphrey ran a small store to support his family. As more children arrived (David was the oldest of seven boys and two girls) the family's financial problems increased. In 1858, when half of San Francisco rushed to the gold strike in British Columbia, the Belascos were among them. David lived in Victoria for seven years, with nary a stint at a monastery or in a circus to lend color to his ordinary boyhood.

The family returned to San Francisco in 1865. David, then twelve, prepared for his Bar Mitzvah, helped his father at his fruit store, and began making a name for himself as star elocutionist and actor at Lincoln Grammar School. At the school's annual exhibition in 1871, he received a first prize for his rendition of "The Maniac," performed costumed in chains, a sponge soaked in red ink hidden beneath the shirt. While still in school, he started writing plays and did odd jobs in San Francisco theaters, including taking small roles.

After he graduated from the eighth grade, he worked furiously to learn his craft. Wrote Timberlake:

He copied scripts, prompt books and parts, . . . he paraded into mining towns of the interior with fly-by-night touring companies and gleaned his knowledge of stage management . . . "on the road." He peddled a patent medicine that had been concocted by his mother; he free-lanced as a reporter and served as a hack play [wright].

Hearts of Oak, written with James A. Herne, was the first of Belasco's plays to attract wide attention. It flopped in New York but was well received elsewhere in the country. His next, *La Belle Russe,* opened at the Baldwin Theatre in San Francisco. In 1882 Belasco went to New York,

David Belasco's flair for the spectacle was apparent in his first play, produced when he was eighteen. Jim Black, or The Regulator's Revenge *had eight acts, over fifty players, and such a realistic street scuffle scene that several older patrons were frightened and the hall nearly set on fire. Courtesy, the William Winter Collection*

In his autobiography David Belasco (1853–1931) relates the tale of how the composer Giacomo Puccini raced backstage after a performance of Madame Butterfly *in New York and begged to be allowed to set the play to music. A very successful opera resulted. Puccini and Belasco collaborated once more on the classic* Girl of the Golden West, *an early production of which is shown here. Courtesy, Museum of the City of New York*

where he worked as stage manager at Madison Square Garden while writing *May Blossom*, which in 1886 became the first of his many smash hits.

From that moment on Belasco worked continually as a playwright, director, and later, producer. Throughout his long career he was involved in the staging of some 400 plays, 150 of which he wrote himself. He was widely praised for his extraordinary attention to realistic detail, elaborate stage settings, lighting, and other special effects. His best-known plays were *Heart of Maryland, The Return of Peter Grimm*, and *Du Barry*. Also widely enjoyed were the two whose plots were later to be transformed into the popular Puccini operas *Madame Butterfly* and *The Girl of the Golden West*. Belasco often worked on plays with western settings: *The First Born*, set in San Francisco's Chinatown; *Rose of the Rancho*, a play about the Mexican border by Richard Walton Tully; and *The Heart of Wetona*, which was built around an Indian theme.

Belasco lived in New York from the 1880s on, but his birthplace remained dear to him. In a letter to his biographer, William Winter, Belasco wrote, "We must meet soon and have good long talks about the golden days in California, *my* California."

Toby Rosenthal, who rose from an impoverished newsboy to an acclaimed painter, also had to relinquish his California home to develop his talent and pursue his career in the arts. The third of Esther and Jacob Rosenthal's four sons, Toby was born in Strasbourg in 1848. He emigrated with his family, first to New Haven, Connecticut, then in 1858 to San Francisco. During Toby's first four years in that frontier metropolis, he joined his two elder brothers and father in the struggle to provide the family with food and shelter. Even while peddling newspapers, delivering fruit, and hawking refreshments in a theater, Toby recalled being fascinated by paintings he saw in saloons and residences. He practiced drawing whenever possible, and at the age of fourteen he enrolled in a drawing class.

"Indescribably happy, I made my way to the first lesson," Rosenthal wrote in his memoirs.

A self-portrait by Toby Rosenthal, one of the first artists from the Far West to enjoy international recognition; courtesy, John Rodes, Altadena, California

in his behalf, the young artist worked unsparingly in Munich, even when suffering from poor health, as he frequently was.

During Toby's student years, his father kept the San Francisco newspapers apprised of his son's achievements. Several months before the twenty-three-year-old artist returned to San Francisco for a nine-month stay, the *Alta California* of March 8, 1871, heralded his visit with a show of communal pride, noting that

Rosenthal was cited as the recipient of a silver medal annual prize for cartoon at the Royal Exhibition at London by the Bavarian Government. His success will be gratifying to his many friends in San Francisco and to our people, who will be glad to know that a young Californian contested nobly at Munich with a student from far-off Greece.

Toby's extended visit in San Francisco was a huge success. The youthful painter was inundated with social invitations and commissioned to paint portraits of a number of San Franciscans.

Four years later, not he but one of his works created a great stir in what the *San Francisco Chronicle* called "the art crime of the century." Rosenthal's painting *Elaine*, inspired by the epic poem *Idylls of the King*, by Alfred, Lord Tennyson, arrived in San Francisco in March 1875 for a public viewing at Snow's and May's Gallery before being delivered to its San Francisco owner, Mrs. Robert Johnson. *Elaine* had already received much praise at showings in Munich, Berlin, Hamburg, and Boston, and San Franciscans were eagerly awaiting what one overly excited journalist called "the greatest painting in the world." Viewers packed the gallery for three days before the painting mysteriously vanished. An outraged public demanded and got action from the San Francisco police. The painting was reclaimed within forty-eight hours from a gang of hoodlums that had engineered the robbery hoping to extract ransom from the wealthy owner of the painting. The slightly damaged work was quickly repaired and placed on view in the gallery for the crowds of curious San Franciscans to see. The following year *Elaine* won a gold medal at the United States Centennial Exhibition held in Philadelphia.

Rosenthal visited his hometown once more

Within a year he was urged to exhibit his student work, which, in fact, was already on display in his proud family's tailor shop window. Encouraged by his admiring friends, his father sent Toby to study with portrait painter Fortunato Arriola for intensive training. Two years later Arriola advised the tailor to send his gifted son to Munich to study with master artists. Possessing only modest means, Toby's parents had to struggle to pay for the costly training. Driven by the desire to succeed and eager to merit the sacrifices made

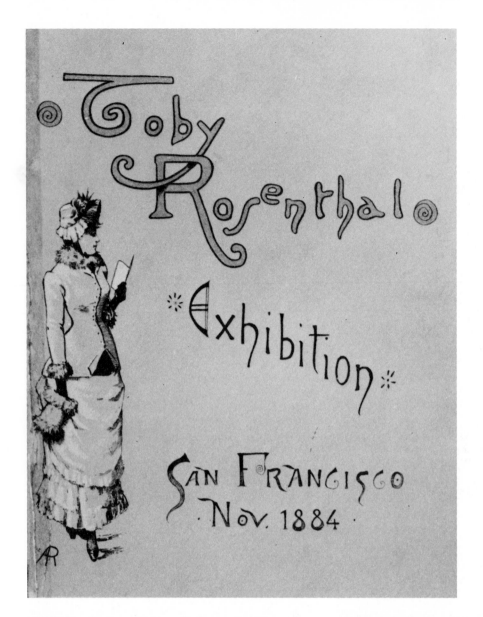

From his first, much-heralded exhibition; courtesy, University Research Library, University of California, Los Angeles

in 1879 and was again cordially received by culture-hungry San Franciscans eager to entertain him and purchase his work. Thereafter he wrote letters and sent paintings to his family and patrons and received a steady stream of visiting Californians in his Munich studio, but he never returned to San Francisco. In 1880 he married Susan Ansbacher, daughter of a wealthy Jewish family of Furth, Germany, and they had three children. The marriage—consummately happy according to Toby—deepened his attachment to Europe. Rosenthal nonetheless considered himself a Californian, and he had his first major exhibit in San Francisco in 1884. Included was his world-famous painting *The Trial of Constance de Beverly* as well as six other paintings gathered from San Francisco owners. Rosenthal continued receiving commissions, mainly for portraits, although by the 1890s his health and self-esteem

were on the wane. Painters who worked in the academic style, as did Rosenthal, had begun losing favor, first with the critics, then with the public, as the attention of art enthusiasts shifted to the new and more exciting works of the emerging modernists.

As the career of one far westerner in Europe ebbed, that of another was about to begin. In the early 1900s Gertrude Stein, figuratively, swam far out to sea, caught an incoming wave, rode it to shore, and planted her flag triumphantly in the twentieth century. Of her abundant achievements, none superseded her early understanding and enthusiastic espousal of the baffling new age. She *sensed* the character of the emerging epoch, said Stein, because she was a westerner and had a pioneer's affinity for the new. Like other westerners who went east (to Paris) to find the timeless West within the mind (as literary

As renowned for her friends as for her novels and essays, Gertrude Stein (1874–1946) promoted and encouraged the work of modern artists and literary giants of the early twentieth century—Matisse, Picasso, Braque, Gris, Hemingway, Fitzgerald—and amassed a fabulous collection of her friends' art. Courtesy, Collection of American Literature, Beinecke Library, Yale University, New Haven, Connecticut

critic William Gass put it), Stein was most extravagantly a westerner when far from home. When she visited Oakland after a thirty-year residence in France, she was dismayed to find that "there was no there there"—certainly not the peppy and pastoral "there" she called Gossols (Oakland) in her autobiographical novel, *Making of Americans.*

Stein described her longtime companion, Alice B. Toklas, the granddaughter of a Jewish forty-niner, to be "as ardently Californian as I."

The pair met in Paris in 1907. Their relationship was partially revealed in the best-selling *Autobiography of Alice B. Toklas*, Stein's rendition of her dutiful but acerbic mate's views of the great and obscure who passed through their ménage.

Gertrude, the youngest of Daniel and Amelia (Kaiser) Stein's five children, was born in Allegheny, Pennsylvania, and was five in 1880 when her family moved west. Her restless father, on arrival a confirmed and fervent westerner, settled his wife and children in a big house on ten acres in an undeveloped part of Oakland, then rushed out to make a killing in mining, the stock market, and real estate. He finally struck it moderately rich after investing in the Omnibus Cable Car Company.

From early childhood on, Gertrude was markedly attached to her brother Leo and with him explored the environs. After their mother died in 1881 and her father followed in 1891, the fourteen-year-old Gertrude's ties to her brother intensified. Leo's intellectual interests and fantasies became hers, particularly the aspiration to be revealed a genius and become enshrined in history. In 1892 Gertrude went to live with her relatives in Baltimore, who were initially amused by the bulky, garrulous, and disheveled girl and who attributed her idiosyncrasies to the fact of her being a westerner. When that arrangement wore thin, Gertrude enrolled at Radcliffe College to be near Leo, who was studying at Harvard University. Three years later, after stops at Johns Hopkins University (she studied medicine briefly) and London (she read novels at the British Museum), the pair, still together, established themselves in Paris, residing at 27 rue de Fluerus. Leo was captivated by modern art and had begun collecting the works of Monet, Renoir, Cézanne, and Picasso. Gertrude, as usual, caught his passion.

They had been living at "27" a year when Gertrude made her first solo effort, a novel she dashed off in two months, called *Q.E.D.* Her second effort was another novel, *Three Lives.* The style she had developed—it was rhythmic, repetitious, and laden with subconscious undertones—elated Gertrude. She was convinced that she had captured the immediacy Picasso hailed

San Francisco natives and next-door neighbors, Harriet Lane Levy and Alice B. Toklas, shown above, went to Paris together in August 1907. Alice met Gertrude Stein, and Harriet returned to San Francisco alone. Courtesy, The Bancroft Library, University of California, Berkeley

as the essence of modern art. Leo despised the first novel, and they argued about it at length. When, despite his objections, she did the second in much the same manner, they continued to wrangle until a schism developed between them.

Alice Babette Toklas was born in San Francisco in 1877 to Emma (Levinsky) and Ferdinand Toklas and was raised in Seattle, where her father was a partner in the firm of Toklas and Singerman. After she graduated from Mount Rainier Seminary, she enrolled in the University of Washington to study music, hoping to become a concert pianist. The year she turned twenty her mother died, and she and her ten-year-old

brother Clarence were sent to live in San Francisco with her widowed grandfather, Louis Levinsky. A glimpse into Alice's life during the ensuing decade was provided by her friend and next-door neighbor Harriet Lane Levy.

Among the ever-present, shifting group Alice remained the only woman there. In spite of her youth, she existed to them as a housekeeper, provider of food and general comfort. Any opinion that she might venture at the table was ignored or sponged out by a laugh . . . her strange austere beauty passed over them unsuspected. Alice was odd, they said, and forgot her. Unnoticed she fled the after-dinner cigar-laden talk of local politics and recovered her identity among congenial circles in the pages of Henry James.

With Harriet and her friends Michael and Sarah Stein, who were Gertrude's brother and sister-in-law, Alice—at loose ends after the death of her grandfather—traveled to Paris in 1907. She met Gertrude for the first time at Sarah's art-choked apartment. Remembered Alice: "She was a golden brown presence, burned by the Tuscan sun. . . . She wore a large round coral brooch and when she talked . . . I thought her voice came from this brooch."

Gertrude was equally attracted to Alice. She invited her on walks and, exhibiting her pleasure, elicited from Alice increasingly bold views. Eventually, she gave her *Three Lives* to read; a work of genius, judged Alice. Gertrude took her new friend to the Stein's summer retreat at Fiesole, Italy, and there she declared herself. Wrote Toklas's biographer, Linda Simon, "What she proposed to Alice was nothing less than marriage. They would live together, Alice as wife, Gertrude as husband." Alice wept, and continued to weep for days, but her answer was a definite yes. With Alice serving as cook, hostess, typist, critic, and proofreader, Gertrude turned out work after work. The forty-year union ultimately yielded a controversial body of novels, plays, poems, essays, and criticism; friendships—enduring and ephemeral—with some of the twentieth century's cultural pathfinders; and the fame that two California girls had craved.

Of all the laudable careers launched by exceptionally talented pioneer Jews in the newfound freedom of the Far West, none towers above that of the famed physicist Dr. Albert Abraham Michelson. The son of a struggling mining camp merchant, Michelson, who helped prepare the ground for Einstein's theory of relativity, in 1907 became the first American to receive the Nobel Prize for science.

Albert, the oldest of the eight Michelson children, was born in Strelno, (Polish) Prussia, in 1852. He was four years old when his parents, Samuel and Rosalie (Przlubska) Michelson, settled in Murphys Camp, Calaveras County, California. Albert's intellectual and creative gifts (he became an artist, a musician, and an athlete, as well as a scientist) were apparent early to his father and to his mother, his first teacher. While still of grammar school age, Albert was sent to live with relatives in San Francisco, where better educational facilities were available. The principal of Lowell Boys' High School, Theodore Bradley, encouraged him to pursue an appointment to the United States Naval Academy, where he could get a fine scientific education at no cost. Years later Michelson recalled his debt to Bradley in an interview:

The principal of the high school . . . was an unusual man. I owe a great deal to the toughness of his training. . . . He took a liking to me, and drilled me very hard, especially in mathematics. I did not enjoy it at the time: it was work! But later I came to appreciate its value.

Interestingly, Albert may have received his appointment because of his Jewish origins and the family's removal to Nevada (the Michelsons resettled in Virginia City in the 1860s). Applying on the Nevada quota, he emerged as one of the top three candidates but lost to the son of an impoverished Civil War veteran with one arm. Inexorable in his quest for an appointment, he traveled by train to Washington, D.C., bearing a letter of strong recommendation from the Nevada congressman:

Had I felt at liberty to be governed by consideration of expediency I should have selected him. His father is a prominent and influential merchant in Virginia City, and a member of the Israelite persuasion, who by his example and influence has largely contributed to the success of our cause, and induced many of his coreligionists to do the same. These people are a powerful element in our politics. The boy who is uncommonly bright and studious is a pet among them, and I do most steadfastly believe that his appointment at your hands, would do more to fasten these people to the Republican cause, than anything that could be done.

The president had filled his allotted slots, and young Michelson was told to go to Annapolis and wait there. After three days, with hope dissolved, he was about to start back to Washington when he received a message informing him of his appointment.

Michelson entered the United States Naval Academy in June 1869. His ingenuity and creativity in problem solving on one occasion led to a charge of cheating. When he demonstrated

*Nobel prize-winning physicist Dr. Albert A. Michelson exhibited zestful originality in di-
verse pursuits, including this self-portrait. When asked why he tackled such difficult physics
experiments, Michelson would embark on a scientific explanation, only to stop and laugh-
ingly admit that "the real reason is . . . it is such good fun." Courtesy, Special Collections,
U.S. Naval Academy, Annapolis, Maryland*

that he had solved the problem in question by
his own method, the case was dismissed. After
graduating ninth in a class of twenty-nine in 1873,
he spent two years at sea, then returned to the
academy as an instructor in physics and chem-
istry under his commanding officer, William T.
Sampson. During this period he married Sampson's niece, Margaret Heminway, with whom he
had two sons and a daughter. The twenty-year
marriage ended in divorce. In 1899 he married
Edna Stanton and with her had three daughters.

Michelson made his first major contribution
at twenty-six. He invented a ten-dollar device
that measured the velocity of light with six times
the accuracy achieved by prior methods. He recorded his discovery in a letter that appeared in
the *American Journal of Science* in May 1878, earning an international reputation. In the ensuing
decade, he developed the epoch-making Michelson interferometer, used to test the relative
velocities of the earth and the ether. His third
major contribution was the extremely original

echelon spectroscope, permitting high spectro-scopic resolution. For these and related achieve-ments, in 1907 Michelson was awarded the No-bel Prize in Physics by the Swedish Academy of Sciences. Throughout his career he received many prestigious honors and awards. From 1901 to 1903 he was president of the American Phys-ical Society; in 1907 he received the Copley Medal from Britain's Royal Society; in 1910 and 1911 he was president of the American Association for the Advancement of Science; from 1923 to 1927 he presided over the National Academy of Science. A plaque was laid and a street was named for him in Strelno, and the United States Navy named in his honor the Michelson Laboratory of the Naval Weapons Center at China Lake, California, Michelson Hall at the Naval Aca-demy, and an oceanographic ship, the USNS *Michelson*. Physicist Robert A. Millikan summed up the significance of Michelson's work, saying,

"The whole development of modern physics is ultimately bound up with Albert A. Michelson's precision of measurement." Millikan also took the trouble to point out that "Michelson received no religious training, had no interest in Judaism, and took no part in Jewish communal affairs."

In this, as in other facets of his exceptional personality, Michelson was extraordinary. Not all but certainly a large percentage of the early Jews in the Far West helped to organize and were active in Jewish religious and ethnic organiza-tions, or sought to maintain their ties to Jewish life in small, temporary groups or as individuals. The difference between their old-world tradi-tions and their radically new lives on the frontier caused considerable conflict in the early years. Presented with the necessity and provided with latitude to change, far western Jews created new forms as diverse as they were hard won.

Chapter Eight

A MATTER OF FAITH

In September 1849 in San Francisco, a reported thirty worshipers gathered in Lewis Franklin's tent store on Jackson Street to observe Rosh Hashanah, the Jewish New Year. This High Holy Day observance was the first known Jewish public worship service held in the Far West. Those who responded to the newspaper item announcing the service were of remarkably diverse origins and stations in life. They came from the United States, England, Australia, Poland, Prussia, and Bavaria. Some of those present were already well-known; others would become so. Among them were Joseph Shannon, future San Francisco County treasurer; Leon Dyer, officer in the Texas War of Independence and the Mexican War and longtime president of the first Baltimore Hebrew Congregation; Ben Davidson, financial agent for N. M. Rothschild and Company; and far western merchants Abraham Watters and Conrad Prag.

Albert Priest, a Sacramento merchant, chanted the Pentateuchal portion of the morning service, not from Torah scrolls—none could be found—but from a printed text. Those who recited the solemn and self-scrutinizing Rosh Hashanah prayers in that new and uncertain setting must have found the experience moving and told others. Ten days later, on Yom Kippur, the Day of Atonement, fifty Jews gathered for a second service.

The next few months in San Francisco were

Congregation Ryhim Ahoovim, Stockton, California, erected in 1855; courtesy, Holt-Atherton Pacific Center for Western Studies, Stockton, California

filled with life-threatening calamities. The city's first big fire razed the canvas-and-frame business district; fifty inches of winter rain slowed trade and construction; and widespread lootings and murders kept law-abiding San Franciscans on constant guard. Yet the first Jew to die was the victim of neither crime nor catastrophe but of a poisonous mushroom. He was Henry D. Johnson, son of an English Jew who had settled in Cincinnati in 1817 and brother of Edward Israel Johnson, who was killed at Goliad during the Texas War of Independence. Johnson's death on December 26, 1849, brought San Francisco's Jews together again, this time to discuss the acquisition of a burial ground as required by Jewish law. As a result of the meeting, a group of English, American, and Polish Jews formed the First Hebrew Benevolent Society to establish and maintain a Jewish cemetery, prepare their dead for burial, and assist the sick and needy. A committee of six headed by Henry Hart swiftly collected $4,000 and purchased cemetery land, two lots stretching from Broadway to Vallejo and from Gough to Franklin streets.

In early September 1850, with the High Holy Days again approaching, a committee calling itself the Kearney Street Congregation and headed by Leon Dyer gathered $500 and rented the Masonic Hall for services. Mrs. Keesing, Mrs. Berg, and Mrs. Simon decorated the room, which on Rosh Hashanah Eve was filled to capacity. Ten days later Lewis Franklin delivered an incisive Yom Kippur sermon. Franklin, a twenty-nine-year-old merchant, had been born in Liverpool

Lewis A. Franklin (1820–1879), a native of Liverpool, England, hosted the first known Jewish service held in the Far West. The event, a Rosh Hashanah service, took place in September 1849 in Franklin's tent store on Jackson Street in San Francisco. Ten days later worshippers returned to observe Yom Kippur. The next year, Franklin delivered a Yom Kippur sermon in a hall on Kearney Street. In the summer of 1851, Franklin moved to San Diego. That fall, he organized the first High Holy Day services in southern California. Courtesy, Norton B. Stern, Santa Monica

into a distinguished Polish Jewish family. Several of his brothers in England were high-ranking members of the leading Orthodox Anglo-Jewish organizations, and one, Jacob, had for five years published at his own expense a periodical opposing the emerging Jewish Reform movement. Dyer invited Franklin, a former business associate, to speak, confident that he was capable of preaching a sermon whose language and content the worshipers would find both comprehensible and uplifting.

Speaking in eloquent English, Franklin dwelt on the opportunities and the temptations to vice facing all new Californians. Like preachers of other faiths that year, he cautioned against runaway materialism. The feverish love of gold, like molten lead, cools and hardens, warned Franklin. He enjoined the worshipers to revere the gift of religious freedom and to use that freedom to practice their creed proudly. In keeping with the occasion, he pleaded for a renewed commitment to Jewish law, specifically the observance of the Sabbath, since few Jewish merchants refrained from doing business on that day. He also noted the common wish of the assembled to establish a permanent congregation and alluded to the obstacles thwarting that desire. There was already dissension among the worshipers, as was revealed in his forceful condemnation of disunity. (A small group had left Rosh Hashanah Eve to conduct their own service according to the Germanic *Minhag Ashkenaz* and, in all probability, had not returned for the service on Yom Kippur.)

The 1850 High Holy Days season concluded with a Simchat Torah service led by Leon Dyer. Afterward Dyer hosted an elaborate dinner at Philip Mann's Boarding House for a select group. Thus ended the short life of the Kearney Street Congregation. Dyer soon returned to Baltimore, and Franklin, who would move to San Diego in the summer of 1851, made no further effort to unite San Francisco Jewry.

Evidence that the breach was widening came on October 2, 1850, when August Helbing and a group of Bavarian Jews organized a second mutual-assistance group, the Eureka Benevolent Society. The "Baierns" claimed the "Pollacks," the Poles of the First Hebrew Benevolent Society, were turning away Bavarian needy. The accused countered with their own complaints. Thereafter, Jewish aid was dispensed along lines of national origin.

Still hoping to bridge their differences and establish a congregation together, members of both factions attended a meeting held in March 1851 at Philip Mann's Boarding House. Abraham Watters, a Prussian Jew, presided. The group made plans for a Passover celebration and initiated a building fund. A follow-up meeting at

Temple Sherith Israel, San Francisco, California, 1857; courtesy, California State Library, Sacramento

the end of the month showed encouraging progress. A total of $4,400 had been collected from 182 contributors living in San Francisco and elsewhere in California. The group met again a week later to elect officers and proceed with their building plans. At this third meeting, however, a bitter quarrel erupted, purportedly over the selection of a *shochet*, a ritual animal slaughterer, required to supervise the butchering and distribution of kosher meat. The Polish faction rejected the candidates offered by the Germanic group, and vice versa. Stubbornly clinging to their old differences (the shochet dispute was but one), they battled beyond the point of compromise. The same night, April 6, 1851, the first *two* congregations in the Far West were formed. Those committed to the Orthodox Minhag Polen—mainly the Poles, British, Americans of Anglo-Polish descent, and some Prussians—left the meeting as members of Congregation Sherith

Israel, while adherents of the Orthodox Minhag Ashkenaz—western and southern Germans, some Sephardic Americans, and at least one Prussian, Abraham Watters—became charter members of Congregation Emanu-El. Some French Jews would also lean toward Emanu-El until they were able to start their own social and religious circle. Within the next decade other groups formed, including the Shomrai Shabath, a coterie of thirty Orthodox Russian and Polish Jews who were strict observers of the Sabbath. However, none matched in size or vitality the first two congregations, which, like sibling rivals, would continue to compete, occasionally cooperate, and, when the need arose, stand together against a common threat.

Due as much to distinctions of class and nativity as to differences of a religious nature, to varying degrees, this schism between the supporters of the Polish rite and those of the Germanic persisted well into the twentieth century. During the early pioneer period, San Francisco was the only community with a Jewish population large enough to support two congregations. Elsewhere the first congregation was usually composed of Jews of various national origins and modes of worship. When more of their coreligionists arrived, some Jews, still bound to their old habits, divided into separate groups.

Although dissimilar in some respects, these trailblazing congregations had two traits in common: they were spontaneous expressions of the predilections of their organizers, and they were voluntary and self-sustaining. In Europe and to some extent in colonial America, religious affairs were regulated by government policies, but in the United States, with religion deemed a private matter, Jews were on their own. The organizations that sprang up in the Far West—*minyanim* (prayer groups), the benevolent and burial societies, and the permanent congregations that evolved therefrom—resembled similar groups east of the Rockies. Yet some distinctive characteristics, inherent at their inception, made these western bodies unique. Like the frontiersmen who created them, they were, even when traditional, less tradition-bound, more flexible, and more a part of the general community than older groups elsewhere. Also shaping them was the frontier ambience itself—spacious, sunny, full of wondrous scenery, simultaneously promising and laden with risk. Far removed from the entrenched European religious communities from which most of them came, their members were free to adhere to the old forms, or, as they emerged, to test new ones. In San Francisco the congregants of Sherith Israel chose to do the former; the members of Congregation Emanu-El, the latter.

One of the more penetrating descriptions of these two congregations was set down by Israel Joseph Benjamin, an able chronicler who came to San Francisco to study that city's nascent Jewish community. Benjamin sailed through the Golden Gate on August 24, 1860, noting for his readers the heavy waves, the cold breeze, the whales, and a "single sea-lion . . . its eyes shining." Surveying the scene and studying records, he swiftly conceded to California great wealth

Wandering Jewish chronicler Israel Joseph Benjamin; courtesy, American Jewish Archives, Cincinnati, Ohio

and beauty and an equal amount of misery. Concerning the state of Jewish affairs, this seasoned observer found much to praise. He was particularly impressed with what the two large congregations had accomplished in less than a decade, and doubted that comparable growth would have been possible in Europe in so short a period.

Benjamin was born in 1818 in Falticini, Moldavia, Rumania, of Yiddish-speaking, Polish Jewish parents. In 1845 he forsook his trade as a lumber merchant to embark on a seemingly quixotic mission: the study of Jewish communities throughout the world. He took his inspiration from Benjamin of Tudela, a twelfth-century scholar who traveled the globe in search of the lost tribes of Israel. To pay for his travels, Benjamin II, as Israel Joseph called himself, sought contributions and subscriptions for the books he proposed to write. By the time he arrived in San Francisco, his *Five Years of Travel in the Orient, 1846–1851,* which he wrote in German, had been published in French, German, and Hebrew, and he was gathering material for his next work, *Three Years in America, 1859–1862.* To his investigative task Benjamin brought an extensive Jewish education; firsthand knowledge of Jewish life in Europe, Africa, and Asia; and solid years of reportorial experience. He was clearly partial to Orthodoxy, and his quill could turn indulgent or vituperative, depending on how his requests for financial assistance were received. But his perceivable prejudices only slightly affected his ability to take measure of a congregation and identify where it fit on the Jewish spectrum.

Sherith Israel, reported Benjamin, had 110 congregants and a handsome, capacious synagogue on Stockton Street. The service especially delighted the peripatetic traditionalist. It followed the "correct Polish Minhag," was strictly

Dr. Henry A. Henry, Temple Sherith Israel, 1857; courtesy, Western Jewish History Center, Judah L. Magnes Museum, Berkeley, California

Orthodox, and was "conducted in the true Jewish manner of our ancient ancestors."

Dr. Henry A. Henry, a fifty-two-year-old native of England, was the rabbi at the time of Benjamin's visit. Henry had been ordained by Orthodox Rabbi Herschell of London and had served as tutor to the great Rothschild family for several years. He had emigrated from England in 1849 and had served congregations in Cincinnati and New York before he came to San Francisco in January 1857 to fill the pulpit at Sherith Israel. An author on Jewish themes, Henry had brought with him the most extensive Jewish library Benjamin had seen in America. The rabbi received the wayfarer warmly and frequently, as did his congregants. Sherith Israel's board gave Benjamin a $250 contribution, with an invitation to ask for more should he need it.

At the larger and more costly Temple Emanu-El, located on Broadway, was Daniel Levy, a cantor and teacher who had translated Benjamin's book on the Orient from German to French. Other than Levy, of whom he was fond, Benjamin saw little to praise at Temple Emanu-El, the first congregation in the West to experiment with the new American Reform practices. His distaste for Reform Judaism occasionally spilled over his professional guard, but he did his best to concentrate on the facts.

Emanu-El's first house of worship, noted Benjamin, had been completed in 1854 at a cost of $35,000, and a new, $100,000 edifice was being planned. The congregation had brought Dr. Julius Eckman, the first congregational rabbi in the Far West, to San Francisco in 1854. (Benjamin failed to note that the scholarly, middle-aged, unwed, and impoverished rabbi lasted but a year in this post.) Rabbi Eckman, a graduate of the University of Berlin, had been ordained by Leopold Zunz, the nestor of modern Jewish scholarship in western Europe. But Eckman hovered between Orthodoxy and Reform, and lacking a well-defined program for change, he proved a poor guide for a congregation of aggressive pioneers in search of rites to match their new lives. According to Benjamin, Dr. Elkan Cohn, who assumed the post in 1860 (and kept it for twenty-nine years), "avers to all Orthodoxy [and] introduced Reform in its place." Cohn, a native of

Left: *The Temple Emanu-El in San Francisco—the Sutter Street Temple—was completed in 1866 at a cost of $134,000. The onion-domed landmark was destroyed in the 1906 earthquake and fire. Courtesy, Norton B. Stern, Santa Monica, California*

Right: *Reform rabbi Dr. Elkan Cohn, Congregation Emanu-El, San Francisco; courtesy, Congregation Emanu-El, San Francisco, California*

Posen, as was Eckman, had studied with renowned Orthodox scholars Rabbi Isaac Eger and Akiba Eger the Younger as well as with German Reformer Levi Herzfeld, and he had earned a doctorate in classics at the University of Berlin. In the United States Cohn had served a congregation in Albany, New York, and was considered a valued supporter of the American Reform movement before he came to Emanu-El. Cohn was well paid at $3,000 a year plus perquisites and swiftly earned respect as a preacher, scholar, and institutional organizer. When Benjamin worshiped at Emanu-El, reforms introduced by the new rabbi were already in practice. Men and women sat in family pews, a shorter service was in use, and there was organ music with a choir.

To convey to his readers the concerns of a modern American congregation, Benjamin included the annual report of 1860 submitted by congregation president Henry Seligman. The president noted congregants' deaths and births, the new members (forty-nine), monthly expenses ($800), and the state of the mortgage (almost paid up). He lavishly praised the work of the new spiritual leader and looked ahead to increased members and larger facilities. In closing his description, Seligman expressed the hope that now that they had "crossed over the treacherous strait [Cohn's reforms], the congregation could resume its past harmony."

As further evidence of the prevailing spirit, Benjamin footnoted that the board, on Seligman's recommendation, had agreed to give him $250, but he had never collected the much-needed donation. A member had tirelessly lobbied against the gift. As a result, reported Benjamin, "there were no less than five sessions held about me that decided now 'aye' now 'nay' until the 'nays' won."

In February 1861 Benjamin set out to cover the rest of the western frontier. By steamer and stagecoach he journeyed through California, the Pacific Northwest, Nevada, Utah, and eastward over the Rockies. Spending days in one place,

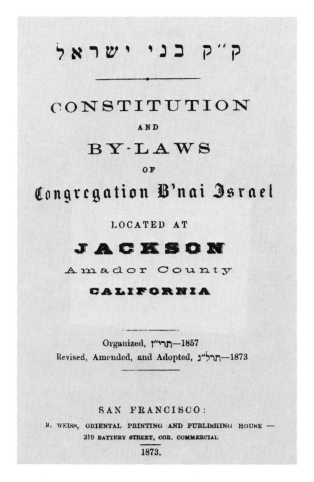

ק"ק בני ישראל

CONSTITUTION

AND

BY·LAWS

OF

Congregation B'nai Israel

LOCATED AT

JACKSON

Amador County

CALIFORNIA

Organized, תרי"ז—1857
Revised, Amended, and Adopted, תרל"ג—1873

SAN FRANCISCO:

M. WEISS, ORIENTAL PRINTING AND PUBLISHING HOUSE —
319 BATTERY STREET, COR. COMMERCIAL

1873.

Courtesy, The Bancroft Library, University of California, Berkeley

hours in another, wherever he stopped he sought out Jewish brethren. Benjamin estimated that in addition to the five thousand Jews living in San Francisco in 1860, there was an equal number elsewhere in California. In the mining-supply center of Sacramento he found five hundred Jewish inhabitants and the Congregation B'nai Israel Synagogue, consecrated in 1852, the first permanent Jewish house of worship in the state. The Jewish population of Stockton, another gold rush supply center, had declined to twenty-six, but the Rhyim Ahoovim Synagogue and cemetery, established there in 1855, were still in use. He also visited the Beth Israel, or B'nai Israel Synagogue in Jackson, but missed the "Bench Berith" (B'nai B'rith) in Placerville, according to

the San Francisco *Weekly Gleaner* issue published September 29, 1858.

Throughout California and the Pacific Northwest, Benjamin discovered pockets of Jewish population. Among the larger and better-organized communities were those in Los Angeles and Marysville, California; Portland, Oregon; and Victoria, British Columbia. Each had approximately one hundred congregants, a cemetery, and a benevolent society. Where Benjamin found Jews but no organization, he summoned his local coreligionists and initiated one. For example, during his brief stopovers in California, the thirty Jews in Mokelumne Hill and the twenty-three in Folsom established benevolent societies with his help.

Crossing the Sierra Nevada by stagecoach, he continued his mission in Virginia City, Nevada, where he counted fifty Jews, and in Carson City, where he found twenty. By the time he reached Salt Lake City, the Jewish presence was running thin. Benjamin found only five Jews there, two of whom had converted to Mormonism. Thereafter he saw no evidence of Jewish activity until his stage stopped at a small oasis near the Rocky Mountains. There he encountered no Jewish people but did come upon a Jewish newspaper, the *American Israelite*, published in Cincinnati and edited by Rabbi Isaac Mayer Wise, founder of the Reform movement in America.

The scarcity of Jews Benjamin witnessed was temporary. As gold mining declined in California, new mineral discoveries and agricultural and trade opportunities opened the vast wilderness between California and Missouri and in the Pacific Northwest from 1860 to 1880. Jews fanned out into hundreds of raw frontier settlements. In new mining boom towns or trade centers, if the Jewish population rose to one hundred or more, rudimentary organizations—minyan, cemetery, and benevolent society—quickly appeared and often resulted in a permanent congregation. In remote villages, camps, and outposts, from one to a dozen or more Jewish settlers marked important religious holidays or milestone events together or, if necessary, entirely alone. Whether these pioneers participated in an organization or a temporary group or prayed alone, their precarious life on the frontier allowed little time for religious observances. Yet thousands maintained their religious identity for decades with not much more than pioneer ingenuity and the wish to remain Jewish. Indeed, some who initially lacked that desire, when afforded the solace of nature and a time for reflection, regained a lost appreciation for Jewish life and thought.

The success of frontier Judaism was in part the result of the laissez-faire outlook concerning religion in the early Far West. In the beginning, non-Jewish frontier busters tended to be curious but baffled by their Jewish neighbors' religious practices. In fall 1865 Denver's *Rocky Mountain News* reported: "Today is some sort of a holiday for the Jewish persuasion, unknown to us Gentiles. Business houses kept by that class in town are closed from 'rosy morn' till dewy eve."

Not long after, though, William Byers of the *Rocky Mountain News* was regularly dispensing Jewish news with ease, as did other frontier journalists, such as the one who noted for the readers of the *Arizona Miner* in September 1880 that "Yom Kipoor" was imminent and the "Israelites of Prescott observe the day by closing their places of business and assemble for worship."

Non-Jews could even be surprisingly helpful. In the fall of 1867, a troubled year for non-Mormons in Salt Lake City, Brigham Young offered the Jews a church building to use for the High Holy Days. The local newspaper reported:

The descendants of Judah assembled yesterday in the Seventies Hall to inaugurate the New Year of 5829 [the year was 5628]. . . . Messers. Wood, Watters, and Ellis were the readers. Mr. Prag blows the shofar, in other words, the ram's horn.

The effectiveness of Judaism in the West was attributable to an even greater extent to the nature of the religion. Judaism was born in the desert, the faith of nomads. After the Jews established a homeland, a temple theocracy developed. The destruction of the temple in Jerusalem, first at the hands of the Chaldeans and later by the Romans, called forth new and mobile institutions—the small synagogue and the acad-

The first known Jewish wedding in the Arizona Territory took place in 1879 in the home of Mrs. H. Solomon of Tucson. The bride was Lillie Marks of Oroville, California, and the groom, Joseph Goldtree, an early Arizona settler. Courtesy, Arizona Historical Society, Tucson

emy. Moreover, a growing body of religious literature emerged—liturgy, commentaries, codes, and responsa—that kept the faith evolving and assisted Jews far from their ancestral home to retain their religious integrity. A simple, democratic, nonhierarchical, and group-centered format developed. Then as today, some prayers were recitable by an individual in solitude, but the core of traditional practice was daily communal worship with a quorum of ten men (Reform and some Conservative Jews now count women as well). Everyone participated, and any knowledgeable member of the assembly could lead, except in the performance of a few rites that required a blessing by a Jew of priestly descent, such as a *Pidyon Ha-Ben* (redemption of the firstborn).

Rarely able to carry out these practices on a daily basis, most pioneer Jews did what they could when they could to preserve their religious ties. In a number of frontier towns a lay leader stepped forward who for years organized and led communal worship and presided at marriage and burial services, which, in accordance with Jewish law, could be conducted by any knowledgeable Jew in the presence of two witnesses.

The first known Jewish wedding in the Arizona Territory was celebrated on June 26, 1879, with the fanfare appropriate to a frontier first. The groom was Joseph Goldtree of Berlin; the bride, Lillie Marks of Oroville, California, the niece of Mrs. H. Soloman, at whose Tucson home the event took place. The *Arizona Daily Star* took pains to report:

The ceremony opened with blessing for the bride and groom recited by everybody belonging to the faith and witnesses of the marriage, after which the silver cup containing wine was given first to the bride and then to the bridegroom. Then the bridegroom took hold of the bride's first finger of the right hand and repeated in Hebrew, "Thou art sanctified unto me with this ring."

The name of the Jewish officiant was not included. It could have been Sam Drachman, who served as lay leader of Tucson Jewry from shortly after he arrived in 1867 until his death in 1911. For his family and many members of the community, no wedding was official without Uncle Sam.

Other Jewish lay leaders in the Far West served their communities as long and as well as Sam Drachman. Nathan and Amalia (Oppenheimer) Colman moved from Denver to booming Deadwood in the Black Hills of South Dakota in 1877. There Nathan opened a tobacco store; the next year he was appointed justice of the peace, a post he held until his death in 1906. Colman officiated at the first "Hebrew" wedding in the Black Hills on November 4, 1879, joining in matrimony Rebecca Reubens and David Holzman. Twenty-six years later, still in good form, Nathan performed the wedding ceremony for

Pioneer infant's grave, Shasta County, California; Hebrew translation: *Here lies buried the boy Elchanan son of Eliakin Brownstein from the city of Red Bluff. Born on the 24th day of the month of 24 Adair in the year 5624 and died the 15th day of Kislev in the year 5625 from the creation of the world. Courtesy, California State Department of Parks and Recreation*

his daughter Anne, the only one of his three daughters to marry. The service was described as "one of the most beautiful and unique ever observed." The bridegroom was identified as a "young businessman well known in Deadwood and Lead [South Dakota]" and the bride as "belonging to one of the oldest and most esteemed of Deadwood's families."

Also worthy of notice are the frontier funerals conducted by these lay leaders. Circumstances surrounding these events often revealed the innermost feelings and attachments of these pioneers and their families. Some peripatetic seekers were brought to rest in a section fenced off for Jews in the local cemetery of the last town they inhabited. For example, Amalia and Nathan Colman and all but one of their children are buried on "Hebrew Hill" in the Jewish portion of Deadwood's Mount Moriah Cemetery. Adjacent are the graves of more pioneer Jews (about forty-four in all) who, along with other denizens of the Black Hills—among them, Calamity Jane (Badge) and Wild Bill Hickok—called Deadwood home.

Other Jews ended their lives in one place but had deeper ties elsewhere. Bertha Strouse, mother of Sheriff Mark Strouse, died in Virginia City, Nevada, on December 24, 1875, and asked to be returned to California to be buried alongside her two sons in the Jewish section of the Mokelumne Hill Cemetery. Another gold rush California resident, Melanie Reeb, who succumbed in Spokane, Washington, in 1912, wanted her remains sent to the Sonora Cemetery in California for burial alongside her husband, Moses. Josephine Sarah Marcus Earp chose as her final stop the Marcus family plot in the Jewish Hills of Eternity cemetery in Colma, California (near San Francisco). She and her common-law husband, Wyatt, who died before her, are buried there side by side. Wrote Josie, by way of explanation: "Wyatt's family were almost all gone and we had no children. My only home was where my parents rest. So I took Wyatt's ashes to San Francisco." A number of others who, like Josie, lived apart from Jewish life also chose to rejoin the flock in death. Gabriel Levy of Signal, Arizona Territory, who had a long liaison with Tula Leivas Eshom and fathered two of her children, chose as his burial site the Levy family plot at a Jewish cemetery in San Francisco.

Some funerals also made it clear that the general community expected Jews to be responsible for their destitute or itinerant coreligionists. A wayfaring tightrope walker fell to his death in Corsicana, Texas, in the early 1900s. The city fathers, believing the man was a Jew, turned over his remains to the leaders of the Jewish community for burial. After some discussion, the nameless performer was interred in the Corsicana Jewish cemetery under a headstone bearing all available information: ROPEWALKER.

Many Jews on the far western frontier belonged to a fraternal organization that made funeral arrangements for its members and, in some places, maintained cemeteries. One such group, the Independent Order of B'nai B'rith (IOBB), was the only Jewish organization in Tucson in June 1883, when Henry Schaber, a sixty-two-year-old businessman, committed suicide there. On June 8 the *Arizona Daily Star* bannered an account of Schaber's death: "TIRED OF LIFE—Shuffling Off This Mortal Coil with Aid of a Bulldog [pistol]." The *Star* attributed the deed to Schaber's despondence over failure to conclude a mine sale for which he had expected to earn a $10,000 commission. Local authorities asked the B'nai B'rith to bury the deceased. The IOBB, it turned out, prohibited the burial of suicides, so the individual members personally raised a collection and escorted the remains at the funeral.

On the frontier, more difficult to adhere to than laymen-led observances were Jewish rites requiring the services of a skilled practitioner (preferably one who had been trained and certified and who was supervised), such as a *mohel*, a circumciser, or a *shochet*, a ritual slaughterer of animals and fowl. Most pioneer Jews took whatever measures were necessary to have their infant sons circumcised, since the failure to do so could not be easily remedied at a later date. Some transported the babies to a mohel in a far-off city. Others were affluent enough to have the practitioner come to them. In November 1866 Abraham Galland, a mohel much in demand on the Pacific Coast, sailed to the Hawaiian Islands to "bring one of [King] Kalakaua's youngest subjects into the fold of Abraham." In April 1872 the Reverend H. Lovenberg of Elko, Nevada, traveled to the City of Saints in order to perform circumcisions on the infant sons of Samuel Kahn and a Mr. Heilbronner.

The majority of these pioneers waited for an itinerant mohel to make an appearance in their community. One of the most widely respected of these circuit-riding mohelim was Dr. John Elsner, who arrived in Denver in 1866. The descendant of a four-hundred-year-old line of physicians, Elsner, a native of Vienna, was educated in Prague and New York. He was graduated from the New York Eye and Ear Infirmary at twenty-two; soon thereafter, he set off with a mining company for Colorado. Elsner became one of Denver's most valued early citizens. In 1870, as the newly appointed county physician, he organized a thirty-nine-bed hospital. He also

Prominent Denver physician and traveling mohel, Dr. John Elsner *(third from left); courtesy, Colorado Historical Society, Denver*

founded the Denver Medical Society, chaired a committee on Colorado diseases, founded and taught at Gross Medical College, and collected specimens that formed the basis of the mineral collection at the state historical museum. Elsner was also a leading figure in Jewish organizations: B'nai B'rith, Temple Emanuel, and the Colorado branch of the Jewish Theological Seminary.

Elsner viewed his duties as a mohel as his religious and professional obligations. He performed circumcisions throughout Colorado, New Mexico, Wyoming, and Nebraska. Between 1867 and 1905 his well-kept records showed 169 entries specifying date, age, and Hebrew names of child and father.

More laborious and, for the majority of early pioneer Jews, less obligatory was the maintenance of dietary laws requiring the services of a shochet. By 1850 the San Francisco Jewish population was large enough to support several. Even a smaller Jewish community would occasionally give the dietary laws high priority and would hire its own shochet. In 1861 Congregation B'nai B'rith in Los Angeles, spurred by lay leader Joseph Newmark, brought Abraham Wolf Edelman from San Francisco to serve as its rabbi-cantor-teacher, mohel, and shochet. As one of his daily duties, Edelman would slaughter cattle and sheep to provide the kosher meat needed by his congregants.

Observant Orthodox Jews in sparsely inhabited or remote areas handled the matter individually or as a family. Their practices often attracted attention and comment. The family of Wolf Sabolsky, who opened a store in Helena, Montana, in the 1870s, provides an example. At Mrs. Sabolsky's death, the *Helena Daily Independent* described her as "probably the most orthodox Jew in the state. . . . So rigid was her observance that she might be said to have been a vegetarian. . . . At times there would be killed for her a chicken according to the rules of her religion, and that was the extent of her meat eating."

Adelaide and Henry Bloch, early Jewish residents of Portland, were remembered as keeping a kosher home long after most of their fellow Jews had given up. After a debilitating bout with diphtheria, however, Adelaide also ceased making the extra effort. A member of a well-known eastern European pioneer clan, Mary (Rachovsky) Kobey also stood out as a model of unswerving piety. She arrived in Colorado in the late 1860s an observant Orthodox Jew and was no less so when she died thirty-five years later. Mary and her equally pious husband, Samuel Abrum, started out with their relatives, the Rittmasters and Rachovskys, in Central City, high in the Rockies. For a period Mary had kosher meat shipped up the mountain from Denver, but because it usually arrived spoiled, the family became vegetarian. As soon as it was possible, the Kobeys, yearning for a traditional Jewish community life, moved to Denver. There, both husband and wife became prominent and useful members of the Orthodox community. Samuel served as a rabbi for Agudas Achim Synagogue, and Mary became a busy midwife.

Free to practice their religious preferences, the early pioneers (1849–1880) fell into four general categories. A small number were professional officiants, lay leaders, and dedicated congregants who devoted a great deal of thought and energy to the building and operation of Jewish religious and communal organizations in the Far West. They drew some support and inspiration from national Jewish bodies once these groups were established: the Board of Delegates of American Israelites, founded in 1859; the (Reform) Union of American Hebrew Congregations, founded in 1873. (The [Conservative] United Synagogues of America was not founded until 1913.) Nonetheless, these local institution builders remained largely responsible for the progress of their self-governing organizations. A second and much larger group wished to remain practicing Jews—some as traditionalists, others as modernists—but were too occupied with their city or frontier enterprises to attend daily, or even weekly, services. Those who were able supported congregations financially; attended important services or meetings; and observed Jewish marriage, birth, and death rites. A third segment lined up on the freethinking side of the then-popular debate between science and religion and refused to belong to any religious group. Instead, many of them joined Jewish social and fraternal organizations, and if they took a spouse of another faith, they tended to retain their Jewish friends and affiliations. Members of a fourth category, few in number, took pains to eradicate their Jewish identity permanently by denial or conversion, evaporating into the crowd.

By 1878 there were twenty congregations in the Far West, twice the number I. J. Benjamin had counted in 1860. For an eighteen-year period in a swiftly expanding region, however, the amount of increase was unimpressive. Some rea-

sons for the organizational slowdown were the Civil War, the ephemeral nature of much of the growth on the frontier, and a widespread depression in the 1870s. When Rabbi Isaac Mayer Wise toured the West in the summer of 1877 seeking support for the American Reform movement, he was enthusiastically received, but he left with promises instead of money. Wise, however, did not despair. He found among the San Franciscans many, indeed, "who were public-spirited and munificent" and left assured that support would be forthcoming at a later date.

During this highly transitional era, some congregations were still struggling to integrate their ill-matched elements. A wide chasm, for example, often yawned between a rudely tutored congregation and their spiritual leader, who might hold a doctorate from a leading European university and have been ordained by a renowned sage. Sometimes, as Harriet Lane Levy described in her book *920 O'Farrell Street*, love spanned the distance. Concealing the names of leader and flock, Levy vividly preserved one of the most positive of these relationships.

The rabbi had left his seat and slowly mounted to the reading desk. Olive-skinned, tall and slender, he looked like a prince of Egypt. A coldly intellectual man, he was curiously misplaced in the orthodox pulpit of a congregation of merchants and shopkeepers. His mental endowment was beyond their need, and when he graciously trained upon them the full strength of his eloquence, it was less for their edification than to give exercise to his own accomplishment. His congregation loved him, reaching with satisfaction toward an erudition beyond their understanding.

Some congregations were shifting from the traditional to the increasingly popular Reform mode during those years. The transition often generated great volatility, at times erupting into embarrassing public displays. One conflict at Congregation Beth Israel in Portland between 1872 and 1880 went from solemn to antic to near tragic. Though more extreme than was usual, the struggle contained the usual seeds of disagreement: an ongoing intracongregational dispute over traditional and Reform worship, agitated factions, a spiritual leader who made up in arrogance what he lacked in credentials, and

Rabbi Moses May and his confirmation class in Portland, Oregon, 1878; courtesy, Oregon Jewish Historical Society, Portland

frontier peoples' unfortunate tendency to be quick on the trigger.

Just before teacher and cantor Moses May was hired to serve as acting rabbi at Beth Israel, a disgruntled group had walked out to form a traditional congregation with Dr. Julius Eckman, formerly of San Francisco's Temple Emanu-El, as their rabbi. One remaining faction expected Rabbi May to establish Reform practice, something another group firmly opposed. In favor of the change, May tried to persuade the board to adopt Wise's *Minhag America* prayerbook and other Reform practices. Rabbi May got his *Minhag America*, but it was ill received, and Orthodox rituals continued to dominate.

Rabbi May's supporters somehow got him reelected for another three years in 1877. A year later, however, his detractors gained control and sought to replace him with an officiant committed to the Orthodox prayer book. Boardroom battles ensued. May was accused of libertine behavior, of impugning the virtue of the women congregants, and of lack of faith. He countered with charges of slander and ignorance.

The hostilities came to a head on a Portland street on September 30, 1880. Congregant Abraham Waldman, who headed the temple's religious school committee, accused May of ungentlemanly conduct. Passing Waldman's store soon after, May shouted through the door, "You're a liar!" When Waldman next saw his spiritual leader, he was in conversation on a street corner. Waldman pounced on him and tore at his coat. May whipped out a pistol and shot at Waldman twice (the bullets went astray). Before May could shoot again, the police interceded. May vanished soon after, and the congregants eventually found their way to Reform under the more temperate Rabbi Jacob Bloch.

Some congregations staunchly maintained their traditional stances. Among them were Ohabai Shalome and Beth Israel, founded in 1864 and 1872, respectively, in San Francisco; and Ahavai Shalom, established in 1872 in Portland. By radical decree or slow accommodation, many more shifted to Reform practices. Some of the more prominent and long-established of them were the first "Polish" synagogue in San

The traditional Congregation Ohabai Shalome was established in San Francisco in 1864. The Moorish-style synagogue was erected in 1898 on Bush Street to accommodate a growing membership. Courtesy, Congregation Ohabai Shalome Collection, Western Jewish History Center, Judah L. Magnes Museum, Berkeley, California

Francisco, Sherith Israel, founded in 1851; and Congregation B'nai B'rith, started in Los Angeles between 1862 and 1863.

In the 1880s a combination of social and economic cross currents energized new Jewish organizational activity. One significant spur was the growth of far western cities. As mining declined and the frontier shrank, Jews and other pioneers moved to expanding urban centers to enjoy the fruits of their success or to nurse their frontier wounds. Newly arriving eastern European immigrants also added significantly to the far western Jewish population. Their presence gave rise to new Orthodox and Conservative synagogues such as Beth Israel (Olive Street Shul) and Sinai Temple in Los Angeles, the former in 1892, the latter in 1906; Beth Hamedrosh Hagadol, Denver, in 1897; and Bikur Cholim, Seattle, in 1891.

More spectacular was the proliferation of Reform temples—reflecting the popularity of the Reform movement in the Far West—and the temple-building boom it inspired. The prime movers in these congregations were among the best-established Jews in the region. On the frontier, they had given up their European or more traditional ways and had been richly rewarded in material gain and power. Grateful and self-congratulating, they loved America and loved being Americans. The Reform movement gave them a way to practice Judaism in American attire, language, and music, expressing their allegiance to their new homeland and to its values. Heightening their interest in Jewish institutions at the time was their recent exclusion from elite Gentile circles. Screened out of high, non-Jewish social echelons, still eager to express their permanence and prominence in the Far West, dy-

Another of San Francisco's early traditional synagogues was Congregation Beth Israel, founded ifn 1872. The imposing house of worship shown above, the congregation's fourth, was completed on Geary Street between Fillmore and Steiner in 1908. Courtesy, Congregation Beth Israel Collection, Western Jewish History Center, Judah L. Magnes Museum, Berkeley, California

namic, well-heeled leaders poured their money and energy into Jewish religious and communal buildings. Manning the building committees were figures prominent in local and state affairs, such as Moses Alexander of Boise, Idaho; I. W. Hellman of Los Angeles and San Francisco; David May and Simon Guggenheim of Denver; Simon Bamberger of Salt Lake City; and Bailey Gatzert of Seattle. Bold entrepreneurs and able politicos, they envisioned a house of worship as a hymn to their triumph in the West, and they spared no expense.

Hymns to Jewish Success

Around the turn of the century, Reform temples rose in middle and upper class neighborhoods in burgeoning cities throughout the Far West. Costly, of eclectic design, these houses of worship were eloquent expressions of Jewish integration and affluence in the Far West.

Temple Emanu-El established in 1889 in Helena, Montana, erected in 1891; courtesy, Montana Historical Society, Helena

Temple Beth Israel, established in 1895 in Boise, Idaho, erected in 1896; courtesy, Idaho Historical Society, Boise

The congregation Beth Israel, established in 1858 in Portland, Oregon, built this temple in 1889. Courtesy, Herbert Bernhard Collection, Beverly Hills, California

As the number of congregations in the Far West increased, so did the competition for suitable spiritual leaders. Before 1840 few ordained rabbis would consider coming to the notoriously irreligious United States. Those who did come might be out of favor at home or in flight from personal problems; or they were missionaries willing to sacrifice a few years to the reclamation of the ignorant, if not downright sinful, American Jews. Between 1840 and 1880 more rabbis, German Reform and Orthodox, were among the tens of thousands of Jews entering the New World. The most desirable were snapped up by congregations east of the Rockies or by the few affluent groups on the West Coast. After the first American rabbinical schools, the Reform Hebrew Union College (HUC), founded in 1875, and the Jewish Theological Seminary, established in 1887, began graduating spiritual leaders, the problem eased. As more rabbis capable of leading a modern, American congregation became available, a coterie of distinguished Jewish spiritual leaders emerged in the Far West. They brought a fountainhead of Jewish knowledge and practice to their congregants and to Jews in surrounding hinterlands. They also provided models of exemplary Jews to the public at large and stimulated interest in human betterment, education, and aid to the needy. Representative of these spiritual leaders were such men as Leopold Freudenthal of Trinidad, Colorado; Rabbi Martin Zielonka of El Paso, Texas; and Dr. William Friedman of Denver.

Leopold Freudenthal was the first rabbi to hold the pulpit at the Reform Temple Aaron in Trinidad, a small coal-mining town on the Purgatoire River in southern Colorado. He arrived in December 1889. His initial rabbinical duty was to lead a dedication ceremony for the unusually handsome, two-story brick and sandstone temple, graced by stained-glass windows vividly illustrating biblical scenes. During his twenty-six years in office, the learned rabbi, a graduate of Heidelberg University, actively encouraged Jewish practice and disseminated Judaic values in this coal and railroad center. Rabbi Freudenthal's duties included counseling, a weekly service, and direction of the Sunday school. Both

the school and his Holy Day services drew people from fifty miles around. Freudenthal also traveled in southern Colorado and New Mexico to officiate at marriages, burials, and circumcisions and to conduct Bar Mitzvah services. Freudenthal's circumcision record book shows he performed the rite on about two hundred Jewish infants. He was also an active Mason and an influential member of the Trinidad School Board.

By the turn of the century, natural gas and oil were cutting into Trinidad's coal profits and slowing business. Many Jewish merchants began seeking a livelier marketplace. As the congregation dwindled, the rabbi agreed to two salary cuts. When he died in 1916, another rabbi briefly held his office. Then one of Freudenthal's dedicated followers, Gilbert Sanders, a member of a pioneer Jewish family of Trinidad and an attorney and respected civic leader, took over as lay rabbi.

Rabbi Leopold Freudenthal (1848–1916) was the spiritual leader of Temple Aaron in Trinidad, Colorado, from 1889 until his death in 1916. Courtesy, Beatrice Sanders, Trinidad, Colorado

Rabbi Martin Zielonka, El Paso, Texas, 1912; courtesy, El Paso Public Library, El Paso, Texas

Freudenthal's sons, Samuel, a prominent Colorado attorney, and Alfred, a surgeon, continued to support their father's temple. When Alfred, a bachelor, died, his $400,000 estate went to Temple Aaron. Sanders, his attorney, created the Alfred Freudenthal Memorial Trust Fund to perpetuate Judaism in the area.

Rabbi Martin Zielonka was twenty-three when he became spiritual guide of Temple Mt. Sinai in El Paso. Born in Berlin and educated in the United States, Zielonka was ordained at the Hebrew Union College in 1899 and had served a Waco, Texas, congregation for a year. In the next thirty-eight active years, he earned the devotion of his congregants, including a small group of traditionalists who remained with Mt. Sinai until a Conservative synagogue formed. He also became "rabbi" to Jews throughout the Southwest who had no other spiritual leader.

Emulating his congregants in this town on the Mexican border, Zielonka became a Spanish-speaking southwesterner. He lent his influence to a variety of causes, including helping to or-

ganize the El Paso Health League and serving as the director of the College of the City of El Paso until 1920.

In 1908 the Central Conference of American Rabbis sent Zielonka to Mexico on a mission that would interest him for the rest of his life. He was to find out how many Jews were living in Mexico and under what conditions, and he was to determine whether Mexico would make a feasible destination for some of the millions of eastern European Jews who were then fleeing their homelands.

This *figura rara,* as one reporter called the rabbi, found a thin scattering of Jews all over Mexico, with an estimated five hundred in Mexico City. Only one small congregation, of Syrian Jews, was in operation, and many others had ceased to acknowledge that they were of Jewish descent. Zielonka was initially enthusiastic about the resettlement of Jews in Mexico: Its natural resources were rich, the climate moderate, and the economic opportunities abundant. During his brief stay, however, the disadvantage of pervasive political unrest caused him to change his mind. The revolution that raged in Mexico between 1910 and 1917 made immigration infeasible. When the conflict ended, however, the B'nai B'rith built on the Jewish settlement work initiated by Zielonka. Thousands of Jews would eventually settle in Mexico, a large number of them personally assisted by Zielonka.

William Stern Friedman, the spiritual leader at Temple Emanuel in Denver for half a century, embodied most of what was praiseworthy and problematic about the American Reform movement. He was an outstanding product of the ideology, skills, and loyalties Hebrew Union College inculcated in its rabbinical students, who were young, bright, idealistic, usually poor, and often orphaned.

Friedman was born in Chicago in 1868; he soon lost his parents and was raised in the Chicago Orphan Asylum. At twenty-one, when he graduated from Hebrew Union, he was already a strong enough leader to guide his first congregation, Denver's sixteen-year-old, conflict-torn Temple Emanuel, out of chaos and into the American Reform camp. In addition to his con-

Rabbi William Stern Friedman (1868–1944), Temple Emanuel, Denver, Colorado; courtesy, Rocky Mountain Jewish Historical Society, Denver, Colorado

gregational work, he swiftly established himself as a leader in charity work and would continue to help the underprivileged, particularly the sick and homeless (Denver had a substantial population of indigent tuberculars), throughout his long tenure. He helped organize and fund the National Jewish Hospital in 1890 and actively served that institution for twenty-five years. From 1890 to 1901 he served as vice-president of the Charity Organization Society, and served on the governing boards of the Colorado Conference of Charities and Corrections and other public welfare agencies.

An eloquent orator and brilliant writer, Friedman expressed his views on a variety of Jewish and general issues. His public utterances and sermons, widely circulated and discussed, rendered him spokesman for Reform Judaism in Denver, and his fervent advocacy of American ideals, prophetic Judaism, and ecumenicism made him a model for all Denver Jews who sought the privileges and responsibilities of full

membership in the mainstream community. His congregants were among the most affluent and powerful in Denver—David May, Simon Guggenheim, and Louis Shoenberg were among them. Friedman's anti-Zionist views earned him enemies, particularly as the need for a Jewish homeland became more pressing. He continued to oppose American Zionism until conditions in Europe in the 1930s convinced him that the establishment of a Jewish state was more crucial than the American Jews' risk of being accused of maintaining a dual loyalty.

While the early pioneers were proclaiming their permanence in the Far West with the construction of costly religious facilities, America's third and largest Jewish immigration commenced. Between 1881 and 1912, eastern Europeans, mostly Yiddish speaking, helped swell American Jewry from a quarter million in 1881 to more than two million in 1910. (Another million arrived before immigration closed in 1924.) Thousands came west, more than tripling the

A Russian Jew illustrated by Frederick Jackson; courtesy, Nostalgia Press, Flushing, New York

size and changing the course and the character of far western Jewry.

These late pioneers (1881–1912) were not the first eastern European Jews to venture into the Far West. As already noted, eastern Europeans—from Poland, Polish Prussia (Posen), Russian Poland, Russia, Latvia, Bohemia, Hungary, and Lithuania—figured prominently among the earliest pioneers in the Far West. They flung themselves into frontier life, built enterprises, started families, held public office, and swiftly Americanized, much like their German-speaking brethren between 1848 and 1880. Some of their number slipped into the German Jewish milieu, which was considered more cultured (Germany's Jews had earlier access to higher ed-

ucation) and was often more affluent. Many more retained their own native affiliation, as their dedication to their largely Orthodox and Conservative institutions attest.

Eastern European Jews who came to the Far West after 1881 tended to adapt more slowly than did their predecessors. One among many reasons was the fact that they had lived in the backwaters of eastern Europe, cut off from the ferment of modern thought. In the late eighteenth century millions of Jews were driven from their homes and forced to relocate in primitive agrarian or trade towns in the undeveloped "Pale of Settlement," a vast, impoverished section of western Russia, and in portions of Poland and the Austro-Hungarian Empire. In 1855 the reforms of Alexander II permitted Jews some access to the awakening Russian society, but after the monarch was murdered by terrorists in 1881, persecution more violent than ever began. The harsh new regime of Alexander III blamed the Jews for the assassination and incited peasant mobs to pogroms. Rioters overran hundreds of Jewish towns, forcing the inhabitants to flee. Flight swelled to a major exodus in 1882 after the passage of the May laws, Alexander III's plan for Russia's five million Jews: one third to be converted, one third to emigrate, and one third to be left to starve.

The majority of those able to leave sailed for American shores. The tens of thousands who arrived annually after 1881 encountered greater obstacles than those faced by earlier immigrants. By the 1880s opportunities on the frontier were diminishing. At the same time, nationwide depressions, from 1883 to 1885, from 1893 to 1897, and again in 1907, stalled the rapidly changing American economy, creating widespread unemployment in towns and cities. Jobless Americans competing for work with a tidal wave of poor immigrants, of whom the Jews were but a fraction, were unleashing their frustration in increasingly angry antiforeigner activity. To ease the tension, national Jewish immigrant aid and relocation organizations diverted thousands of new arrivals to other than East Coast ports or assisted them out of overcrowded eastern cities and helped them to settle in less-congested sec-

National Council of Jewish Women Picnic, Denver, Colorado, circa 1895; courtesy, Rocky Mountain Jewish Historical Society, Denver, Colorado

tions of the country, including the Far West. Many more eastern Europeans, seeking entrepreneurial opportunities, surged west on their own. But times were hard everywhere, even in the underpopulated new region, and far westerners, non-Jews and Jews alike, were less than welcoming to the newcomers.

Apprised of their brethren's plight, far western Jews gathered rescue funds, organized mass meetings, and wrote letters of protest. They wanted to help the eastern Europeans, but not in the Far West, where, as one San Francisco rabbi put it, "the unabsorbable Russians" might undo the work of two generations. Despite efforts to halt them, the immigrants arrived and settled—some in agricultural colonies, but the majority in far western cities. Once the impoverished newcomers, dressed in bedraggled Old World attire, were attracting attention on the streets of their new hometowns, established Jews expended considerable effort to help them adjust by teaching them English, American manners, hygiene, and employable skills.

Too poor, insular, or pious to dwell among the general population, many immigrants gathered together in Jewish quarters, miniatures of New York's Lower East Side, in run-down sections of the region's cities. There, in the mild and sunny Far West, they reconstructed the in-

stitutions they had forged in their *shtetlach* or in urban Jewish quarters in the chilly Pale. The pious formed small, diverse congregations within the mandatory walking distance from their dwellings, while other community-minded organizers swiftly started mutual aid, fraternal, and burial societies, as well as local branches of Zionist, anarchist, Socialist, Communist, and various other international political movements.

Among the earliest of these Jewish quarters was the West Colfax section of Denver, where the Jewish population ballooned from 260 in 1877 to 15,000 in 1912, largely because of the influx from eastern Europe (a sizable percentage were tuberculars and their families). By 1906 many of San Francisco's 10,000 eastern European immigrants were living South of Market or on San Bruno Road. Jewish sections also sprang up in Los Angeles, where Yiddish-speaking newcomers caused the Jewish population to jump from 2,500 in 1900 to 10,000 in 1912. The first enclaves formed around Temple Street and Central Avenue. By 1910, 15 percent of the eastern Europeans had crossed the Los Angeles River and were living in Boyle Heights, where the largest Jewish community in the Far West would flourish between World Wars I and II.

In time the newcomers would demonstrate they had no less ability, energy, or ingenuity than

Sherith Israel—the Tenth Street Shul—was established in 1899 in West Colfax, Denver's Jewish quarter. The Orthodox congregation bought the handsome stone structure from a church group and remodeled it. Named a historic landmark in 1976, the building, now the Emanuel Gallery, is situated on the campus of Auraria Higher Education Complex. Courtesy, Rocky Mountain Jewish Historical Society, Denver, Colorado

In 1906 Fannie E. Lorber and Bessie Willens organized the Denver Sheltering home to care for the dependent children of destitute tuberculars, most of them eastern European immigrants. The above photograph shows the home's twenty-six residents and their attendants, circa 1912. Courtesy, Rocky Mountain Jewish Historical Society, Denver, Colorado

the early pioneers. Yet in their backgrounds and in the obstacles confronting them, they were different. These eastern Europeans were not simply less Westernized when they arrived, they were also more bound to *Yiddishkeit,* Jewish culture. Moreover, they had fewer skills and fewer opportunities. A minority fanned out into small, bustling cities, such as Helena, Montana, Phoenix, and El Paso, and like their predecessors, some rapidly developed substantial enterprises. Many more kept to the larger Jewish population centers, where they were obliged to start in marginal businesses dealing in junk, secondhand clothing, and groceries, all on a small scale. Others clerked in stores or used their old-world crafts to serve their Jewish-quarter neighbors as cobblers, butchers, bakers, fishmongers, and carpenters. They yearned to test their known talents, uncover new ones, and advance in an open society. And they did, often taking a generation to accomplish what earlier pioneers achieved in a decade or two. There were benefits in this slower acculturation: gradual integration, as op-

posed to the swift immersion of those who preceded them, helped them to retain more of their Jewish heritage.

In the Far West, as elsewhere in the nation, an ongoing "family" quarrel sometimes simmered, sometimes boiled, between the *Yiden,* eastern European immigrants, and the *Yahudim,* the established American Jews. As one *Yid* argued, "Where is it written that the Yahudim should lead, and the Yiden should follow?" Some emissaries were always able to carry messages between the two and occasionally unite both camps in behalf of a crucial cause. But, few, if any, envisioned that a vital fusion would occur once the latecomers joined their predecessors in their middle-class institutions or that each of the factions would be able to bring to this union qualities the other lacked. The earlier pioneers, for example, had extensive mainstream experience to share with the more segregated eastern Europeans, while later arrivals reintroduced authentic rituals and customs that many of their predecessors had modified or abandoned.

The "Yiddish public," for whom Madame Regina Prager was scheduled to perform on April 2 and 3, 1912, was several thousand strong that year and, according to the prima donna's publicity man, yearning for Old Country entertainment. Courtesy, Seattle Jewish Archives Project, Suzzallo Library, University of Washington, Seattle

By 1912 far western Jewish life—most visible in its communal buildings—was reminiscent of a vast construction site with no perceivable master plan. Scattered across the landscape were costly onion-domed and spired temples; substantial but less pretentious synagogues; parlor and storefront places of Jewish worship; and piles of lumber, stacks of bricks, and buckets of mortar awaiting still another construction crew. Other signs of widespread Jewish presence were evident in the burial grounds, meeting halls, social clubs, educational and health facilities, settle-ment houses, orphanages, and homes for the aged that had sprung up throughout the region. Like other facilities constructed at top speed in the Far West, these Jewish institutions were spurred more by heartfelt desire than by systematic planning and foresight. Few if any of the builders imagined that while dealing with their modest and immediate Jewish needs, they were also laying the communal groundwork for a major Jewish population center.

Rapid growth and size would not be the only traits of this new American Jewish ingathering.

Eva and Jacob Boscoe started the Star Bakery in 1907 to serve the needs of Jewish immigrants living in Denver's West Colfax district. By 1912 the bakery was making citywide deliveries in a shiny, new black truck. Courtesy, Rocky Mountain Jewish Historical Society, Denver, Colorado

From its inception, the character of far western Jewry was unlike any other. "We do things differently out here," was the way one journalist describing Jewish life in the Far West put it. Some of those differences are attributable to the unique circumstances shaping this early Jewry.

One key element was the far western landscape—vast, remote, sparsely inhabited, and dramatically diverse, encompassing sun-scorched deserts, rainy forests, a long sunny shoreline, and snow-covered mountain ranges. Its spaciousness, hospitable and healthy climate, awesome beauty, and numerous natural recreational areas encouraged Jews to live a more robust life than most had previously known. Compounding the physical benefits was the psychological revitalization observed to be an inherent part of the wilderness experience from biblical times forward. (In Judaic literature, the wilderness is, among other things, the symbol of a place to caste off slavish ways and start anew.) Born on a remote frontier and nurtured on the roots of American democracy, this Jewry, particularly in the early years, integrated into the new region with unprecedented speed and with an exuberance that is still discernible.

Another personality-shaping force was the character of the Jews who responded to the lure of the West. By temperament, they were among the more adventuresome and independent of their kind. As a result, they mingled more with people of diverse religions, races, and cultures and tended to absorb more of the customs of their non-Jewish neighbors than did Jews who kept to circumscribed communities. Often underlying their neighborliness were the social and political ideologies that had inspired them to abandon their home soil and rush westward in search of first-class citizenship in a new and freer region. Dreams of a better self and a more humane society continued to color their views.

Still another element, more tangible and consequently stronger, was the seemingly unlimited possibility of financial gain in the Far West. Economic development, sped by new industrialization and rising capital, created opportunities in every corner of the wide frontier. For the daring, enterprises held out the promise of an immediate foot in the door, and also, in the spirit of the times, a chance at the key to the treasurehouse. Utilizing their entrepreneurial skills, the majority of pioneer Jews—penniless when they arrived—in one to three decades were entrenched in the middle class, and a small percentage had won a place in what passed for peerage in the Far West—the new rich. As a result, pioneer Jews and their descendants expected their new life to be clothed in abundance—if not today, then tomorrow.

Also important were the influences traceable to a mandated freedom of religion in the United States, and a relaxed attitude about religious observance in the Far West. With government banished from spiritual concerns, far western Jewish institutions, like those elsewhere in the nation, were self-supporting, self-governing, and voluntary. With neither state nor social pressures to impose membership, even where congregations were numerous, a significant number of pioneer Jews did not join them. Instead, some belonged to secular ethnic organizations. Others, remaining unaffiliated, preserved their Jewish identity as individuals.

Earmarked by these and other less apparent forces, it seems quite natural that the Jews of the Far West were, and continue to be, self-defining and self-defending, individualistic and communal, innovative and conserving, group-minded and pluralistic. Until recent years, far western Jews have lacked a sense of themselves as a Jewry, largely due to an ignorance of general and Jewish regional history, which has been slow taking shape. As they grow more familiar with the character and the development of the region and the significant role their pioneer predecessors played in it, Jews of California, Utah, Nevada, and so forth, are gaining a deeper sense of their shared past. They are also beginning to recognize that the distance they traveled from European tradition has not made them of necessity lesser Jews, but different Jews. As its self-knowledge and self-esteem grow, America's newest Jewry is moving toward its own stance. To date it is still unarticulated. When far western Jewry does speak, its words are likely to bear the markings of its formative years in an iconoclastic age in an emerging region and dwell more on the future than on the past.

EPILOGUE: 1912

When the territorial period ended in 1912, approximately one hundred thousand Jews and an unassessable number of far westerners of secret or partial Jewish descent resided in the Far West. More than half were ensconced in burgeoning coastal cities, but a significant minority continued to dwell in smaller urban centers in the interior and in outlying agricultural, ranching, and mining districts. Occupying every walk of life, they ranged from magnate to mendicant, from intellectual and artist to rough-hewn illiterate, from social and political kingpin to solitary stray, from the meticulously observant to the scoffing apostate, and from the Spanish-speaking crypto-Jew with centuries on far western soil to the Yiddish-speaking tenderfoot with three days in the "vild Vest." Present, too, although less apparent, were signs that a creative interplay of cultures—imported and far western—was under way, as a last brief look at these pioneer Jews and their concerns will attest.

By 1912 most descendants of the secret Jews who had settled in south Texas and New Mexico in the late sixteenth and seventeenth centuries had lost touch with their Jewish roots and were thoroughly integrated into the Hispanic American Catholic mainstream. Amazingly, a dedicated few had remained stubbornly attached to their faith. Eulogia "Loggie" Carrasco, a resident of Albuquerque who was reared in a crypto-Jewish home, speaks openly of the customs and beliefs of the secret Jews of New Mexico. According to Carrasco, 1912 was a landmark year for these proud holdouts.

"*Nuestro gente,* our people," as this small and habitually circumspect circle refers to themselves, "viewed statehood—granted to the New Mexicans in 1912—as their long-awaited redemption," says Carrasco. They infused the cel-

Clelia Sanches (1900–1972), who became the wife of Antonio Carrasco, was a descendant of a seventeenth-century crypto-Jewish New Mexican family. As a schoolgirl she participated in Statehood Day festivities in Santa Fe on January 6, 1912. She and her classmates recited a poem written by their teacher Don Manuel Sena, who also had early Jewish roots in New Mexico. Entitled La Bandera Sin Mancha *("The Unstained Flag"), the poem paid homage to the American flag, which was never defiled by the Spanish Inquisition. Courtesy, Loggie Carrasco, Albuquerque, New Mexico*

ebration with their own, still largely secret meaning and took pains to recount the events of Statehood Day (January 6, 1912) to their children. Her mother, Clelia Sanches Carrasco (one of the 259 descendants of sixteenth-century land grantee Don Fernando Sanches y Chavez who in 1971 were granted heirs' rights to their forebear's New Mexican lands) often described the statehood festivities to Loggie when she was a child. Clelia was a twelve-year-old schoolgirl living in the tiny crypto-Jewish community of La Vega del Monte, ten miles south of Albuquerque at the time. Her teacher Don Manuel Sena, also a crypto-Jew, wrote a poem for his pupils to recite at the program commemorating statehood in Santa Fe, the new state capital. The title of the poem was *La Bandera Sin Mancha*, ("The Unstained Flag"). Recalled Loggie:

My mother taught me the poem and explained its meaning as Don Manuel had to her and the other children of La Vega del Monte. Ever since *nuestro gente* had been expelled from Spain, said my mother, we have yearned for that day when we could live in freedom under a flag unblemished by the stain of the Spanish Inquisition. After some three centuries of secret dedication on New Mexican soil, statehood transformed our wish into a reality.

By the early years of the twentieth century, a still small but growing number of non-Hispanic far western Jews were also joining the Christian majority by conversion or simply by taking a non-Jewish spouse. For some the act resulted in permanent estrangement from Jewish life. Many more continued to circulate with ease in both Christian and Jewish communities.

Such appears to have been the case of Phoenix merchant Baron Goldwater, his Episcopalian wife Josephine, and their children, who were reared in their mother's faith. On February 14, 1912, for example, this couple had the pleasure of watching their two-year-old son Barry steal the show as ringbearer at the Jewish wedding of Hazel Goldberg and Joseph Melczer. The ceremony, which, coincidentally, took place on Arizona Statehood Day and was ever after linked to that event in the minds of the participants, was an important occasion in Phoenix's small but vital Jewish community. The bride was the grand-

daughter of early Arizona pioneers Augusta and Hyman Goldberg, and the daughter of Carrie and Aaron Goldberg (who like his father was an early Arizona merchant and a territorial legislator). The groom was a member of a more recently arrived but by then well-established family that had come to Phoenix in 1892 to set up a wholesale liquor distributorship. According to a front-page story in the *Arizona Republican* on

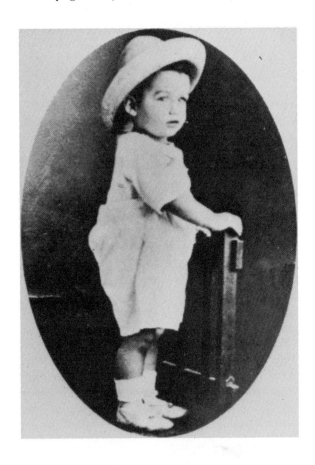

Barry Goldwater, age two, circa 1911. During the third quarter of the twentieth century Goldwater became Arizona's leading statesman and one of the chieftains of the conservative wing of the national Republican party. In 1964 Goldwater ran a losing race for the United States presidency and is now serving his fifth term in the Senate. Courtesy, Goldwater Collection, Arizona Historical Foundation, Hayden Library, Arizona State University, Tempe, Arizona

February 18, 1912, one hundred and fifty guests had crowded into the flower-bedecked Phoenix Women's Club to witness the afternoon wedding. The bridal party, attired in "the most elaborate creations of the dressmaker's art," included the bride's cousins Reba Heyman and Ruth Dorris, whose fathers together had formed the Dorris-Heyman Furniture Company, and the offspring of other (Jewish) Phoenix businessmen. The reporter noted that "Master Barry," dressed in a chaplet of silver leaves and rosebuds, negotiated the aisle carrying the wedding ring and two calla lilies. Comfortable in Jewish and in Christian society then, as thereafter, the future senator from Arizona identified with and drew support from both communities.

Wholly oblivious to statehood celebrations and sumptuous social events that year was a group of Yiddish-speaking agricultural colonists cultivating a portion of the southern Utah desert. These immigrants, chafing at their lot in overcrowded, economically depressed eastern cities, heard Russian-born, back-to-the-soil enthusiast Benjamin Brown speak, or read his article "Why Can't We?" (regenerate ourselves by farming) and joined his independent Agricultural and Colonization Association. The group was preparing to follow their "new Moses" to a site near Deming, New Mexico, when Philadelphia rabbi Joseph Krauskopf, founder of the National Far School, persuaded them to consider Utah instead. In Utah, said Krauskopf, a Jewish community that included such men as Simon Bamberger, Samuel Newhouse, and Herbert Auerbach would assist their precariously undercapitalized association. There, too, the state officials, most of them Mormons and well disposed toward Jews, could be of aid.

As the rabbi predicted, Utah officials were helpful. The state had just completed an irrigation project in the Gunnison Valley, one hundred and fifty miles south of Salt Lake City, and was looking for new settlers. They offered Brown's association liberal terms—six thousand acres at $45 per acre on a twenty-year loan, with no down payment. A pioneer contingent of the one hundred and fifty-member group arrived in the fall of 1911 to establish the settlement they named Clarion Colony. The first year was discouraging: two irrigation canals broke; an initial attempt at drilling a well failed; and the light soil proved difficult to irrigate; but these hardy idealists pressed on undaunted.

On June 14, 1912—a red-letter day at Clarion and throughout the Gunnison Valley—Governor William Spry, Rabbi Charles J. Freund, and other well-wishers motored down from Salt Lake City to view the new farmers' accomplishments and cheer them on. At a high-spirited luncheon at the colony, speakers ignored the disappointments of the first year and focused on the group's promising future. The governor expressed his certainty that the Jewish newcomers would join hands with hospitable old-timers—much in evidence at Clarion that day—to make Gunnison Valley "one of the most delightful spots in the state."

The colonists contended with their stubbornly unirrigable acreage until 1915, when the land was repossessed. Disappointed with agriculture, but not with the region, most Clarionites sought more rewarding opportunities in far western cities. Last to leave the Gunnison Valley was Nathan Brown, brother of the founder, and his family. After the colony collapsed, Brown acquired ninety acres in the environs and farmed on his own until 1927, when he and his family moved to Los Angeles.

Other new immigrants striving to retain their own values as they adapted to life in the Far West were the Sephardic Jews from the Balkans and adjacent countries who had settled in Seattle. Eight hundred strong in 1912, theirs was the largest Sephardic settlement in the United States outside of New York City. Descendants of the Jews of Spain and Portugal, these Sephardim spoke Judeo-Spanish (Ladino)—Spanish laced with Hebrew, Greek, Turkish, and Arabic—and were fiercely loyal to their Iberian past and to the customs of their adopted home communities. They refused to mingle, not only with the traditional eastern Europeans and the Reform Jews, but also with *los ajenos,* ("outsiders"), Sephardim who were natives of countries other than their own. Each group formed its own religious organizations and mutual aid societies.

(By 1914 the majority had joined the Jews of Rhodes in their Ezra Bessaroth synagogue or the Jews of Turkey in their Bikur Cholim synagogue.) Admonishments to violators of communal mores and quarrels between splinter groups occasionally (via a Seattle correspondent) reached the pages of *La America,* a Judeo-Spanish newspaper published in New York. On January 2, 1912, for example, a harsh scolding was directed at a young Seattle Sephardi from Turkey. After a few years in Seattle, the man had sent for a bride from his hometown. By the time the woman arrived, however, the prospective bridegroom had fallen in love with someone else and refused to honor his obligation to her—a breach of ethics that earned him censure.

By 1912 the eastern Europeans who had settled in Denver had achieved a numerical majority and a well-entrenched power base in the Jewish community of that city, then home to 15,000 of the 16,308 Jews in Colorado. The big news that year was the organization of the Central Jewish Council of Denver, composed of thirty-four Jewish religious, philanthropic, educational, and social organizations. The aim of this nonpartisan, nonpolitical federation as set forth in its constitution was "to further the cause of Judaism and to promote concerted action by the Jews of Denver in respect to all matters of Jewish interest." The unspoken purpose of the council was to mend an eight-year rift that began in 1904 when a committee of eastern Europeans, Dr. Charles Spivak among them, organized the Jewish Consumptives Relief Society. The group was soon in conflict with the established National Jewish Hospital of Denver, guided by powerful American Reform leader Rabbi William Friedman of Temple Emanuel. When the council met on August 26, 1912, to elect officers, representatives of the National Jewish Hospital were on hand, but Friedman was noticeably absent. Orthodox Rabbi Charles E. H. Kauvar of Beth Hamedrosh Hagadol synagogue was chosen founding president by the council's eastern European majority. One of the council's first acts was to stage a mass meeting in protest of the massacre of Jews in Balkan countries where hostilities leading up to the Balkan Wars (1912–1913) had recently erupted.

In Los Angeles, 1912 was also a year of vis-

Solomon Calvo, right, at the Water Front Fish and Oyster Company, Seattle, circa 1903. Calvo was among the first of the Sephardic Jews of Rhodes, Turkey, and Greece who settled in Seattle in the early 1900s. He arrived in New York in 1902, and was told by a Greek acquaintance that if he took a westbound train to the end of the line he would find a city that was exactly like his beloved birthplace, Marmara. Courtesy, Seattle Jewish Archives Project, Suzzallo Library, University of Washington, Seattle

ible progress in the growth of Jewish community facilities. Through the combined, though rarely joint, efforts of the highly motivated eastern European newcomers and Los Angeles's established Jewry, a number of permanent organizations and institutions were initiated or expanded. That year the Federation of Jewish Charities was founded; a new Jewish Orphans' Home (later Vista Del Mar Child Care Agency) was completed in Huntington Park; and the Southern California Jewish Consumptive Relief Society (which gave rise to the Duarte Sanitarium, forerunner of the present-day City of Hope) was initiated. By that year eastern Europeans had established a beachhead east of the Los Angeles River in Boyle Heights and were attracting to that burgeoning Jewish quarter community facilities from older sections of the city. The Kaspare Cohn Hospital for Consumptives had moved from Carroll Street in the Angeleno Heights section and was in operation as a Jewish general hospital on Stephenson Avenue (Whittier Boulevard) at the southeastern tip of Boyle Heights. The Congregation Talmud Torah, founded in 1905 downtown on Rose Street, in 1912 moved to Boyle Heights, where it became known as the Breed Street shul. Two years later, the Jewish Home for the Aged on Rose Street relocated in larger quarters on South Boyle Avenue in Boyle Heights.

Across town, that same year, without fundraising speeches or fanfare, Jesse Lasky, a San Franciscan and a former vaudevillian, and a few associates founded an important new industry. Taking the advice of his brother-in-law Sam Goldfish (later Goldwyn), Lasky set out to make a feature-length film based on the hit play *The Squaw Man.* Lasky, working with playwright-actor Cecil B. DeMille, came to Los Angeles in search of an outdoor western locale and inexpensive quarters for the Jesse Lasky Feature Play Company. The pair scouted the City of the Angels until an abandoned barn on a two-acre site at Vine Street and Selma Avenue caught their eye. Its owners, prominent southern California realtor Jacob Stern and his wife, Sarah, a member of the Laventhal family, early Los Angeles Jewish pioneers, lived on an adjacent site in a sprawl-

ing, California-style stucco home set in a lushly landscaped tropical garden. (Their five-acre plot was bounded by Hollywood Boulevard, Vine Street, Selma Avenue, and Ivar Street—later the heart of Hollywood.) Stern agreed to rent Lasky the barn for $25 a month on a month-to-month basis (brother-in-law Sam had cautioned Lasky not to make any long-term commitments). The film, *The Squaw Man,* the first feature film made in America, was completed the following year on a budget of $15,000. A historical plaque, which now marks the site where the Stern barn housed Hollywood's first studio, credits as the makers of the film Jesse Lasky, Samuel Goldwyn, and Cecil B. DeMille. A few years later, the same trio joined Adolph Zukor to form Paramount Pictures.

Although Los Angeles was clearly on its way both as a metropolis and as a Jewish center, in 1912 San Francisco was still indisputably both the New York and the Jerusalem of the Far West. Six years after it had been all but demolished, first by an earthquake and fire, then by citywide corruption scandals, the Golden Gate City, rebuilt and regenerated, was eager to move on to an even more glittering future. The Jews of San Francisco continued to add their lights and shadows to the chiaroscuro of the city. Possibly the most notorious—and certainly the most discussed—man in San Francisco that year was lawyer and deposed political boss Abraham Ruef. From May 21 to September 5, 1912, his memoirs, written in his San Quentin cell and appearing daily in the *San Francisco Bulletin,* were digested and debated from the Embarcadero, on the East Bay, to the Cliff House, on the Pacific Ocean.

A formidable contender for the most respected San Franciscan that year was M. C. "Max" Sloss, the youngest son of California forty-niner and Alaska Commercial Company founder Louis Sloss. In 1912 Max Sloss at age forty-three was in his seventh year as a justice of the California State Supreme Court. His reputation for brilliance and scrupulous honesty, earned during his student days at Harvard Law School and his early years as a junior member of a San Francisco legal firm, had won Sloss a superior court judgeship in 1901 at only thirty-one years of age. He had quickly gained renown as a first-rate jurist

The celluloid Wild West was born in 1912, some years after the real Wild West had been tamed. That year, future movie moguls Jesse Lasky, his brother-in-law Samuel Goldfish (Goldwyn), and Cecil B. DeMille organized the Jesse Lasky Famous Feature Play Company in Los Angeles to make The Squaw Man, *the first full-length movie ever made in America. Courtesy, Jesse Lasky, Jr.*

who relished the most challenging cases. When a vacancy appeared on the State Supreme Court in 1906, California governor George C. Pardee had been quick to offer him the seat, and in 1910 California voters had validated that choice by reelecting Sloss to the bench for a full twelve-year term. (He would resign in 1919, however, on his fiftieth birthday, to return to private practice.) As one of three liberal justices on the court in the stormy Progressive years, Sloss would ultimately author 583 "careful, lucid" opinions, many of which—those addressing labor relations and water rights, in particular—are now considered landmarks of California law.

A quiet man of gentle, kindly temperament, Judge Sloss presented a striking contrast to his vibrant, outspoken wife, the former Hattie Hecht, a five-foot-tall dynamo who helped found the National Council of Jewish Women and the California Social Welfare Commission and who headed dozens of philanthropic and cultural activities. Yet he lacked neither Hattie's zeal for public service nor her devotion to the city's Jewish community. In 1912 Sloss began his fourth year as president of the Pacific Hebrew Orphan Asylum and Home Society and his third as head

of the Federation of Jewish Charities, formed in 1910 when the city's Jewish agencies pooled their fund-raising efforts. In performance of his duties, Sloss presided at all important Jewish community functions in 1912. The most auspicious was the cornerstone-laying ceremony on August 14 for the $250,000 reconstruction of the earthquake-damaged Mount Zion Hospital.

After 1912 the magnetic pioneer nucleus—composed of dynamic individuals and groups much like those just described—continued growing, annually attracting thousands (and in some years, tens of thousands) of Jews into the region. In 1968, according to *American Jewish Yearbook* figures, some three-quarters of a million Jews were in residence. More than five hundred thousand of those counted lived in greater Los Angeles, which had become one of the world's major Jewish population centers. Uncounted was another large number of unaffiliated Jews, part Jews, former Jews, and the descendants of Jews, many of whom identified themselves as wholly or partly Jewish and who were, overtly or tacitly, contributing to the unique character of Jewish life in the Far West.

By then, this once-overlooked Jewry had attracted the attention of a small army of historians. Some studies had been completed, and more were under way, on individual pioneers, families, institutions, and communities. This is the first region-wide study to reach publication. Others will undoubtedly follow as interest in the western Jewish experience grows. Mounting data have begun to provide answers, and even more, to pose new, far-reaching questions. Were there forces other than those usually cited that swept Jewish seekers west? How has this long and variegated Jewish presence affected the regional lifestyle? What role will far western Jewry play in Jewish history? Although responses will be slow in the making, the fact that these questions are being asked in itself signals an important advance. Only a few years ago, the mention of western pioneer Jews typically evoked a blank but amused: "Were there any?"

BIBLIOGRAPHY

In preparing this regional study, we drew upon bibliographies, periodical indexes, catalogs of manuscripts, general and Jewish historical and sociological works, as well as state, community, institutional and family histories and biographies. We also used diaries, reminiscences, letters, oral histories, business and public records, and articles from the general and the Jewish press. We have listed herein those primary and secondary sources that have most facilitated and enriched this work.

Source Books

Agresti, Olivia Rossetti. *David Lubin: A Study in Practical Idealism*. Berkeley and Los Angeles: University of California Press, 1941.

Bancroft, Hubert Howe. *California inter Pocula*. San Francisco: History Co., 1888. Pp. 372–74.

———. *History of California*. San Francisco: History Co., 1884–90. 7 vols.

———. *Native Races*. San Francisco: A. & L. Bancroft & Co., 1886. 5 vols. 5: 77–78.

Baruch, Bernard. *My Own Story*. New York: Henry Holt & Co., 1957.

Bean, Walton. *Boss Ruef's San Francisco*. Berkeley and Los Angeles: University of California Press, 1952.

Belasco, David. *The Theatre Through Its Stage Door*. 1919. Reprint. Bronx, N.Y.: Benjamin Bloom, 1969.

Benjamin, I. J. *Three Years in America*. Philadelphia: Jewish Publication Society of America, 1956.

Bentwich, Norman. *For Zion's Sake: A Biography of Judah L. Magnes*. Philadelphia: Jewish Publication Society of America, 1954.

Billington, Ray Allen. *The Far Western Frontier, 1830–1860*. New York: Harper & Brothers, 1956.

Borthwick, J. D. *Three Years in California, 1851–1854*. Edinburgh and London: William Blackwood, 1857.

Breck, Allen Dupont. *Centennial History of the Jews of Colorado, 1859–1959*. Denver: Hirschfeld Press, 1960.

Brooks, Juanita. *The History of the Jews in Utah and Idaho*. Salt Lake City: Western Epics, 1973.

Carvahal, Luis de [the Younger]. "Autobiography" and "Letters and Last Will and Testament." Translated by Martin A. Cohen. In *The Jewish Experience in Latin America*. New York: KTAV Publishing House, 1971. 2 vols. 1: 243–312.

———. *The Enlightened: The Writings of Luis de Carvajal El Mozo*. Edited and translated by Seymour B. Liebman. Coral Gables: University of Florida Press, 1967.

Carvalho, Solomon Nunes. *Incidents of Travel and Adventure in the Far West*. Philadelphia: Jewish Publication Society of America, 1954.

Chavez, Father Angelico. *Origins of New Mexico Families in the Spanish Colonial Period, 1598–1820*. Santa Fe, N.M.: Historical Society of New Mexico, 1954.

Cleland, Robert Glass, and Putnam, Frank B. *Isaias W. Hellman and the Farmers and Merchants Bank*. San Marino, Calif.: Huntington Library, 1965.

Cohen, Martin. *The Martyr: The Story of a Secret Jew and the Mexican Inquisition in the Sixteenth Century*. Philadelphia: Jewish Publication Society of America, 1973.

Connelley, William Elsey. *Doniphan's Expedition and the Conquest of New Mexico and California*. Topeka, Kans.: William Elsey Connelley, 1907.

Cray, Ed. *Levi's*. Boston: Houghton Mifflin Co., 1978.

Cross, Ira. *Financing an Empire: History of Banking in California*. 4 vols. Chicago: S. J. Clarke, 1927.

Davis, John. *The Guggenheims: An American Epic*. New York: William Morrow Co., 1978.

Dimont, Max I. *The Jews in America*. New York: Simon & Schuster, 1978.

Earp, Josephine Sarah Marcus. *I Married Wyatt Earp: The Recollections of Josephine Sarah Marcus Earp*. Edited by Glenn G. Boyer. Tucson: University of Arizona Press, 1976.

Fairfield, Asa Merrill. *A Pioneer History of Lassen County.* San Francisco: H. S. Crocker Co., 1916.

Fierman, Floyd S. *Some Early Jewish Settlers on the Southwestern Frontier.* El Paso: Texas Western College Press, 1960.

Frank, Herman W. *Scrapbook of a Western Pioneer.* Los Angeles: Times-Mirror Press, 1934.

Freudenthal, Samuel J. *El Paso Merchant and Civic Leader from the 1880s.* Edited by Floyd S. Fierman. El Paso: Texas Western College Press, 1965.

Glanz, Rudolph. *The Jews of California from the Discovery of Gold until 1880.* New York: Walden Press, 1960.

Glaser, Lynn. *Indians or Jews? An Introduction to a Reprint of Manassah ben Israel's "The Hope of Israel."* Gilroy, Calif.: Roy V. Boswell, 1973.

Graves, J. A. *My Seventy Years in California, 1857–1927.* Los Angeles: Times-Mirror Press, 1928.

Greenleaf, Richard. *The Mexican Inquisition of the Sixteenth Century.* Albuquerque: University of New Mexico Press, 1969.

Gregg, Josiah. *Commerce of the Prairies.* Norman: University of Oklahoma Press, 1954.

Harris, Beth Kay. *Towns of Tintic.* Denver: Sage Books, 1961.

Harris, Leon. *Merchant Princes.* Reprint. New York: Berkley Books, 1979.

Hawgood, John. *America's Western Frontier.* New York: Alfred A. Knopf, 1967.

Higham, John. *Strangers in the Land: Patterns of American Nativism, 1860–1925.* New York: Atheneum, 1969.

Hopkins, Ernest J. *Financing the Frontier: A Fifty Year History of the Valley National Bank, 1899–1949.* Phoenix: Arizona Printers, 1950.

Johnston, Samuel P., ed. *Alaska Commercial Company, 1868–1940.* San Francisco: Edwin E. Wachter, 1940.

Kohlberg, Ernst. *Letters of Ernst Kohlberg (1875–1877).* Edited by Walter L. Kohlberg. El Paso: Texas Western Press, 1973.

Kohut, Rebekah. *My Portion.* New York: Thomas Seltzer, 1925.

Kramer, William M. *Emperor Norton of San Francisco.* Santa Monica, Calif.: Norton B. Stern, 1974.

———. *The Western Journal of Isaac Mayer Wise.* Berkeley, Calif.: Western Jewish History Center, Judah L. Magnes Memorial Museum, 1974.

Kramer, William M., and Stern, Norton B. *San Francisco's Artist: Toby E. Rosenthal.* Northridge, Calif.: Santa Susana Press, 1978.

Lamar, Howard R. *The Reader's Encyclopedia of the American West.* New York: Thomas Y. Crowell Co., 1977.

Lesinsky, Henry. *Letters Written by Henry Lesinsky to His Son.* Edited by Albert R. Lesinsky. New York: Albert R. Lesinsky, 1924.

Levinson, Robert. *The Jews of the California Gold Rush.* New York: KTAV Publishing House, 1978.

Levison, J. B. *Memories for My Family.* San Francisco: John Henry Nash, 1933.

Levy, Harriet Lane. *920 O'Farrell Street.* New York: Doubleday and Co., 1947.

Liebman, Seymour B. *A Guide to Jewish References in the Mexican Colonial Era, 1521–1821.* Philadelphia: University of Pennsylvania Press, 1964.

———. *The Jews in New Spain: Faith, Flame, and the Inquisition.* Coral Gables, Fla.: University of Miami Press, 1970.

Litman, Simon. *Ray Frank Litman: A Memoir.* New York: American Jewish Historical Society, 1957.

McDonald, Frank V. *Notes Preparatory to a Biography of Richard Hayes McDonald.* Cambridge: At the University Press, 1881.

McDougall, Ruth Bransten. *Coffee, Martinis, and San Francisco.* San Rafael, Calif.: Presidio Press, 1978.

McDowell, Edwin. *Barry Goldwater: Portrait of an Arizonan.* Chicago: Henry Regnery Co., 1964.

Mack, Gerstle. *Lewis and Hannah Gerstle.* New York: Profile Press, 1953.

Magnes, Judah L. *Dissenter in Zion: From the Writings of Judah L. Magnes.* Edited by Arthur A. Goren. Cambridge, Mass.: Harvard University Press, 1982.

Magnin, Cyril, and Robins, Cynthia. *Call Me Cyril.* New York: McGraw-Hill Book Co., 1981.

Mankowitz, Wolf. *Mazeppa: The Lives, Loves, and Legends of Adah Isaacs Menken.* New York: Stein and Day, 1982.

Marcus, Jacob Rader, ed. *The American Jewish Woman: A Documentary History.* New York: KTAV Publishing House, 1981.

———. *Memoirs of American Jews.* Philadelphia: Jewish Publication Society of America, 1955. [Contains memoirs of Toby Rosenthal, Jesse Seligman, and Morris Shloss.]

Meketa, Jacqueline. *Louis Felsenthal: Citizen-Soldier of Territorial New Mexico.* Santa Fe: Historical Society of New Mexico, 1982.

Muir, Ross L., and White, Carl J. *Over the Long Term . . .: The Story of J. and W. Seligman and Company.* New York: J. & W. Seligman & Co., 1964.

Narell, Irena. *Our City: The Jews of San Francisco.* San Diego: Howell-North, 1980.

Newmark, Harris. *Sixty Years in Southern California, 1853–1913.* Los Angeles: Zeitlin & Ver Brugge, 1970.

Newmark, Leo. *California Family Newmark.* Santa Monica, Calif.: Norton Stern, 1970.

Nodel, Julius J., and Apsler, Alfred. *The Ties Between: A Century of Judaism on America's Last Frontier.* Portland, Oreg.: Temple Beth Israel, 1959.

Parish, William J. *The Charles Ilfeld Company: A Study of the Rise and Decline of Mercantile Capitalism in New Mexico.* Cambridge, Mass.: Harvard University Press, 1961.

Paul, Rodman W. *Mining Frontiers of the Far West.* Albuquerque: University of New Mexico Press, 1974.

Perkins, William. *Three Years in California: William Perkins' Journal of Life in Sonora, 1849–1852.* Berkeley and Los Angeles: University of California Press, 1964.

Postal, Bernard, and Koppman, Lionel. *A Jewish Tourist's Guide to the United States.* Philadelphia: Jewish Publication Society of America, 1977.

Rischin, Moses, ed. *The Jews of the West: The Metropolitan Years.* Waltham, Mass.: American Jewish Historical Society, 1979.

Robinson, W. W. *Los Angeles from the Days of the Pueblo.* San Francisco: California Historical Society, 1959.

Rosenbaum, Fred. *Architects of Reform: Congregational and Community Leadership, Emanu-El of San Francisco, 1849–1980.* Berkeley, Calif.: Western Jewish History Center, Judah L. Magnes Memorial Museum, 1980.

——. *Free to Choose: The Making of a Jewish Community in the American West.* Berkeley, Calif.: Western Jewish History Center, Judah L. Magnes Memorial Museum, 1976.

Rothmann, Frances Bransten. *The Haas Sisters of Franklin Street.* Berkeley, Calif.: Western Jewish History Center, Judah L. Magnes Memorial Museum, 1979.

Schappes, Morris, ed. *Pictorial History of the Jews in the United States.* New York: Marzoni & Munzell, 1958.

Scholes, France V. *Troublous Times in New Mexico.* New York: AMS Press, 1977.

Shapiro, Amy. *A Guide to the Jewish Rockies.* Denver: Rocky Mountain Jewish Historical Society, 1979.

Sharfman, I. Harold. *Jews on the Frontier.* Chicago: Henry Regnery Co., 1977.

——. *Nothing Left to Commemorate: Pioneer Jews of Amador County.* Glendale, Calif.: Arthur H. Clark Co., 1969.

Simon, Linda. *The Biography of Alice B. Toklas.* New York: Avon Books, 1977.

Simpson, Lesley B. *Many Mexicos.* 3d edition. Berkeley and Los Angeles: University of California Press, 1963.

Sonnichsen, C. L. *Tucson: The Life and Times of an American City.* Norman: University of Oklahoma Press, 1982.

Soule, Frank, et al. *The Annals of San Francisco.* 1855. Reprint. Palo Alto, Calif.: Lewis Osborne, 1966.

Sprigge, Elizabeth. *Gertrude Stein: Her Life and Work.* New York: Vintage Books, 1960.

Starr, Kevin. *Americans and the California Dream.* New York: Oxford University Press, 1973.

Stein, Gertrude. *The Autobiography of Alice B. Toklas.* 1933. Reprint. New York: Vintage Books, 1960.

Stern, Norton B. *The Franklin Brothers in Gold Rush California.* New York: KTAV Publishing House, 1976.

Stern, Norton B., ed. *The Jews of Los Angeles: Urban Pioneers.* Los Angeles: Southern California Jewish Historical Society, 1981.

Stern, Norton B., and Kramer, William M. *Morris L. Goodman: The First American Councilman of the City of Los Angeles.* Los Angeles, n.p., 1981.

Stewart, Robert E., and Stewart, M. F. *Adolph Sutro.* Berkeley: Howell-North Publishing Co., 1962.

Stocker, Joseph. *Jewish Roots in Arizona.* Phoenix: Tercentenary Committee of the Phoenix Jewish Community Council, 1954.

Sturhahn, Joan. *Carvalho: Portrait of a Forgotten American.* Merrick, N.Y.: Richwood Publishing Co., 1977.

Taylor, Rosemary. *Chicken Every Sunday.* New York: Whittlesey House, 1943.

——. *Riding the Rainbow.* New York: Whittlesey House, 1944.

Thomas, Lately [pseud.]. *A Debonair Scoundrel.* New York: Holt, Rinehart & Winston, 1962.

Timberlake, Craig. *The Bishop of Broadway.* New York: Library Publishers, 1954.

Toll, William. *The Making of an Ethnic Middle Class: Portland Jewry over Four Generations.* Albany: State University of New York Press, 1982.

Torquemada, Father Juan de. *Monarquía Indiana.* 1615. Reprint. Introduction by Miguel Leon Portilla. Mexico City: Biblioteca Porrua, 1969. 3 vols. 1: 22–27.

Turner, Frederick Jackson. "The Significance of the Frontier in American History." In *The Turner Thesis,* edited by George Rogers Taylor. Lexington, Mass.: D. C. Heath & Co., 1972.

Uchill, Ida. *Pioneers, Peddlers, and Tsadikim.* Boulder, Colo.: Quality Line Printing, 1957.

Vorspan, Max, and Gartner, Lloyd P. *History of the Jews of Los Angeles.* San Marino, Calif.: Huntington Library, 1970.

Wartenberg, Henry. *Los Angeles Jewry in 1870.* Santa Monica, Calif.: Norton B. Stern, 1977.

Watters, Leon L. *The Pioneer Jews of Utah.* New York: American Jewish Historical Society, 1952.

Webb, James Josiah. *Adventures in the Santa Fe Trade, 1844–1847.* Southwestern Historical Series, edited by Ralph P. Bieber, vol. 1. Glendale, Calif.: Arthur H. Clark Co., 1931.

Williamson, Ruby G. *Otto Mears, "Pathfinder of the San Juan": His Family and Friends.* Gunnison, Colo.: B. & B. Printers, 1981.

Wilson, Carol Green. *Gump's Treasure Trade: A Story of San Francisco.* New York: Thomas Y. Crowell, 1965.

Winter, William. *The Life of David Belasco.* New York: Moffett, Yard, 1918.

Wolf, Edwin, II. *Rosenbach: A Biography.* Cleveland and New York: World Publishing Co., 1960.

Wolf, Simon. *The American Jew as Patriot, Soldier, and Citizen.* Philadelphia: Levytype Co., 1895.

Zarchin, Michael M. *Glimpses of Jewish Life in San Francisco.* San Francisco: Michael M. Zarchin, 1952.

Periodicals

Aaron, Sam. "An Arizona Pioneer: Memoirs of Sam Aaron." Edited by Jacob Rader Marcus. *American Jewish Archives* 10 (October 1958): 99–120.

Abrahamsohn, Abraham. "Interesting Accounts of the Travels of Abraham Abrahamsohn to America and Especially to the Gold Mines of California and Australia." 1856. Reprint. Translated by Marlene P. Toeppen. *Western States Jewish Historical Quarterly* 1, April 1969: 128–45; 1, July 1969: 182–95; 2, October 1969: 44–70; 2, January 1970: 106–16.

Alschuler, Al. "The Colmans and Others of Deadwood, South Dakota." *Western States Jewish Historical Quarterly* 9 (July 1977): 291–98.

Angel, Marc. "History of Seattle's Sephardic Community." *Western States Jewish Historical Quarterly* 7 (October 1974): 22–30.

Badt, Gertrude N. "Milton Benjamin Badt." *Northeastern Nevada Historical Society Quarterly,* summer 1978, pp. 92–112.

Blumenthal, Helen. "The New Odessa Colony of Oregon, 1882–1886." *Western States Jewish Historical Quarterly* 14 (July 1982): 321–32.

Boxerman, Burton Alan. "Kahn of California." *California Historical Society Quarterly* 55 (winter 1976–77): 340–51.

Carrico, Richard L. "Wolf Kalisher: Immigrant, Pioneer Merchant, and Indian Advocate." *Western States Jewish Historical Quarterly* 15 (January 1983): 99–106.

Chavez, Father Angelico. "New Names in New Mexico." *El Palacio* 64 (September–October 1957): 291–318, and 64 (November–December 1957): 367–80.

Clar, Reva. "First Jewish Woman Physician of Los Angeles." *Western States Jewish Historical Quarterly* 14 (October 1981): 66–75.

Cohen, Henry. "Henry Castro, Pioneer and Colonist." *American Jewish Historical Quarterly* 5 (1897): 39–43.

———. "The Jews in Texas." *American Jewish Historical Quarterly* 4 (1896): 9–19.

———. "The Settlement of the Jews in Texas." *Publications of the American Jewish Historical Society* 2 (1894): 139–56.

Coleman, Julie L. "Some Jews of Early Helena, Montana." *Rocky Mountain Jewish Historical Notes* 2 (March 1979): 1–2, 5.

Cooley, Everett L. "Clarion, Utah, Jewish Colony in 'Zion.'" *Utah Historical Quarterly* 36 (spring 1968): 113–31.

Cowan, Max P. "Memories of the Jewish Farmers and Ranchers of Colorado." *Western States Jewish Historical Quarterly* 9 (April 1977): 218–25.

Cutter, Charles H. "Michael Reese: Parsimonious Patron of the University of California." *California Historical Society Quarterly* 42 (June 1963): 127–44.

Ellsworth, S. George. "Simon Bamberger: Governor of Utah." *Western States Jewish Historical Quarterly* 5 (July 1973): 231–42.

Fierman, Floyd S. "The Drachmans of Arizona." *American Jewish Archives* 16 (November 1964): 134–60.

———. "Frontier Career of Charles Clever: From *Guten Tag* to *Buenos Dias*." *El Palacio* 85 (winter 1979–80): 2–6, 34–35.

———. "The Goldberg Brothers: Arizona Pioneers." *American Jewish Archives* 18 (April 1966): 3–19.

———. "The Impact of the Frontier on a Jewish Family: The Bibos." *American Jewish Historical Quarterly* 59 (June 1970): 460–522.

———. "The Spiegelbergs: Pioneer Merchants and Bankers in the Southwest." *American Jewish Historical Quarterly* 56 (June 1967): 370–435.

Fireman, Bert M. "A Bar Mitzvah Message from Prescott, Arizona, in 1879." *Western States Jewish Historical Quarterly* 12 (July 1980): 344–51.

Friedenberg, Albert M. "Solomon Heydenfeldt: A Jewish Jurist of Alabama and California." *Publications of the American Jewish Historical Society* 10 (1902): 129–40.

Glazer, Michele. "The Durkheimers of Oregon." *Western States Jewish Historical Quarterly* 10 (April 1978): 202–9.

Goldberg, Isaac. "Reminiscences of Isaac Goldberg." Edited by Harriet Rochlin and Fred Rochlin. *Western States Jewish Historical Quarterly* 2 (April 1970): 172–90.

Goldberg, Richard B. "Michael Wormser, Capitalist." *American Jewish Archives* 25 (November 1973): 161–206.

Goldwater, Barry M. "Three Generations of Pants and Politics in Arizona." Speech delivered to a meeting of the Arizona Historical Society, Tucson, 3 November 1962. *Journal of Arizona History* 3, no. 3 (autumn 1972): 141–58.

Gradwohl, Rebecca. "The Jewess in San Francisco—1896." *Western States Jewish Historical Quarterly* 6 (July 1974): 273–76.

Hafen, LeRoy F. "Otto Mears, 'Pathfinder of the San Juan.'" *Colorado Magazine* 9 (March 1932): 71–74.

Hornbein, Marjorie. "Dr. John Elsner, a Colorado Pioneer." *Western States Jewish Historical Quarterly* 13 (July 1981): 291–302.

Hoyt, Edwin P. "The Guggenheims, Giants of Mining." *Denver Post*, 4 December 1966.

Jones, Hester. "The Spiegelbergs of New Mexico." *El Palacio* 35, nos. 15–17 (10, 17, 24 April 1935): 81–89.

Kaplan, Michael. "Colorado's Big Little Man: The Early Career of Otto Mears, 1840–1881." *Western States Jewish Historical Quarterly* 4 (April 1972): 117–45.

Kelson, Benjamin. "The Jews of Montana." *Western States Jewish Historical Quarterly* 3 (January 1971): 113–20; 3 (April 1971): 170–89; 3 (July 1971): 227–42; 4 (October 1971): 35–49; 4 (January 1972): 101–12.

Kramer, William M., and Stern, Norton B. "A. Levy of the Bank." *Western States Jewish Historical Quarterly* 7 (January 1975): 118–37.

———. "Early California Associations of Michel Goldwater and His Family." *Western States Jewish Historical Quarterly* 4 (July 1972): 173–97.

———. "A Search for the First Synagogue." *Western States Jewish Historical Quarterly* 7 (October 1974): 3–21.

———. "Some Further Notes on Michel Goldwater." *Western States Jewish Historical Quarterly* 5 (October 1972): 36–39.

Landau, Francine. "Solomon Lazard of Los Angeles." *Western States Jewish Historical Quarterly* 5 (April 1973): 147–57.

Leaphart, Susan. "Frieda and Belle Fligelman: A Frontier City Girlhood in the 1890s." *Montana* 32 (July 1982): 85–92.

Levey, Samson H. "The First Jewish Sermon in the West: Yom Kippur, 1850, San Francisco." *Western States Jewish Historical Quarterly* 10 (October 1977): 3–15.

Levi, John Newmark, Sr. "This Is the Way We Used to Live." *Western States Jewish Historical Quarterly* 4 (January 1972): 71–85.

Levinson, Robert E. "American Jews in the West." *Western Historical Quarterly* 3 (July 1974): 285–94.

Levy, Daniel. "Letters about the Jews in California, 1855–1858." *Western States Jewish Historical Quarterly* 3 (January 1971): 86–112.

Liebman, Seymour. "Research Problems in Mexican Jewish History." *American Jewish Historical Quarter* 54 (December 1964): 165–80.

Livingston, John. "Cotopaxi Colony." *Rocky Mountain Jewish Historical Notes* 1 (June 1978): 1–2, 6.

McKee, Irving. "The Shooting of Charles de Young." *Pacific Historical Review* 16 (1947): 271–84.

Marks, Bernhard. "A California Pioneer: The Letters of Bernhard Marks to Jacob Solis-Cohen (1853–1857)." Edited by Jacob Solis-Cohen, Jr. *American Jewish Historical Quarterly* 44 (September 1954): 12–57.

Mayer, Alexander. "Letters of a California Pioneer: Alexander Mayer." Edited by Albert M. Friedenberg. *Publications of the American Jewish Historical Society* 31 (1923): 134–71.

Meyer, Eugene. "My Early Years." *Western States Jewish Historical Quarterly* 5 (January 1973): 87–99.

Narell, Irena. "Bernhard Marks: Retailer, Miner, Educator, Land Developer." *Western States Jewish Historical Quarterly* 5 (October 1972): 26–38.

Newmark, Marco. "Pioneer Merchants of Los Angeles." *Historical Society of Southern California Quarterly* 24, no. 3 (September 1942): 77–97; 25, nos. 1–2 (March–June 1943): 5–65.

Noel, J. Thomas. "W. Wilberforce Alexander Ramsay, Esq., and the California Gold Rush." *Journal of the West* 12 (October 1973): 563–75.

O'Dell, Roy. "Jim Levy, Gunfighter." *Tally Sheet: English Society of the Westerners* 27, no. 3 (April 1980): 53–61; no. 4 (July 1980): 78–84.

Parish, William J. "The German Jew and the Commercial Revolution in Territorial New Mexico, 1850–1900." *New Mexico Historical Review* 35 (January 1960): 1–29, 35; 35 (April 1960): 129–50.

Ridgeway, William. "Solomon, Emigrant from Germany, Builds Small Empire in Gila Valley." *Sheriff Magazine*, April 1959, pp. 50–52.

Rischin, Moses. "Beyond the Great Divide: Immigration and the Last Frontier." *Journal of American History* 55 (June 1968): 42–53.

Rochlin, Harriet. "Brides for Brethren." *Arizona Post*, 26 December 1980.

———. "Enterprising People: Pioneer Jews of Arizona." *Arizona Post*, 5 September 1980.

———. "My Mother-in-law's Kitchen." *Arizona Post*, 23 October 1981.

———. "One Jew Stopped in Caborca." *Present Tense*, winter 1975, pp. 68–72.

———. "Pioneer Jews of Arizona." *Hadassah Magazine* 58 (October 1977): 14–15.

———. "Report from Los Angeles: Fiddlers on the Freeway." *Present Tense* 5 (summer 1978): 20–21.

———. "Solomon's Territory." *Westways*, April 1979, pp. 27–31, 86.

Rochlin, Harriet, and Rochlin, Fred. "The Heart of Ambos Nogales." *Journal of Arizona History* 17 (summer 1976): 161–80.

———. "Tracking Leopold Ephraim." *Western States Jewish Historical Quarterly* 1 (January 1969): 75–85.

Rollins, Ralph. "Life Story of Black Jack Newman." *Mining Journal*, 30 August 1928.

Rollins, Sandra Lea. "Jewish Indian Chief." *Western States Jewish Historical Quarterly* 1 (July 1969): 151–63.

Rosenwaike, Ira. "Leon Dyer: Baltimore and San Francisco Jewish Leader." *Western States Jewish Historical Quarterly* 9 (January 1977): 135–43.

———. "The Parentage and Early Years of M. H. de Young: Legend and Fact." *Western States Jewish Historical Quarterly* 7 (April 1975): 210–17.

Rubinoff, Michael W. "C. E. H. Kauvar: A Sketch of a Colorado Rabbi's Life." *Western States Jewish Historical Quarterly* 10 (July 1978): 291–305.

Rudd, Hynda. "Auerbach's: One of the West's Oldest Department Stores." *Western States Jewish Historical Quarterly* 11 (April 1979): 234–38.

———. "Samuel Newhouse: Utah Mining Magnate and Land Developer." *Western States Jewish Historical Quarterly* 11 (July 1979): 291–307.

———. "The Unsinkable Anna Marks." *Western States Jewish Historical Quarterly* 10 (April 1978): 234–37.

Santos, Richard G. "Mexican-Americans: A Jewish Background?" *San Antonio Express*, 2 July 1973.

Scarlach, Bernice. "Abe Haas, Portrait of a Proud Businessman." *Western States Jewish Historical Quarterly* 12 (October 1979): 3–25.

Schackel, Sandra. "The Charles Ilfeld Company: A Perspective on a New Mexico Mercantile Family and Their Long-lived Firm." *El Palacio* 87 (spring 1981): 18–24.

Scheider, James G. "Otto Mears—Pathfinder of the San Juan." *Westerners Brand Book* 21 (January–February 1975): 81–83, 87.

Sloss, Frank H. "M. C. Sloss and the California Supreme Court." *California Law Review* 46 (December 1958): 715–38.

Stanley, Gerald. "Merchandising in the Southwest: The Mark I. Jacobs Company of Tucson, 1867–1875." *American Jewish Archives* 23 (April 1971): 86–102.

Stern, Norton B. "Abraham Mooser, First Jewish Businessman of Santa Monica, California." *Western States Jewish Historical Quarterly* 1 (April 1969): 109–27.

———. "California's Jewish Governor." *Western States Jewish Historical Quarterly* 5 (July 1973): 285–87.

———. "Mayor Strauss of Tucson." *Western States Jewish Historical Quarterly* 12 (July 1980): 347–69.

———. "Myer Joseph Newmark." *Western States Jewish Historical Quarterly* 2 (April 1970): 136–71.

———. "Notes on a Virginia City Police Chief." *Western States Jewish Historical Quarterly* 12 (October 1979): 89–91.

———. "Toward a Biography of Isaias W. Hellman." *Western States Jewish Historical Quarterly* 2 (October 1969): 27–43.

Stern, Norton B., and Kramer, William M. "Arizona's Mining Wizard: Black Jack Newman." *Western States Jewish Historical Quarterly* 11 (April 1979): 255–64.

———. "The First Jewish Organization, the First Jewish Cemetery, and the First Known Jewish Burial in the Far West." *Western States Jewish Historical Quarterly* 11 (July 1979): 318–24.

———. "The Polish Jew in Posen and in the Early West." *Western States Jewish Historical Quarterly* 10 (July 1978): 327–29.

Sterne, Adolphus. "Diary of Adolphus Sterne." Edited by Harriet Smither. Serialized in *Southwestern Historical Quarterly*, 1926–35.

Toll, William. "Fraternalism and Community Structure on the Urban Frontier: The Jews of Portland, Oregon—a Case Study." *Pacific Historical Review* 47 (August 1978): 369–403.

Viener, Saul. "Surgeon Moses Albert Levy: Letters of a Texas Patriot." *Publications of the American Jewish Historical Society* 46 (September 1956–June 1957): 101–13.

Voorsanger, Jacob. "The Beginning of the First Jewish Hospital in the West: Mount Zion in San Francisco." *Western States Jewish Historical Quarterly* 7 (January 1976): 99–101.

Weyne, Arthur. "The First Jewish Governor: Moses Alexander of Idaho." *Western States Jewish Historical Quarterly* 9 (October 1976): 21–42.

Winestine, Belle Fligelman. "Mother Was Shocked." *Montana: Magazine of Western History* 24 (July 1974): 70–79.

Winn, Karyl. "The Seattle Jewish Community." *Pacific Northwest Quarterly* 70, no. 2 (April 1979): 69–74.

Zuber, W. P. "Captain Adolphus Sterne." *Quarterly of the Texas State Historical Association* 2, no. 3 (January 1899): 211–16.

Manuscripts and Archival Materials

Adler, Adam. "Life of Lewis Adler by A. W. Adler, His Son." Irma Adler Franquelin Collection, Oakmont, Calif.

Appel, Nathan Benjamin. Papers. Hayden Library, Arizona State University, Tempe.

Appel, Ron. Interview by Fred Rochlin. 6 August 1983. Rochlin Collection, Los Angeles.

Barth, Solomon. Biographical sketch. Hayden Library, Arizona State University, Tempe.

Bartlett, Washington. Statement, and biographical sketches by library staff, 1886–1890. Bancroft Library, University of California, Berkeley.

Bernstein, Jean W.; Feldman, Dorothy R.; and Smith, Mildred A., eds. "Biographical and Historical Sketches of the Jewish Citizens of Cheyenne, Wyoming." 1968. American Jewish Archives, Cincinnati.

Blaine, Lamb. "Pioneer Jews in Arizona, 1852–1920." Ph.D. dissertation, Arizona State University, 1982.

Board of Delegates of American Israelites and the Union of American Hebrew Congregations. "Statistics of the Jews of the United States." 1880. Hebrew Union College Library, Cincinnati.

Braden, Amy Steinhart. "Child Welfare and the Community Service." Typescript of an oral history conducted by Edna Tartaul Daniel. 1965. Regional Oral History Office, Bancroft Library, University of California, Berkeley.

Brooks, William E., to Anna Parker Merriam Brooks. 4 August 1904. William E. Brooks Letters, 1903–1906, Arizona Collection, Arizona State University, Tempe.

Carrasco, Loggie. Interview by Harriet Rochlin and Fred Rochlin. 8 July 1981, Albuquerque, N.M. Rochlin Collection, Los Angeles.

Cline, Scott. "Community Structure on the Urban Frontier: The Jews of Portland, Oregon, 1849–1887." Master's thesis, Portland State University, 1982.

Dalin, David Gil. "Public Affairs and the Jewish Community: The Changing Political World of San Francisco Jews." Ph.D. dissertation, Brandeis University, 1977.

Dean, Patricia. "The Jewish Community of Helena, Montana: 1866–1900." Honors thesis, Carroll College, 1977.

Drachman, Moses. Reminiscences. Arizona Historical Society Library, Tucson.

Drachman, Sam. "Arizona Pioneers and Apaches." 1885. Arizona Historical Society Library, Tucson.

Eckstein, Joanna. Typescript of an oral history conducted by Meta Kaplan. 25 July 1975. University of Washington Library.

Flax, Sam. Typescript of an interview conducted by Belle Marcus. 3 November 1976. Rocky Mountain Jewish Historical Society, Denver.

Fleishhacker, Mortimer, Jr., and Fleishhacker, Janet Choynski. "Family Business and the San Francisco Community." Typescript of an oral history conducted by Ruth Teiser and Kathryn Harroun. Regional Oral History Office, Bancroft Library, University of California, Berkeley.

Floersheim, Irma Belle. Interview by Harriet Rochlin. 9 July 1981, Springer, N.M. Rochlin Collection, Los Angeles.

Freudenthal, Wolf. Reminiscences. Courtesy of Betty Ramenofsky.

Gelfand, Mitchell Brian. "Chutzpah in El Dorado: Social Mobility of Jews in Los Angeles, 1900–1920." Ph.D. dissertation, Carnegie-Mellon University, 1981.

Goldmann, Jack B. "A History of Pioneer Jews in California, 1849–1870." Master's thesis, University of California, Berkeley, 1940.

Goldsmith, Bernard. Dictation. Bancroft Library, University of California, Berkeley.

Haas, Elise Stern. "The Appreciation of Quality." Typescript of an oral history conducted by Harriet Nathan. 1972. Regional Oral History Office, Bancroft Library, University of California, Berkeley.

Haas, Walter A., Sr. "Civic, Philanthropic, and Business Leadership." Typescript of an oral history conducted by Harriet Nathan. 1976. Regional Oral History Office, Bancroft Library, University of California, Berkeley.

Heilner, Sigmund A. "The Diary of Sigmund A. Heilner, 1859–1861." Oregon Historical Society, Portland.

Ilfeld, Charles. Papers. William Parish Collection, Special Collections Library, University of New Mexico, Albuquerque.

Ilfeld, Fred. Interview by Fred Rochlin. 6 December 1982, Beverly Hills, Calif. Rochlin Collection, Los Angeles.

Jacobs, Frances. Papers. Rocky Mountain Jewish Historical Society, Denver.

Jaffa, Adele S. Papers. Western Jewish History Center, Judah L. Magnes Memorial Museum, Berkeley, Calif.

Kahn, Edgar Myron. "Early San Francisco Jewry." 1955. Bancroft Library, University of California, Berkeley.

Karsh, Audrey. "Hannah Schiller Mannasse: San Diego Resident, 1863–1913." Serra Museum Library, San Diego Historical Society.

Koshland, Daniel E. "The Principle of Sharing." Typescript of an oral history conducted by Harriet Nathan. 1971. Regional Oral History Office, Bancroft Library, University of California, Berkeley.

Koshland, Lucille Heming. "Citizen Participation in Government." Typescript of an oral history conducted by Harriet Nathan. 1971. Regional Oral History Office, Bancroft Library, University of California, Berkeley.

Larralde, Carlos Montalvo. "Chicano Jews in South Texas." Ph.D. dissertation, University of California, Los Angeles, 1978.

Lesinsky, Charles, III. Interview by Harriet Rochlin. 23 August 1981, Los Angeles. Rochlin Collection, Los Angeles.

Levison, Alice Gerstle. Reminiscences. Typescript of an oral history conducted by Ruth Teiser. 1973. Regional Oral History Office, Bancroft Library, University of California, Berkeley.

Levy, Benjamin. "Isaac Levy, His Family, and Friends." Rochlin Collection, Los Angeles.

Magnes, Judah L. Papers. Western Jewish History Center, Judah L. Magnes Memorial Museum, Berkeley, Calif.

Marshall, Audrey. "Southwest Jewish Traders." Special Collections, University of Arizona Library, Tucson.

Morrow, Delores. "A Voice from the Rocky Mountains." Master's thesis, University of Montana, 1981.

Myers, Bertha. "Cheyenne's First Dry Goods Merchant Brings Home a Bride." Typescript of an oral history conducted by Alice M. Shields. 1936. Statewide Historical Project, Wyoming State Historical Research and Publications Division.

Parkhill, Forbes. "The May Story." 1952. Courtesy of the May Co.

Polock, Lewis. Papers. American Jewish Archives, Cincinnati.

Ramenofsky, Betty. Interview by Harriet Rochlin. 17 June 1977, Phoenix. Rochlin Collection, Los Angeles.

Ramenofsky, Betty. "The Solomon Family." Courtesy of Betty Ramenofsky. Rochlin Collection, Los Angeles.

Righter, Robert. "The Life and Public Career of Washington Bartlett." Master's thesis, San Jose State College, 1963.

Sanders, Beatrice. Interview by Harriet Rochlin and Fred Rochlin. 10 July 1981, Trinidad, Colo. Rochlin Collection, Los Angeles.

Schutz, Max, Jr. Interview by Harriet Rochlin and Fred Rochlin. 8 February 1981, Redondo Beach, Calif. Rochlin Collection, Los Angeles.

Schwabacher, Edna, and Schwabacher, Morton. Typescript of an oral history conducted by Meta Kaplan, Karyl Winn, and Jacqueline Greenberg. 19 July 1973. University of Washington Library.

Seligman, Jesse. Dictation. Bancroft Library, University of California, Berkeley.

Silverman, B. D. "A Short History of Clarion, the Jewish Colony in the State of Utah." Courtesy of Lillian Brown Vogel.

Sloss, Louis. Dictation. Bancroft Library, University of California, Berkeley.

Solomon, Adolph. Interview by Harriet Rochlin. 20 February 1978, Santa Monica, Calif. Rochlin Collection, Los Angeles.

Solomon, Anna F. Reminiscences. Special Collections, University of Arizona Library, Tucson.

Solomon, Isidor Elkan. Autobiography. Hayden Library, Arizona State University, Tempe.

Solomons, Selina. Papers. Bancroft Library, University of California, Berkeley.

Sutro, Adolph. Papers. Bancroft Library, University of California, Berkeley.

Taichert, Milton. Interview by Harriet Rochlin and Fred Rochlin. 6 July 1981, Las Vegas, N.M. Rochlin Collection, Los Angeles.

Vogel, Barbara. "Clarion's Call." 1962. Courtesy of Barbara Vogel. Rochlin Collection, Los Angeles.

Weinstock, Lubin, and Co., Sacramento, Calif. Scrapbooks, 1902–1904, 1920–1923. Western Jewish History Center, Judah L. Magnes Memorial Museum, Berkeley, Calif.

INDEX

CREDITS